HOPE, LAUGHTER, SURVIVAL

On The Refugee Trail

Eileen Kay

to Peter,

happy trails!

Eileen

Also by Eileen Kay

Noodle Trails, a Travel Memoir
Fair Trade, Dung Trade and Travels in Thailand and Beyond

Noodle Trails 2: My Secret Century in Budapest

Noodle Trails 3: Nothing Went to Plan and Other Silver Linings – From Thailand to Hungary and more

HOPE, LAUGHTER, SURVIVAL

On The Refugee Trail

from Africa via Ukraine to Hungary and beyond

Noodle Trails 4, travel memoir

Eileen Kay

SABRE BOOKS LONDON

First published in Great Britain in 2024.

1. Travel (Hungary, Ukraine)
2. Memoir, Autobiography (Eileen Kay)

British Library Cataloguing in Publication Data: a catalogue record for this title is available from the British Library.
A US Library of Congress Catalogue Card Number is on file.

Paperback ISBN 978-1-9161470-4-1
Ebook ISBN 978-1-9161470-3-4

Cover design: Nanjar Tri Mukti @ Nanjart
Front cover photo: Miss Speaker (left to right: Devotion, Princess, Mark Rimmell, Eileen Kay, Focused, Speaker)
Author's photo: Steve Best

To all the daisies pushing through concrete to sunlight,

every day

CONTENTS

EARLY SPRING 2022

Across Four Quarters of The Globe

1. Everyone and His Dog Leaves Ukraine for Budapest

Thursday 24 February 2022, Snake Island, Ukraine

An audio recording went viral of Ukrainian State Border Guards on Snake Island under attack from the Russian Navy. They'd received the following radioed message: "This is a Russian warship. I propose you lay down your weapons and surrender to avoid bloodshed and unnecessary victims. Otherwise you will be bombed."

The Ukrainian side's reply was, by most translations, "Russian warship, go fuck yourself."

The BBC reported this with a prissier "Go to hell", and later with "Get lost", neither of which I believe. Even Google Translate was not that coy. I felt sure the first version was closer to the original, but it's just a hunch.

Experts, see for yourself: Русский военный корабль, "иди на хуй". [1]

Snake Island is a 40-acre rocky island owned by Ukraine in the northwest Black Sea, near Romania. It's mostly empty except for a military outpost, has no snakes any more, but is strategically a hugely important hub. Whoever controls that island and its surrounding waters controls all shipping routes connecting Ukraine to the rest of the world. Across that water, about 300 km (186 miles) to the east is Crimea, which was controversially annexed by Russia in 2014. If Russia controlled both Crimea and Snake Island, they'd control all that part of the Black Sea, and almost all access to Ukraine. Then all of Ukraine could easily be starved. Nothing could come or go. Ukraine had to hang on to that island, to keep access to the port of Odesa.

On the first day of the 2022 war, after the above verbal exchange, Russian warship *Moskva* opened fire and destroyed most of Snake Island, taking control.

All thirteen Ukrainian guards were presumed dead. This was reported widely by most major news sources, but Russia claimed they were alive and well, having surrendered. Who could we believe?

The initial battle took on legendary significance and so did that first verbal exchange. At first, I found no details about the radio operator who must have savoured the privilege of delivering the now-famous message. Here, let's nickname him Radio Guy. I applaud whoever gave the order, but envy his being the one to actually say it. He was an able spokesman for his people. What's more, soon those words became a national slogan on Ukrainian billboards, T-shirts – and later, on a postage stamp.

The Ukrainians fought back with humour and attitude, along with the usual weapons.

Russia had thought a simple radio message would let them take this island, and just a few days more would be enough to grab the rest of Ukraine. That's not what happened. There were lots of Radio Guys out there. There was a nation full of them, and this had just been announced to the world.

A Short Word About Bad Words

Overall, there's not much swearing in this book. But, there is a lot in this next section, which you're free to skip if such things don't entertain you. This book only contains one or two other wades through a swearing swamp, but you will receive fair warning beforehand and a clear route of detour. For example, here, you might skip to the next heading. Later on, in the book, if there's a surprise or two, that should be survivable.

About Radio Guy's message to "go fuck yourself", other translations might include such turns of phrase as: fuck off, fuck you, fuck me, get fucked. There are also equivalents like: up your ass, shove it where the sun don't shine.

Obviously there are endless variations involving other orifices, people's mothers and their genitalia, plus a world of straightforward possibilities such as: bite me, eat me, suck me/it/that, and so on. But in the end, it all just means "No" and "Go Away".

It's entertaining hearing scholars discuss these things seriously, by the way.

While we're in Eastern Europe, I'm told it's generally typical to swear profusely and strongly. Many Hungarians have confirmed this to me. With each other, they swear all the way through any normal day, far more than your average English speaker. Also, their swearing is harsher and more violent. It was described as an explosion due to cultural frustration, living in a place with such a long history of misery and miscommunication.

A proper scholar researched this for me, but I haven't enough space here to list all the Hungarian curses in common usage. A surprising number involve a horse's penis and someone's rectum. Or various parts of your mother.

There is a large cultural difference worth noting. English speakers might say "bullshit" or "horseshit" to denote things that are wrong, false, stupid or otherwise disliked or unwanted, whereas your average Hungarian will call such things "horsedick". English subtitles on Hungarian movies don't usually say that. [2]

So, this entire culture is swearing all day in the background of this story, but almost never in this particular text.

One last item: When Russia invaded Ukraine, there was a protest rally in neighbouring Budapest, of about a thousand people, during which they projected a message in light, onto the Russian embassy. The message they projected was in Ukrainian, and it was exactly the same as Radio Guy's message. [3]

You are now safe from bad words for a while, but not from bad news about bad events, however irony and sarcasm try to deal with it.

A Message From The Current Residents of This Fair City

Come to beautiful Budapest! Whoever you are, you can make all kinds of new friends, some of whom had never heard of the place, and yet here they are.

In this charming, pretty and endlessly interesting city of over a million people, many more people than that passed through recently and probably will never come back. Some of them long to return, to visit fond new friends. Others couldn't wait to leave and never gave it another thought.

You might have touching, moving, deep encounters. You might renew your faith in human kindness. There will be laughter, of course. There's always laughter, sooner or later. It might be warm, or desperate, or sharp, or dark, but there will be laughter. Sarcasm, irony and all forms of humour will be some of your best friends in times like these.

You might make precious connections who never leave your life again. However, most people will disappear and you will never learn what happened. If you've ever stood on a train platform during a manic and panicky rush hour, imagine three months of that and you'll get a feeling for our spring season here this year.

On the one hand, the menu may offer confusion, frustration, guilt, annoyance, sleeplessness, a strain on your budget, sharp paranoia, aggressive arguments, increased hatred of all outsiders, and either disgust or pleasure at how this kind of situation can be exploited for profit and political manipulation.

Or, on the other hand, there might be extraordinary joy.

You may experience the paradox that a crisis can bring out the best in people.

In wartime, there can be gemstones. And new allies. And also, great soup.

I was yearning to return to Budapest – that lovely, loveable city, where I'd been so happy. I'd spent most of the last six years there. I loved the place but not its winter. So, I'd been away in a warm place to escape all that. Working online allows such opportunities. I was reading about Hungary's neighbour

Ukraine being invaded by Russia. I was trying to follow that story as best I could, which was not easy. Who could you believe? But I was heading for some kind of dramatic epicentre, with my ticket back to Hungary and my little rented flat and temporary home there. I did not know what I was getting into, and it looked chaotic and scary.

Meanwhile, "I intend to help with the refugee aid network" was what I said to friends, with no idea what this meant. It was a seed of an idea, and everything starts with a seed. I've volunteered for all kinds of things in my life, so this would just be the latest effort on that score. I'd seen on the news the horrendous crowds of people waiting to escape falling bombs, trains filled with frightened people standing upright, packed like sardines. Budapest was being overwhelmed with one human tidal wave after the next with every train and bus that arrived. It was an All Hands On Deck situation. In a couple of weeks, once I got there, I'd join them, somehow. I had no idea how, so that was the first search.

24 February 2022, Ukraine

Miss Princess, medical student

> *I was studying medicine and had completed four and a half years of my studies. This was in Vinnytsia, a town in central Ukraine. I was woken up by the sound of bombs at the Vinnytsia military base, and the building shook.*
>
> *The first day of the invasion was chaotic. We were advised to stay and keep calm, and we were still having classes on the day of the first bombing. There were a*

lot of people outside; everyone was trying to buy food and get water to store.

I decided to leave for western Ukraine. I could stay with my brother there. It was close to the Hungarian border. I left immediately, on 24 February, the same day I heard the sound of the bombing. I wanted to cross the border into Hungary. There was only one train ticket left for that day and I immediately booked it.

I had a small bag on wheels. I left everything behind except my documents, winter jacket, a few clothes, laptop, wig. The only train available to Uzhhorod that I booked was cancelled but I was already at the train station. It was very crowded. There was a curfew so I couldn't go back. [4]

It was late February, and I was getting ready to return to Budapest. In the earlier part of this year, I finished writing my third volume of memoirs, which was mostly set in Budapest, and was looking forward to its publication in a few weeks – on my birthday, as it happened. In the meantime, I was already working on the fourth volume, set in Thailand – my continuing wacky, amusing, lizard-filled adventures over twenty winters spent there. Then the world drama had a plot twist: Russia invaded Ukraine, and I was heading straight to one of Ukraine's immediate neighbours. Eventually that story would take priority. The book of funny lizard stories would have to wait.

I trawled the internet to see how Budapest was helping, which groups were doing what, where I might jump in to volunteer once I got there. I was only semi-retired and still working part-time. That meant I was free part-time too. It looked like everyone was doing something. In fact, it was beautiful and amazing how many of us stepped up, one way or another. It was mostly small groups doing small things – but lots of them. Hungarian grannies were bringing baked goods to the train station. All sorts of people stopped on their way to work to hand out water, sandwiches, blankets. It reminded me of the Ukrainian woman who downed a Russian military drone by throwing a bottle of tomatoes at it, and became an inspirational icon as a result. Everybody did their bit, with whatever they had, even tomatoes. Let's call her Tomato Woman and let's not forget her exemplary attitude.

Throughout my lifetime, I've volunteered in hospitals, hospices, community groups – and before you vomit, as you should, at such self-righteousness, please let me quickly add this was not purely altruistic service, certainly not in my younger years. Most of it was fantastically, enjoyably social. These are great ways to meet people, quite apart from serving a good cause, even if that's a cover story. It can be real and honest too, believe it or not. There are friends, companions, drinking buddies, hook-ups, romances, plain boring old good neighbours and more to be had. You might be surprised how well these activities function as matchmaking and dating centres, much cheaper than nightclubs or bars. It never worked for me in that way, but has done for many others, and probably will continue. If you don't meet people through a religious group, this can be a morally righteous second choice for finding a date, with no guilt and fewer rules.

For me, that was then and this was now. I write to you now as a grey oldie who gave up the henna habit years ago. I now wore my honest grey hair and did my honest grey duty. I was also wondering, as I sometimes do, about what I want on my long-range track record. I could not help asking myself, what in the world would I do in their shoes? What if my building was bombed and I ran for a train, with little or no luggage? This idea left me dumbstruck. I had no answer, from my safe, blind, privileged "where shall we eat tonight?" and "I get away for the winter" point of view. I'd be desperate for help, that I am sure of. That's probably why so many of us pitched in. Also, privately, in the long run, I didn't want to recall laziness or excuses when I looked back on this era and these shocking events which were happening right under our noses. Which side of history did you want to be on? I was hearing that question more and more these days. I wanted it on record that I did not shirk from doing something, at least a little bit, or at least trying to do a little bit. I had to do at least a tomato's worth.

Thursday 24 February 2022, Ukraine

Mr Devotion, medical student

> *I was studying medicine at Zaporizhzhia State Medical University in eastern Ukraine. I'd almost finished the first year of my studies.*
>
> *We first heard about the invasion the day it happened, on 24 February 2022. We heard a sound, and we heard students rushing to the bunkers. It was through friends that we found out what had happened. They told me the Russians had attacked. Up until the moment Kyiv was attacked, our school assured us of no reason to panic.*

We had to move to the bunkers every time my university felt concerned for our safety. There were sirens to warn everyone to go hide there. This happened three to five times each day. Sometimes, we were there for two to five hours. We had to buy and bring food and water, because we did not know when we'd get out. It was terrifying.

There were more than 200 people in there. For the first two days, it was very crowded and sweaty. I sat on the ground. Sometimes we couldn't charge our phones to contact our loved ones. We were tired and hungry. It was a fearful and sad time. The number of students reduced each day as this went on. Most of the students ran away to take trains out of the country because the airports had been shut down.

I left three days later, on the 27th. I left behind almost everything – clothes, books, kitchen equipment. I just carried a few clothes and my documents in a small backpack with some food.

A couple of weeks before I was scheduled to return, I joined every possible online group on this theme in Budapest, and there were many. Many individuals criticised the Hungarian government for doing too little and too late. They did let people in, however, which was more than Poland was doing. The Polish border policies were selective along racial lines, according to many eyewitness accounts. [5]

Ultimately, one wondered what was going on. Big news sources always made me feel like a lot was not being reported. Sadly, with individuals and small groups, my Hungarian language skills were not up to much. Fortunately, there was a huge international community in Budapest. It leapt into action, and that, thank heavens, was in English. To be precise, being a very international community, it was a blend of many inventive versions of English, and that's one of my favourite soups. Although I could see online that many Hungarian groups were at work – civic, church, all sorts – I'd never be much use to them. I couldn't even read their updates. I went to lots of web pages hoping for an English version, but found few, if any, of those. The Hungarian sites added Ukrainian plus Russian or German versions. The international sites offered English plus Ukrainian and Hungarian or Russian or something else, and sometimes it went on and on.

However, we could feel a million individuals across the area trying to mobilise, trying to organise, doing their best in a mess.

Later, many would commend the Hungarian people for how they responded – not the government, but the people. The government got mixed and controversial reviews at first, which then got worse as time went on. The thousands of individual citizens who helped left a moving legacy. It felt like the main help went family to family.

Budapest is not a massive metropolis. It has a little over 1.5 million people. When more than 100,000 refugees poured in during that first week, the entire city felt it, and they knew that more were coming. Everything was chaotic. Photos of the hordes arriving showed them even more confused and distressed than when they left Ukraine. At least then, once they'd escaped the bombs, they'd evaded immediate danger. But once they crossed the border, a million new challenges arose. Where would they sleep, how would they eat, what in the world would happen next? There was no centralised place or organisation to answer any such questions.

I was flying into not a flood but a series of floods.

Monday 28 February 2022

Short Detour To Snake Island, Ukraine [6]

The heroes on Snake Island who stood up to the Russians became international icons, but at the time the fighting broke out, radio contact was lost, and they were all reported dead by many different media outlets (BBC, *Guardian*, *New York Post*, *Newsweek*, CBS and many more). Their "proof" was that there was a loss of communication, and much of the island suffered damage to its infrastructure, although the Russians did not admit to it.

Are you 100 per cent persuaded this means they were definitely killed? No? If radio contact was cut off, how does that verify anything? It verifies nothing, by definition. Mainstream journalism assumed they were dead and spread the word. They were not, in fact, dead. It looked probable. But, a few days after the attack, the Ukrainian Navy confirmed that all survivors were being detained by the Russian Navy. Across all media, corrections were published.[7] Later it was confirmed by many sources that the men did not surrender but were forcibly captured, then freed a month later in a prisoner exchange.

One had to question everything more and more. Do you really have proof? Did you just suspect something but state it as true? Should you really publish a guess as a fact? It was like thoughtless gossip but more dangerous.

Russia would control that island for the next few months.

Meanwhile, other people closer by were trying to proceed with medical school, a better cause.

<u>Mr Focused, medical student</u>

We'd heard about the attempted invasion the year before, in December 2021, but didn't take it seriously, until the first bomb hit. It was on 28 February 2022, in the morning, I heard a loud sound, and my apartment building (in Kyiv) was shaking heavily, and I heard people screaming and running. I noticed that above my apartment, it was destroyed – hit by a bomb. No lives were lost but many were injured. I was only two apartments below. I felt the terrible shake which destroyed walls and electrics.

The next day, I moved to west Ukraine. I tried to see if things would get better but it only got worse. My parents were scared and advised that I find somewhere safe. My university also insisted we evacuate before the war spread. I decided to leave by bus, through the Hungarian border town of Zohany, a couple of days later, on 2 March.

I left behind all my clothes, shoes, electronics. I left practically everything. I carried with me two backpacks, one with a few clothes and another with my documents.

<u>Miss Speaker, medical student</u>

I was studying medicine in western Ukraine. I want to be a surgeon. I first heard the news on the internet, then my friends spoke about it too because they also learned the news. At first, I didn't believe it. It all felt like a joke.

But, I saw bombing. I saw buildings damaged. I saw the first building bombed by the first strike because it was close to my house. The houses nearby were all shaking, and people were screaming. I left Ukraine about a week later, in early March. My school insisted we flee the country. A bus was provided by the school, but we had to pay $50 to enter it. I left everything behind except for a few clothes in a bag and my documents.

Budapest, All That Week

With the war's first eruptions, many individuals with aid on their mind were focused on sending things to the border. It would hit the city later. There were the usual arguments about what to do, what to send. Experienced organisations gave good advice based on long years of experience – which of course, many people ignored.

Everyone wanted to get rid of unwanted clothes, yet some escapees had enough to carry already. Surplus clothing mountains often appear in such situations. They can be a nuisance and an obstacle. At the border, they needed tents, sleeping bags, first aid equipment, storable food and water. Still, there were individuals who collected old and unwanted clothing, packed a car, headed for the border and increased the clutter and chaos. One person even claimed to be advertising the location of an obscure crossing where you could – against all advice – cross into Ukraine and deliver things directly. How they got back was quite another question. But that's what a few maverick individuals were encouraging.

When the refugees poured into Budapest, at first many individuals cooked food and brought it to their nearest train station. They showed up with home-baked goods, sandwiches, soup, tea and coffee, and toys and chocolate for kids. They walked up and down the long lines of arrivals, offering their donations. It was both practical and touching. Later, this would be forbidden by the government, who only allowed store-bought items, nothing home-made, reportedly due to hygiene rules that would not be relaxed even during an emergency. One volunteer said it was not that the government did nothing, but rather that they were being actively obstructive to delivering basic aid, like food. They were accused of controlling who could sell and profit from it.

At the two main train stations, Nyugati (Western) and Keleti (Eastern), the Red Cross and Migration Aid set up tables near the train platforms. The first provided key emergency help with water, food and medical care. The second had an astonishing long list of local residents, citizens as well as non-Hungarians living there, who were offering spare beds in their homes and food, assisted by a fleet of volunteers who ferried arrivals to these locations. It had the feeling of a massive spontaneous beehive – but certainly not as organised.

Besides these two big groups, there were a great many smaller groups somehow sharing out the tasks.

Outside of the stations, all manner of help outposts were springing up in schools, neighbourhood groups, religious groups, in small and large NGOs, as well as from families, single old lady pensioners like myself, just about anybody – but however confused this beehive was, everyone agreed on one thing: the government appeared to be doing nothing, or was even getting in the way.

It was not just the street-level grapevine that had the impression that the government was idle. Word on the media grapevine was also saying that the Hungarian government was doing very little.

On the one hand, the government set aside HUF600 million (€1.5 million) to help refugees fleeing Ukraine. This was not including independent donations from Hungarians. [8]

However, CGTN reported that critics accused the government of failing to organise a structured response to the influx of refugees in the early weeks. Most efforts then came from civilian volunteers and support groups. Refugees mostly got help from "people who come to support – there's not much centralised" help. [9]

BNE IntelliNews said Hungary was unwise to write off the possibility of an invasion, that they had no shelters, no information, nothing for refugees, who were sometimes left at the mercy of "drivers offering trips to Budapest for €100–€150, ten times the train ticket price". [10] There were other reports of refugees paying people to drive them over the border but once paid that driver disappeared.

To be fair, on social media, I saw dozens of honest offers by individual citizens who for weeks did nothing but drive back and forth to the border, bringing supplies there to donate, bringing people back and feeding them too, all at their own cost. There was an amazing amount of that kind of thing, plus of course the unsurprising minority of those who prey on the vulnerable. But overall, the feeling was that decades of Soviet and Russian abuse of the Hungarians had inspired many of them to take these Ukrainian cousins into their cars, into their kitchens and onto their living room sofas.

Just to balance out that heartwarming scenario, there were those who said that the Hungarians only helped because Ukrainians are similar, meaning that they are white, and in 2015 Hungarians rejected non-white people escaping the war in Syria. There will be more on that later.

Wars will always have their profiteers. There was a guy who collected money saying it was for wheelchairs. There were other such attempts. It was like the film *The Third Man,* where Harry Lime steals penicillin from military hospitals and sells diluted versions on the black market.

Nevertheless, what I witnessed was a ton of straightforward helpfulness. Most of us felt this was touching and encouraging. We saw hope everywhere, spreading like daisies through concrete.

Thursday 3 March 2022

It was extremely hard to know what was going on, officially. Whatever was happening in the Hungarian government, they tended to work behind closed doors anyway, even to the EU, which sent them money and sometimes had trouble finding out how it was spent, it has been alleged more than once. There were plenty of conflicts on that score. The fact Hungary was still in the EU at all was even being questioned, and continues to be increasingly.

Meanwhile, internet groups were awash with messages such as:

> *Help, family of 7 and 1 dog, here 2 weeks, then go Berlin. We can pay but not like hotel. Dog is small and nice.*

Hello, our flat can host 1 mother & 1 child to share double bed. We are allergic to dogs, very sorry.

These poured in every hour, and families got matched up in their thousands with another family to stay with. As just one example, a public group called "Open Houses for Ukrainians in Budapest" said "If you are fleeing from Ukraine and have nowhere else to go, you can find free beds offered by fellow Hungarians in their Budapest homes". There was many a household that hosted one family after the next, for months and months. There were over four thousand members, and there were still posts helping people needing help, into the autumn of 2023.

Also, from the start of the war and the initial exodus, there were an amazing and touching number of beloved dogs that simply could not be left behind by their Ukrainian owners.

Maybe they'd learned their lesson on that score back in 1986, after the disastrous accident when one of the reactors in the Chernobyl Nuclear Power Plant in Ukraine, then part of the Soviet Union, exploded. Tens of thousands of people were evacuated and told to leave their pets behind. There were reports of howling pet dogs trying to join their families on buses but being pushed off by soldiers. The dogs ran after the buses as far as they could. Later, soldiers shot most of them, in an apparent effort to lower the spread of contamination. Of course, some dogs escaped and survived. Their descendants are there in droves. Thirty years later, there were an estimated 900 stray dogs in that 2,600 sq km (1,000 sq mile) area labelled the Chernobyl Exclusion Zone. [11]

That exodus and mass migration was in 1986. This time, in 2022, people were bringing their dogs with them. Special permission was requested from state veterinary officials to allow pet dogs to cross borders, and special permission was granted.

The building where I lived when I spent time in Budapest did not allow dogs of any kind. They barely managed to tolerate one cat in a communal garden, although clearly this queenly creature was barely tolerating the rest of us on her land. I was so sure the building would not allow refugee guests of any description, I did not even ask. I was also nervous about it, living on my own. Embarrassingly, this was also ironic and cowardly, because in this area, on this very street, there were many safehouses that had hidden Jewish people from being murdered by Nazis in the Second World War, including our cousin Jolán (1896–1980), right on this same street. I had living cousins who knew and loved Jolán – and from their stories, I felt I knew her too.

[By the way, allow me a note on accents, diacritical marks and the difference between writing Jolán and Jolan: in my previous books I anglicised everything because I was overwhelmed by Hungarian spelling, and also I knew that most English readers wouldn't mind or even know. This time, in honour of all the Hungarians who have helped refugees, I shall honour all Hungarian dots, dashes and accents.]

Our gutsy, cool and popular cousin Jolán was a pianist and teacher who lost job after job because of tougher and tougher laws restricting Jews from almost any form of work. When they started killing Jews outright, she hid in a cellar a mere few blocks from where I wrote these words. After the War, she emerged from that safehouse in Budapest XIII and returned to her building in district VIII. It was still mostly standing, which was unusual at the time. She'd been renting a small studio flat where her big piano nearly filled the whole place. Space was so tight, she unrolled mats at night and slept with her feet under the piano.

When she returned, she found a family of three was squatting in the flat. Many people never got back into their homes ever again. But somehow, she regained entry and joined them – all of them in the one room, all of them sleeping with their feet under the piano. Then, her only surviving relative arrived. This was her sister's son – my second cousin Andreas, whom I've visited many times and had many long talks with, now ninety-five at the time of writing. He still looks at me sometimes and remarks fondly that my hair is just like Jolán's, especially the way I sweep it off my temple. He was just sixteen when he showed up at his Aunt Jolán's door, fresh from the death camps of Nazi Germany, Auschwitz and Dachau, where he lost both his parents. Once liberated, he joined others who stole a train and rode back to Budapest, reversing the awful, infamous train journey that first brought them there.

He saw Jolán's place was full and reluctantly turned away, but she pulled him in, insisting this was ideal – it would drive the family out, she hoped. Eventually it did – after she trotted around the city with them to find a new place for them. Then young Andreas stayed and they both slept with their feet under the piano. She helped him finish secondary school and start university. She also helped him get his previously confiscated house back, and this financed his future. She became a very effective second mother to him, sending him off to escape into Austria to the American Zone's Displaced Persons camp, where his daughter Vera was born. That family line now comprises my Vienna Cousins, as I dubbed them and will refer to them from here on.

Andreas and Vera told me a lot about Jolán, whom they loved and admired. They always smiled when reminded of her. Jolán was tough as old boots, as the Brits say, and I'm said to look and act like her, which I take as a big compliment. We both started out as piano teachers, we both adored the world of books and literature, and we both admired gutsiness, so I'm hoping some gutsiness runs from her DNA to mine.

I'd love to think I'd defy Nazis and hide their intended victims in my one-room studio flat. But I wasn't showing strong signs at the moment. Unfortunately, there were many reasons I was the wrong profile to provide accommodation like this, just now. I headed for another theme, one of my favourites: food.

A short aside about blood sugar issues and inconvenient skinniness: To avoid punching people, I need to eat often, regularly and carefully. I have a million digestive issues. When hungry, my body chemistry panics. I have friends who warn newer friends that when I say I need to eat, they must listen and act immediately. I need to eat within thirty minutes of that warning "or she'll tear your arm off," said one of them. Joking aside, the idea of real hunger was awful beyond my comprehension, and certainly beyond my experience. So, as a foodie, a full-on overindulged food enthusiast, I could attest that whatever else is happening in life, we all need to eat. I may not be able to do much, but whatever it is, it'll be on a food theme. I'll be in a kitchen, nearby a kitchen or delivering groceries to a kitchen. The kitchen is the centre of any universe.

Overall, what I felt at that time was that the whole scenario presented a huge puzzle. It was horrendously complicated, unclear, uncoordinated and uncentralised. But, like anyone else, I too was a piece of the puzzle now splattered across our city. So, where did I fit best? This was the question. In search of the answer, I continued a routine of trawling the online groups that were proliferating. This produced a list of places to visit and check out, once I got there. I had an itinerary. I'd be arriving back in Budapest on the very day of the Spring Equinox. That seemed a good sign. I'd planned that long ago, liking the image of flinging seeds into spring and starting a new project. When suddenly this city was in crisis, I didn't change the ticket or the date but I changed the project and my priorities. This return trip now had added purpose.

2. Churches, Challenges, Chaos

March, Week 1, Budapest

I experience a strong sense of ambivalence and a rush of volatile mixed emotions whenever I must face a church or anything like one. I have a long, strong and valid history of scepticism, if not outright avoidance of, any institution of any of the organised religions, be they ashrams, temples, churches or anything even cousinly to them. In this case, I made an exception, at a safe distance, but it turned out to be a short-lived collaboration. I was not the only one. Let's call this hypothetical entity the Amen Church.

When the first tidal waves of refugees hit Hungary from Ukraine in 2022, one thing became clear. Ukrainians were receiving a great deal of help but Africans and Asians living, working and studying in Ukraine who also had to flee, were being discriminated against. International students especially were slipping through the aid net and being abandoned and stepped over, in this emergency.

In Budapest, the Ghanaian Students Association in

Hungary (GASH) had a few members who were acquainted with people at the Amen Church. The student association responded quickly to the crisis, and convinced the church to open their doors and offer space where refugees could shelter after their gruelling journey. GASH knew of about 200 fellow Ghanaian students who were on their way. There would soon be more.

The student group set up and ran everything, on the church's premises. Facebook and WhatsApp groups of all kinds were whirled into existence, and volunteers and help started to come in.[1]

GASH created a refugee help centre, which was launched on 2 March.[2] It was staffed by over 200 volunteers – Americans, Africans, other foreigners studying in Budapest, also some who fled Syria and stayed in Budapest – and they had extra sympathy.

Some of the students said they'd rather be helping than studying. There are times one must take action, and thoughts and/or prayers are not enough.

Ukrainians were officially welcomed with instant work permits and free support such as transport, tuition and student visas at many universities. This was not the case for tens of thousands of Africans and Asians who'd been working or studying in Ukraine. They were shunted aside, sometimes literally and physically shunted off trains in favour of white people.

I never heard anyone, anywhere in the world, express dismay at the amount of generous aid that went to Ukrainians in 2022, much of which may well be continuing for all we know at the time of publishing. However wonderful people are being to Ukrainians now, those who fled the war in Syria in

2015 did not benefit from the same generosity of spirit or aid – or indeed anything. In fact they faced persecution, accusations of criminality and terrorism. Now in 2022, these international students at Ukrainian universities were fleeing the same bombs as their white peers and neighbours and were not getting help. What's more, they faced some ugly discrimination.

From an aid point of view, these particular refugees deserved some prioritising. They needed a break. Thousands of Africans in Ukraine were studying medicine. Ukraine attracts many foreign students and has a strong reputation for medical courses. Plus, expenses are lower than in Western European nations. Now these tens of thousands of African and Asian students fled their Ukrainian universities for safety in Hungary, and Hungary let them in – unlike Poland, which turned many away altogether, sometimes when they were on foot for days in freezing February. Some slept for days once they arrived in deeply traumatised states. The Africans started sharing their experiences online using the hashtag #AfricansinUkraine. [3]

Shelter volunteers met new arrivals at the train station, even in the middle of the night, to bring them to the centre where there was always hot food on the stove, like stew or scrambled eggs. There were toiletries and donated clothes. There was help finding accommodation, registering with the immigration department and planning their next steps.

They found students who would share their dorm rooms. They found families that shared their flats.

One local Hungarian volunteer knew people in local government, and persuaded them to offer housing to international students in student dorms in Budapest and nearby Gödöllő, also in nursing homes in the towns of Peterdy and Erd. GASH registered African students on the computer to tell embassies who wanted to fly home.

There was a big network of volunteers behind all of this. None of it had any connection to the national government.

One coordinator said that, initially, it was more difficult to get donations because many of their guests were African and Asian, while another coordinator added that when the antipathy towards African refugees melted away, help and goodwill poured in.

Foreign students fleeing Ukraine told CNN reporters they faced segregation and racism at borders.[4] Non-Ukrainians had an extra hard time, were separated from others, were made to wait in train stations and at the border, standing in the cold for hours as white people were sent ahead.

They were ordered off the public transit bus at a checkpoint between the Ukraine and Poland border. The bus drove off with only Ukrainian nationals on board.

A student at a university in Lviv was left stranded as they tried to enter Poland.

Other students reported that over ten buses came, and they watched all the other people leave on those buses. They thought that after all the Ukrainians were taken over the border, they would be next. But they were told there were no more buses and they had to walk. This was in a bitterly cold February, when they hadn't slept for about four days.

An Indian fourth-year medical student reported that there were three check posts to go through to get to the border where a lot of people were stranded. They didn't allow many Indians to go through, making them wait; only 30 Indians per 500 Ukrainians got across.

Then it was 4–5 km from the first checkpoint to the second. Ukrainians were given rides in taxis and buses while all other nationalities had to walk.

There were also allegations of violence – that guards pushed, kicked, punched and insulted the international students.

African representatives on the UN Security Council condemned these reports of discrimination at the Ukrainian border at a meeting at the UN HQ in New York. The African Union said it was "disturbed" by reports of segregation against Africans in Ukraine, which it described as "shockingly racist and in breach of international law". The fifty-four-member bloc urged countries to show empathy and support to all people fleeing war, regardless of their racial identity.

Ukrainian border authorities denied these allegations.

In general, international students found a better welcome in Hungary, and many have praised the response of Hungarian citizens and residents, thanking them over and over again. It was for many a scary but moving, unforgettable, life-changing historical event, the kind that leaves a stamp on everyone. This mass migration from Ukraine proceeded in a deeply personal way, step by step, family by family, dorm by dorm. And, a lot of this revolution happened in kitchens.

What astonished me was that many of these organisers and volunteers were also holding down their day jobs. I used to live like that, juggling two if not three jobs, in my twenties and thirties, but certainly not now. Now I had to be realistic. However, the volunteers around me were inspiring, and it was invigorating to be around such positive energy. This was in addition to the inspiring resilience of people in crisis and how they survive.

Later, one volunteer would look back and comment that in that first month, at the shelter, there was actually a fun atmosphere between volunteers and student refugees especially. He said there were great conversations, smiley people, that some of those students were so full of life, vibrant, wonderful, and there was so much real connection.

The student group was exemplary and leading the way. I realised that I could, perhaps, order food online to be delivered to them and their helpers, even from where I was, far away on the other side of the planet. At this point I was still in Thailand, soon to return to Hungary. I already had a delivery account set up with a Budapest supermarket, from when I was there last year. That could work. That was a plan.

Saturday 5 March 2022

I sent a message saying, "Hello, I am returning to Budapest in a couple of weeks. I'll come and help. Meanwhile I can send food supplies."

In all the chaos, however, this proved easier said than done, with the best will in the world from all concerned. I procured a few phone numbers and contact names, but in the overwhelming mayhem, contact was difficult, let alone making practical plans.

A lot of us were trying to help but we felt more like dogs chasing our own tails. Most dogs, however, will eventually run out of steam and lie down. For a while. Until the next round.

Sunday 6 March 2022

I tried again, texting, "I can order groceries and send them. I need the full address, a phone number, and I will send things from your latest list on Facebook."

I went to their list. The day's priorities were a double

burner hotplate and slippers for the shower. Other than that, they only needed half a million things, which momentarily short-circuited the brain. But, I focused on food. That would be the main theme. It narrowed down my own chaos a bit, which was helpful. I persisted, and messaged them again: "I can arrange a delivery if I have the phone number of someone sure to be there to receive it."

The stupid practicality of it was that to get a large delivery there, safe and sound, the delivery people needed a contact name and number of someone who would sign for it. Without that, a nice big fat food delivery could go astray or get returned while the supermarket would not even take the order without that. The volunteer brigade was a swirling, stressed-out beehive, so it took some doing, but I eventually got the info, did the order and checked that it got there. It got there.

You can't expect efficiency in the middle of a flood, after all. But, to sail that metaphor as far as possible: if you want to distribute life jackets, don't fling them into a raging river and watch them float away.

One had to persist, nonetheless.

I sent a small donation to what appeared to be the Amen Church's accommodation fund – although strictly speaking, it was not their fund, but was in the name of one individual. That was a bit confusing. Some limited light would be shed on that, later on. In any case, my budget wouldn't allow many more such donations. When the economic budget got tight, I'd be parcelling out time and skills, not cash or goods.

It happens with these crises – wars, floods, earthquakes, anything. Aid rushes in at first, maybe for a month. In the second month, it recedes like a tide. In the third month there are only scraps on the sand. The news cycle moves onto a new beach, and this one is forgotten, like so many gawking tourists. But more to the point, experts often say it's better to give a smidgen every month, not just a blob at Christmas.

I could offer a different kind of gift, a bit of commitment and follow-up. It had to be realistic, not overly ambitious, doable and – what was the cool buzzword, newish to me? – sustainable. I needed a longer-range project that was sustainable.

Soon I'd be coming home to Budapest. Then I'd have a look around. I just wanted to get there, and sniff things out, like a quiet but relentless bloodhound.

Hundreds of thousands of other people were heading there too, for all kinds of other more desperate reasons.

Monday 7 March 2022

African, Asian and other international student refugees continued to pour into Budapest, with all of the others. Now their own phone networks were alerting them to GASH's project, their soup, their sympathy and their helpers. New arrivals could text ahead asking to be met and volunteers continued to collect and take care of them. The stews kept stewing. The eggs kept scrambling. The donations trickled in and made it all possible – for another month, anyway. Emergency rations. This was when we thought the war might last a month, maybe two.

The man who started the crowd-funding on his own was not officially linked to the church. He clearly knew a lot of people who trusted him. He raised thousands for an accommodation budget. Most people arriving in Budapest in those first few weeks were not there very long. They stayed perhaps a week, or a few weeks at the most. They caught their breath, contacted someone somewhere else to take them in, maybe even long term, and then they got their tickets as soon as possible. This man organised those crucial first days for many, many people. It was achieved with the trust and donations of friends.

When the war first broke out, there was free travel to other parts of Europe by bus or by train. This information was posted at the two main train stations, Keleti and Nyugati. If any refugee was paying for tickets in those early days, they didn't have to. There was free travel for those in need – although that would change in a month or so.

Still, it did not go unnoticed that many of these people bought tickets. These were the "nice refugees" with money, that mainstream journalists were starting to mention, pointing out these were white people, professionals, Christian, just like us (i.e. just like that reporter). They had nice suitcases. They bought tickets sometimes because they could and they were not aid leeches. They were not the usual type of refugee, or anyway, they were better than the Syrians. There were loads and loads of comments along those lines, all across the world's mainstream media.

That sort of reporting by nice middle-class white folks was starting to emerge in all sorts of places. It seemed to generate a lot of warm sympathy for war victims, but not all of them, obviously. Only the ones with nice suitcases and looking like those pale reporters.

Tuesday 8 March 2022

There was a bizarre, almost surrealistic lift in spirits and pride when the citizens of Budapest rose to the challenge, despite the hard situation. Historically, Hungarians have typically excelled in cynicism, black humour, grumpiness or melancholia. It was often a bit grey, inside and out. But here, there was an intense, shocking, beautiful sense of community, a purpose, where just about everyone helped somehow. Some people said that they'd never seen anything quite like it – not since September 11, 2001 when the Twin Towers fell in New York.

Hungarians knew all too well about Soviet-style aggression and tyranny, and in that sense were sympathetic kindred spirits to the Ukrainians. There was some irony when there were public appeals for anyone who could speak either Ukrainian (few) or Russian (many, albeit they might be grumpy about it). All Ukrainians had to learn Russian, though not vice versa. In Hungary, until 1991 Russian was the main foreign language taught in school, often unwelcome and under duress. So Hungarians may have hated the background to this skill, but now their knowledge of the Russian language could be put to a very good use. Many Russian-speaking Hungarians hosted families who spoke only Ukrainian and Russian.

The biggest difference between 2001 and now was the internet. Back when the Twin Towers fell, Facebook had not yet been founded. In 2022, it was more than flourishing. It made millions of small and large mercies possible and quick, and linked people across many languages. It was there and on WhatsApp and similar phone platforms that communications buzzed. That's also where people felt they could trust each other. That's where they got their news – for better or for worse.

Friends texted friends of friends of friends and found spare rooms for thousands of new arrivals, each day. Individuals posted needs and total strangers answered. Single mums took in other single mums with kids, one set after the next. It was extraordinary, and most of it came from ordinary individuals and families. Someday there may even be a statistic indicating that these individuals, collectively, did more to help than many of the formal organisations and, in the first month, certainly more than the government.

Beautiful humanitarian activities took place in that church building, mostly organised by GASH and their friends and other newly-arriving individuals not connected to the church but hearing about the shelter. The church kept separate, officially, and their name was not to be used when individuals raised funds.

As one example, when crowd-funding was set up by one particular person, a well-trusted individual, money flowed in. These funds seemed to come from two groups of donors: people who knew him directly and trusted him, and others who knew someone else who knew him and trusted him, which became a source of trust by proxy. I was in that second group. We had enough trusted mutual friends that I decided he was a sort of unmet cousin twice removed, and I had lots of these. I admired what these people were doing. It gave me hope. I was starting to zero in on my piece in this puzzle. I somehow felt I was on the right trail. I just had to persist and keep my radar scanning.

Later, like others, I too organised a private fundraiser as an individual. In this case, when I advertised it, I was contacted by this church and instructed not to mention their name in any context. There was no connection anyway, so that request seemed odd, to me. But, I didn't say their name, and I won't. I was never told why, and despite some puzzlement, I promised to comply. I can usually comply when a religious group wants nothing to do with me.

To end on a fine note, Gabriel Asante, president of GASH, received an African Hero Award in the USA for the work he did in Budapest in 2022.

Amen to that.

3. Budapest Wasn't Ready: What and Where is Erd?

Late February 2022, Ukraine

<u>Devotion</u>

I took a taxi from my hostel to the train station with my friends. There were about thirteen of us, all from the same church. On this trip, the main struggles were within Ukraine. It was a panic; everything was disorganised. The main wait was in Zaporizhzhia, we were there for over three hours. Then we waited in Lviv about an hour and a half. In both of those stations, we sat vigilantly, prepared to enter any train heading where we needed to go. When it was almost time, we would rush to the entrance of the trains.

We managed to get seats. It was very crowded. Some people could only stay on the walkways all through the journey. A lot of people couldn't get seats.

We had some money and food, and shared whatever we had. We did not have any access to money or real food as we went along. We survived on snacks we had got days before. The cashpoints weren't working when we were in Zaporizhzhia and we weren't close to cashpoints during the journey.

We slept in Uzhgorod before taking a train to Chop and then from Chop to Záhony, the border crossing. We were there about an hour. We crossed the border to Hungary, we bought train tickets and my passport was stamped. At that point, I felt safer. There was no struggle, no troubles with transport after that.

The overall journey from our homes in Ukraine took about two and a half days. The next stop was Budapest.

<u>Princess</u>

Princess was trying to get from east Ukraine to west, to her brother.

The train that I booked was cancelled but I was already at the station and couldn't go back home. There was a curfew. The train station was crowded. An evacuation train to Lviv came, which I entered. My ticket from Lviv to Uzhgorod was cancelled twice; I had to buy another ticket at the ticket office. I waited four hours in Lviv. My journey from Lviv to Uzhgorod was about six hours.

I had a seat. The train was empty. There were about

six people in my car, which could accommodate twenty to thirty people. I had food, my card and some cash. Other people had problems with ATMs, food or water. The overall journey to Budapest took about twenty-four hours.

Maybe I had no problems because it was the first day of the invasion.

<u>Speaker</u>

When I was trying to leave Ukraine, I saw POC [People of Colour] prevented from boarding trains, to let white people go first. Most black people had to force their way in.

I saw POC taken off the trains, to let white people on. I would have been taken off, but I was protected by a Ukrainian family who claimed we were travelling together.

I saw and experienced these things, and heard similar stories from people I trust.

I arrived in Budapest on 3 March, early in the morning. I was scared and did not know what would happen next.

<u>Focused</u>

I heard of black people who were thrown off trains leaving Ukrainian cities. I also heard about racist acts on the border of Poland, when they left black people and people from Third World Countries to wait in the cold for hours and later sent back.

I didn't experience so much difficulty because I left early. But, even then, my train was cancelled multiple times, and they were chasing black people out. I had to hide so they couldn't find me. But I travelled with a Ukrainian family from my same apartment building so they grouped us together. That train was so crowded, there was no space to sit or even stand.

I had about $100 and no food. There was no chance to get any food along the way. ATMs were not paying out. The trip took about twenty-four hours.

March, Week 1, Budapest

The city-wide messy beehive that was Budapest in those weeks did not seem to have any central coordination. You could spend hours upon hours on the internet and end up going in circles. It was frustrating not knowing what to do or who to trust. In the emergency melee, of all the different appeals thrown at the general public, one distinction would emerge again and again. It was the trust factor that ruled over all other considerations, sometimes to a fault. On the one hand, there were official groups and verified organisations. On the other hand, there were individuals who were total strangers, who seemed to mean well, who asked you to trust them, and who did not say who or where they were, or what they'd do with what you sent them.

If you knew them, you might say yes. If not, what then? Who did you trust with a donation? The question of who you trusted became a constant theme.

There was another discrepancy. Organisations were clear about what they needed, but donors didn't always listen.

Donors brought whatever they wanted rid of, unwanted gifts like odd ugly sweaters from Christmas or just plain rubbish.

What do you do with unwanted gifts? I am usually polite but discreetly throw or give it away, wishing it luck finding a happier recipient via a charity shop in a part of town the donor doesn't frequent.

From another angle, I used to wholesale giftware. I used to sell Fair Trade jewellery and other imported goods to gift shops around the UK. I am sincere about the nature and challenge of gift-giving, having given this a lot of thought, personally and professionally. I believe the heart of gift-giving is to seek out what that other person wants, loves or needs. This is quite apart from setting your budget, which I maintain should be minimal. What will put a smile on their face? I mean *their* face, not yours. It's remarkable how many people do not approach it this way.

However, here we were not talking about cute little luxury gifts, but basic needs. Online, there ensued regular pleas from NGO spokespeople for potential donors to remember several things:

- Whatever money you can give, spread it over the year, not just once at Christmas, or not just for the first month of an ongoing crisis.
- Please ask what the recipient needs.
- Please don't give things that haven't been requested.
- Please, before you say anything, ask what the other party wants.
- Please ask first.
- Please?

These reminders were ongoing. Were they being heard? Maybe not.

I did some informal research into the international community in Budapest, which was strong. I already belonged to nearly all of the English-speaking groups in, near or about Hungary. I had a look at the three biggest groups, and put the word "donations" into the search box. Before the invasion, these were the sorts of requests for donations I found, roughly paraphrased and in random order:

- I am an unidentified do-gooder asking for money for an unidentified children's home, or home for the elderly, or dog shelter, or just people who seem to need it, as I decide, and no details are provided.
- Where can I donate my long, long hair to wig-makers who help people who are bald after chemotherapy or other diseases?
- Let's help a street guy who sells dolls; he seems nice.
- Please donate clothes for models doing my fashion shoot and video.
- Which second-hand shops take half-used lipsticks and other soiled make-up?
- I need boxes to move house.
- My dog hates the dog food I bought in a huge sack – who wants it?
- I am moving house; there's plenty for free, but get here today.
- I want to donate blood but I want to get paid for it.

Most of the above examples stopped after the war started, except for the first one: there was a strong increase in the number of nice-sounding total strangers asking you to make donations of clothes or money, without much further information. Some, of course, were scammers.

The trust issue was everywhere but that wasn't the only thing. We all had to deal with impractical or uninformed idiots too.

But, soon, once I actually got back to the city and visited some of the places offering refugee support, I could answer the various enquiries I received from friends and colleagues far away, willing to donate but unsure who to choose. They wanted an eyewitness, their own trusted reporter on the ground. They knew me and asked for recommendations. I appreciated that vote of confidence. I'd report back and was looking forward to it.

The list of commodities everyone was after: trust, information, food and shelter, not necessarily in that order.

Meanwhile, online I was all over the place, but still not actually back in Budapest. Not yet.

Devotion

> *The first place we went was to the Embassy. We registered another day at Hungarian immigration. A few of their staff could speak English.*
>
> *We were given a Certificate of Entitlement to Temporary Residence. It was like an A4 sheet of paper written in Hungarian with the stamps, signatures, dates and personal details. It was for thirty days. It was not clear whether we could take employment or not, but I don't think so. It wasn't possible for them to explain things clearly. It was very crowded and it all took a long time. I was the last person they answered*

that day.

At that time, it was about settling down and finding a place to sleep, something to eat, and the rest. I didn't ask. It took until night-time when the Embassy was about to close and a lot of us didn't have a place to sleep.

We were in Budapest for about three days. My church friends from the journey and I all got separated at the Embassy. We scattered to all different accommodation.

Focused

After crossing the border, we continued into Budapest. Honestly, I was terrified because I didn't know what would happen next from there. A church took us in, fed us and searched for accommodation for us. Shortly they got something in a town called Erd, organised by them and the mayor of Erd.

After this accommodation was found for us, a boy and two Hungarian ladies from the church took us close to Erd, to the train station, where the mayor of Erd came to pick us up.

Speaker

I'd heard negative reviews about the Polish border, so I didn't go there.

The bus took us through the border and into Budapest. The border was so crowded. We waited inside the bus in line, just standing, for twenty-four hours before we got through. It took those who wanted to go to India to the airport. I had no money and no food. I used the last of the money for the bus.

When we arrived in Budapest, it was early and I was scared. A Hungarian lady helped us. She was a friend of one of the guys with us. We went to immigration that day, and finished the registration the next day. At immigration, they spoke English. They gave us a thirty-day visa. They said transportation in the city was free, for the time.

They explained we could only work with a work permit. [In reality, these were hard to get and took many months plus strong sponsorship by an employer. It was highly unlikely they'd ever see one here. Ukrainian nationals got them automatically.]

After immigration, we went to look for accommodation or a place to spend the time. We searched Airbnb, apartments and hotels, but they were too expensive. No one helped us with this. We did this ourselves.

The church helped us find temporary accommodation. We were taken to Erd. We were eight people. I knew some of them already, from the bus ride.

There was no contact from the Nigerian Embassy, then or ever.

Friday 4 March 2022, Erd, Hungary

In Erd, they were housed in a nursing home for the elderly, which handed over some spare rooms. Someone connected to the church succeeded in persuading the mayor of Erd to find this spare space. There was no kitchen and no food, but there was somewhere to sleep. So, the students were taken there but not exactly told where they were going, or why.

Princess

Princess arrived with her brother a bit later than the others. Later, Princess and Speaker would spend a lot of time together. They were the only women among many men. They sometimes held hands and clung to each other like sisters.

> *We left 2 March and arrived [in Budapest] the next day. All I felt was tired. But there was someone there to help, friends of friends that I did not know. There was no one from the Nigerian Embassy. I was with my brother and his friends.*
>
> *For a few days, I slept at the house of a Christian sister (a Jehovah's Witness). I ate three times a day at her place. Later we (my brother and I) went to a hotel, just before we went to Erd [about two weeks later].*
>
> *It was just my brother and me. When I arrived in Erd and saw the place, I was nervous, but the place was OK.*

Speaker

> *I was scared. At first it looked scary, like a hospital or a lab. Like a hospital that was not approved by the government yet. I was afraid that we would be experimented on. Those fears were gone a day after. There were about ten of us there in total.*

Devotion

When we first arrived there, when we first saw it, we thought it was a hospital or something. We felt scared, thinking it was an asylum. We were willing to sleep at the train station until we were assured it wasn't an asylum.

After they left us there, there were a couple of people from the church who communicated with us. Of the others in Erd, only a few went to the church.

I didn't meet the others (Speaker, Focused, Princess) right away. We were at the same location for a while but we were not in the same building so it took time before we met – even after I had moved to the building where they were located. I think it was on 28 March we all met.

That same day the students met each other in Erd, coincidentally, was also my sixty-fifth birthday. I went to my Vienna Cousins who fed me luxuriously well. I had not yet met these students, who at that time were not eating much at all. That would get fixed, but not until later.

Focused

When we first arrived in Erd, I was scared because the town was far from Budapest. The facility we were taken to looked scary, although it was a home for the elderly. It was ash in colour and looked deserted.

The inside was painted white with transparent windows. We were taken upstairs and there were different rooms with stretchers. There were toilets and showers but no kitchen.

We were the first set of refugees to arrive there. Later, other people came. No one communicated with us after they left us there.

4. Challenges, Covid, More Challenges [1]

March, Week 2, Budapest

Week 2 felt quite different to week 1 – for everyone I spoke to. It was a city-wide feeling, and beyond, way beyond. Before, there was a possibility the war might be squashed fairly quickly. There was less hope of that now. Another 100,000 people poured into Budapest from Ukraine. Most would be gone in a week or a month at most. But others looked for ways to stay, or work, or study, or find some other solution, some other place to go, some way to try to pay for it.

There was a huge proportion of mothers with small children. They spoke less now of when they could go back. They had to decide whether or not to put their kids into local schools. These kids were welcomed, despite some language barriers, but what it represented was painful for the families.

We'd entered a new stage of the crisis. It was much more likely this was a migration and relocation, rather than a temporary refuge before going home. Going home would have to wait, perhaps indefinitely.

Back at the church, I messaged someone new, because the first contact, Miss J, was at home, sick and exhausted. She tested positive for Covid. She said it was inevitable, that a thousand people had come through in the last two weeks. It was chaotic, and needs were changing by the hour.

She steered me to a WhatsApp group full of eager, good, generous volunteers that, ironically, was even more crazily chaotic, so much so that later she advised me to steer clear of it altogether. I did and was glad that I did. Things were disorganised enough.

Texts were now flowing:

J *There was discussion yesterday about the space and kitchen. It's a very small basement space with no ventilation. It's a Covid pit. Two volunteers tested positive. We may remove food from the space, because we don't want everybody to hang out there all day.*
But things are changing daily, that's why I'm telling you, thanks for your work and support!!! Can't wait until you are here ... in two weeks?

E *Yes – can I send anything now?*

J *We don't need any deliveries. Don't even have enough bodies to receive deliveries, everyone is so overwhelmed. But thank you. We need bodies to help escort new arrivals to the Nigerian embassy.*
I'm snowed under. And taking a Ukrainian family in tonight. Wife, husband, 8 year old, and

grandmother.

E *You are a good egg. I have no space but will help in other ways.*

J *Am I a Cadbury Creme Egg? I only want to be a Creme Egg.*

E *Sure!*

This was a reference to the most popular treats for kids arriving. A Creme Egg is chocolate with a pale sweet centre that looked like a soft-boiled egg. Also popular were Kinder Eggs, a hollow chocolate egg with a little toy in the middle. It was getting near Easter season, so eggy chocolates were favoured.

Soon, the church was calling specifically for non-cooked food items. They wanted to stop cooking there. They asked us to send picnic food, food in tins, things that would last and didn't need cooking. I scrubbed the previous order and sent the requested sandwiches, fruit, tinned produce, juice and milk, breakfast oat-and-nut bars, cleaning materials and toiletries.

Thursday 10 March 2022

Mothers and children were leaving Ukraine in their droves, while fathers were required to stay behind.

When President Volodymyr Zelensky declared martial law on 24 February 2022, in response to the Russian invasion, all able-bodied men from eighteen to sixty years old were forbidden to leave the country. [2]

J was blogging stories of people she'd met.

One woman wailed that her husband knew computers, not

fighting. He'd never held a gun. He was their sole breadwinner but not now. There were men back in Ukraine hiding from both the Russian and Ukrainian armies.

> *"A hungry mother and son arrived too late for the free lunch, but a volunteer took them to a nearby restaurant, out of her own pocket. They left Kyiv a week ago. Today was their fourth day in Budapest. They didn't know the city at all or anyone, or how long they will stay, or where they will go next."*
>
> *"One family was half way through their journey to Germany, to a sister. They hoped their empty flat in Kyiv didn't get destroyed. They hoped one suitcase each was enough. They hoped his 84 year old mother could make the journey. They hoped the other parents left behind will somehow manage. Tomorrow, they leave."*

A young British man with his Ukrainian girlfriend: "The train was mostly women and children, or older men. Some men did try to get on the train with their families, but the ticket inspectors and security were very strict, everyone had to show their papers. I have my UK passport, so I was OK. But it was horrible to watch fathers being torn away from their children, some were forcibly removed off the train, some were beaten up because they didn't want to leave. There was so much crying and yelling. Men are required to stay in Ukraine to fight. Those who tried to stay on trains were called 'cowards' and 'traitors' for trying to leave Ukraine. It was terrible."

Stories were pouring out everywhere, and so were helpers, feeders and listeners – in spirit, cousins and good neighbours.

New groups and new apps were popping up all the time. Some of them cross-referenced new arrivals with homeowners open for guests, organising connections by common language.

There also emerged a popular phone app reporting air raid warnings in Kyiv, then in other locations. Red meant bombs were dropping. Green was safe. Red air raid warnings were every few hours. The screenshot covered one day at a time.

At this point, it was official in my mind – in fact, in my heart and soul and from head to toe: I was in dire need of a sense of humour, which seemed to have wandered off. That's never a good sign. In my notes at this point was written in large letters, "Where are the jokes? Please, where's a sense of humour? Where are Hungary's comedians, political cartoonists? Clowns, jesters and fools – but also ordinary people joking around every day, to stop from tearing their hair out in frustration?"

We needed more of the spirit of Tomato Woman and Radio Guy. We needed satire of any kind, we really did. I know I speak for many. Somewhere out there in that overrun city, Hungarians were making savage jokes, I was sure of it. Now, if only someone could translate.

Saturday 12 March 2022

One had to try to stay positive, and this was no small challenge. I was clinging fast to any and all of the political satirists that were available. I listened to them every evening and it kept me going. It was like water in a desert.

In general, my nightly fixes were usually Samantha Bee, Stephen Colbert, Seth Myers, Trevor Noah and *The Daily Show* (especially Jordan Klepper in Hungary), John Oliver and always Jon Stewart – and yes, that was alphabetic on purpose. There was always *Saturday Night Live,* thank heavens, and later came podcast "*Pod Save the USA*. Plus, David Letterman even interviewed President Zelensky.[3] Then, from the UK, there was Russell Howard, Nish Kumar, Rachel Parris, Mark Steel, Mark Thomas; TV programmes like *The Mash Report, Mock the Week* and *Have I Got News For You*, plus radio's *The News Quiz.* I was glued to podcast *Pod Save the UK*, with Nish again and Coco Khan. If you know of new ones, please write to me. We need this river.

I have often found that I cannot watch straight and serious news for very long without the very real possibility of sliding into depression about our species at its worst. Yet for some reason I feel a duty to watch, to not cover my eyes. I'm not very strong-stomached about this. What I can manage usually follows this template:

- The government said this.
- Their opposition said that.
- This repeats endlessly, in what you could call bullshit-tennis.
- Is there a joke somewhere, please?

On US TV, I've heard it said that because an entertainment programme containing political comedy gets far bigger ratings than the usual news, and because there's far more money at stake, the result is that far stricter lawyers are involved. This kind of political comedy is fact-checked more diligently than those who give us The News, mainstream-style. In terms of the traditional US fear of expensive lawsuits, and plain economics, it's a plausible theory: therefore, a comedian's facts may be more trustworthy than a newsreader's. In general, I'd continue to get my news from comedians and my inspiration from Tomato Woman.

Sunday 13 March 2022

Volunteer burnout began. There were volunteer superstars doing amazing amounts of good work, running on only a few hours of sleep each night. This was not, as they say, sustainable. Many of us had learned this the hard way, over many decades, and I was finally getting the hang of that sort of realism.

It's amazing how many volunteers risked their day jobs, but some did. These were the fountains of energy that left the rest of us in the dust. Still, we weaker puny types could contribute too. Tortoises also get there in the end, like in Aesop's fable. It all adds up, in a total village effort.

From J's Blog

> *About a week ago, CNN broke the story of international students trapped in Sumy, Ukraine.*[4] *Some finally escaped and arrived in Budapest. They were received like celebrities of bravery.*
>
> *They spent a night on the train, when they had to turn out all lights and not use phones. They had to hide in darkness and silence, to not be noticed, for fear of being Russian bomb targets.*
>
> *Many students want to stay and to continue their medical school education in Europe.*
>
> *They want to complete their education and to return to their home countries as doctors.*

However, those dreams are in limbo.

For some, the only or best choice they have is to return to their home countries."

The Nigerian Embassy provided an evacuation flight this past Friday, for their citizens in Budapest. Some students have chosen to go back home.

Others were scared to go back because lately their country had been filled with intense violence, terrorism and internal warfare. In a little while, I'd be meeting medical students in much the same boat as these. But in the meantime, they were invisible, stuck and hungry in a town called Erd.

Monday 14 March 2022, Snake Island Update [5]

There's mild but comedy swearing in this section and the next one.

The Ukrainian Post Office issued a commemorative postage stamp to pay tribute to their armed forces, and in particular to the heroes of Snake Island.

The now-iconic postage stamp had few words on it, and certainly not the original quotation spoken by Radio Guy. Some people considered his words obscene. Others were celebrating. The image was a drawing of the view from the island, with a Ukrainian soldier facing the sea and a huge Russian warship. His arm is raised and he's giving the enemy vessel The Finger.

This is also known as giving the middle finger, flipping the bird or flipping someone off. It's the visual equivalent of saying what Radio Guy said.

The stamp soon became known as the "Russian Warship, Go FCK Yourself" stamp. Its release was announced by Ukrainian First Deputy Foreign Minister Emine Dzhaparova. It was chosen by public vote, winning out over twenty other designs.

This limited edition postage stamp sold out immediately and became a collector's item, reselling for $100 each.

Bad Word Warning: An Informal History of Giving The Finger [6]

At its most basic – you might say at heart – it's a symbol of contempt in many cultures, but occasionally in some contexts can be used humorously or playfully.

The gesture dates back to ancient Greece and Rome. It can represent a phallus or a finger up an anus. Either way it's meant to degrade and insult, intimidate and threaten, or mock and ridicule. In the case of representing an erect penis, some people slightly raise the two fingers next to the middle one, to represent testicles. It's also been employed as a defence against evil, or the so-called evil eye.

There's an assortment of references in classical literature, art and philosophy:

In ancient Greek comedy, it was an insult against anyone submitting to anal penetration. Farting in someone's face would get the same sort of laugh. Socrates called the gesture "boorish and stupid".

In ancient Roman sculpture, it was known as the "infamis digitus", and it was used to ward off evil.

In Latin, it was known as the digitus impudicus, meaning "the shameless, indecent or offensive finger".

Other classical references abound throughout Western European history, and this is without even venturing eastwards.

In terms of modern infamy, there are far too many instances to list even a fraction of them. Many athletes, politicians, public figures, musicians, actors and other celebrities have had their moments that only flipping the bird could express, but one instance is noteworthy. The first known photograph of someone giving the finger was in the USA, when Boston Braves baseball pitcher Charles "Old Hoss" Radbourn bestowed it upon a photographer in 1886 during a team photo. This is significant historically, photographically, athletically and comically.

Not all stories ended well. A Malaysian man was bludgeoned to death after giving the finger to a motorist following a car chase. A Pakistani man was deported by the United Arab Emirates for the gesture, which violated indecency codes. In 1968, when the USS *Pueblo* was captured by North Korea, US crewmembers gave the finger in forced photo ops, and were later subjected to extremely severe beatings.

In the case of Snake Island, at first no one thought the Ukrainian soldiers were being beaten because most people assumed they were dead.

The Finger has had less dangerous political applications too. In the free-speaking USA, it's been used by both protesters and those they were protesting against. In the 1960s, activist Abbie Hoffman used it against the now-infamous 1968 USA Democratic Convention. Ronald Reagan, as California's Governor, used it against protesters.

In 1976, Nelson Rockefeller used it against hecklers and it became known as "the Rockefeller gesture". In 1982, Canadian

Prime Minister Pierre Trudeau used it against protesters and it became known as the "Trudeau salute".

In 2017, a lady named Juli Briskman was bicycling along, when Donald Trump's motorcade passed her, and she gave it the finger. A photograph went viral, and she was forced to resign from her job. However, two years later she was elected to public office, to join the Board of Supervisors for Loudoun County, Virginia.

Top prize goes here:

In 2023, a Canadian man stood accused of criminal harassment and uttering threats in a courtroom in Quebec. Judge Dennis Galiatsatos wrote, "It is not a crime to give someone the finger … Flipping the proverbial bird is a God-given, Charter-enshrined right that belongs to every red-blooded Canadian. It may not be civil, it may not be polite, it may not be gentlemanly. Nevertheless, it does not trigger criminal liability." Mr Neall Epstein, the accused, was acquitted.

And finally, The Finger has been culturally enshrined by being given its own emoji (Unicode 1F595), available in a reasonable array of skin tones.

Tuesday 15 March 2022, Meanwhile, Back in Budapest

<u>J's blog: Update from Budapest:</u>

> Local Facebook and WhatsApp groups were full of offers to drive refugees from Hungary to other EU countries. Individual volunteers were driving in the family car to the border, to drop off supplies and offer free rides back to their countries.

One volunteer saw this: “Leaving Friday 7 am for Switzerland, seven seats available, drop off at Swiss refugee centre to be processed, please PM me for reservation for seats (preferably women and children). If not full, we will go to the train station tomorrow to offer directly.”

She tried to convince five sets of mothers with children to consider leaving for Switzerland this Friday. None of them were tempted. They did not know anyone there. They were afraid of being too far from their home.

“Tomorrow, I will look for more free ride opportunities to other EU countries and ask my network of Ukrainian mothers if any want to be packed and be ready to go at a moment’s notice.”

Tuesday 15 March 2022

The church’s kitchen got shut down, officially and for good. They’d been doing their best to cook for the hungry hordes, but it became impossible. It was declared an official health hazard, especially when kitchen staff started getting Covid and disappearing. No more cooking was allowed. We supporters were still sending the requested sandwiches, pre-wrapped and never home-made – that was a government decree. All food had to be purchased from shops. It would be cynical to suggest that this was a health and safety policy overreach. Current patterns suggested that the profit factor was involved. Allegedly. Just a theory, a guess, a tomato not thrown.

In the meantime, another facility was going from strength to strength in feeding the refugees, and this was The Workshop. They were about to get a huge influx of interest in their free lunches and other offerings.

This was a Ukrainian restaurant in the centre of the city. They were usually open in the evenings, but they turned themselves into a refugee centre during the day as "a safe space for refugees to hang out". There was free breakfast, lunch and drinks, and there was a pool of volunteers and interpreters.

It was open all day, six days a week. Refugees could use free WiFi, print documents, find accommodation, connect with family and friends, and even sometimes work remotely, if possible.

Everyone streaming into the church for a meal was redirected there – once it was clarified that when they said refugees from Ukraine, they meant anyone fleeing the bombs, not just Ukrainians. Politics to one side, all of them needed some help. Some places offered help to Ukrainians but not to anyone else. One had to ask.

Wednesday 16 March 2022

In the meantime, refugees continued to pour into Budapest. They poured and poured and poured in. It's all anyone could talk about. That's why some of the following was considered absurd:

On this day, Prime Minister Viktor Orbán said that "in the next three days, the government will organise how to continue[!] to assist those in need…" The exclamation mark was added by the researcher who found that quote, because no one saw the government providing any assistance to anyone in need, not in that first month. This researcher found out that they gave money to churches and the Red Cross, but offered no manpower or admin help at all, expecting these two groups to organise and handle everything themselves, while coordinating with many completely unsupported groups.

And of course, there was always the question of whether or not that money ever reached its intended destination. This was a constant suspicion in this part of the world.

Mr O. continued that the war was not calming down, rather it was expanding. It was baffling to hear this presented as news, a few weeks after the fact had become startlingly obvious to everyone else.

He added that, as the war expanded, there was a risk that more people would arrive in Hungary the following week. This too, was a statement of the obvious. By now everyone knew there were more coming. It was inevitable, not "a risk". He was a few weeks late yet again.

He concluded that this would pose a huge challenge to the country, but it was already posing a huge challenge. Why was this statement so belated?

Why was I asking such a naïve question?

Was he blowing hot air, more double-speak?

Yes of course, and I needed a short break from it.

One night that week, falling asleep with my laptop on my belly, I drifted into memories of long ago, of my childhood, in the primary school years. You could say these childish daydreams were my earliest searches, in this case for usefulness projects – not the doable, small-scale, sustainable and realistic projects I was currently in search of, but completely overinflated, imaginary superhero sorts of projects.

A favourite wishful daydream back then was to become a philanthropist, before I'd ever heard that word. The idea was to travel around the globe, plunking hospitals wherever they were needed. I pictured that literally. I imagined flying around and hurling whole hospitals out of planes, flinging them perfectly into place in a convenient area of each town or city, all full of staff and gear, all ready to go, functioning instantly and humming like a well-oiled machine.

I also used to imagine plunking a fortune into an account that funded all these hospitals' needs for one hundred years, as well as employing staff to sort out how they would pay for the next hundred years.

This was after the earlier, pre-school activity of re-branding a doll named Tammy – a sort of Barbie clone. I got rid of her apron and her cocktail dress, renamed her Supergirl, dressed her with a cape, rugged clothes and sensible boots, and sent her flying all over the place, rescuing people from floods and earthquakes. Maybe some landslides too.

It's sad to say that with regard to some of these aims and themes, I lacked the ability and the will to pursue and acquire the mountains of money required, quite apart from other superpowers.

Meanwhile, in present-day challenges, the search continued for usefulness – a project that was realistic, not overwhelming, doable and perhaps not just emergency help, but longer-range help of some kind. I didn't know exactly what that meant, but I meant to pursue some sort of answer.

I wasn't there yet, although I was there in spirit.

SPRING EQUINOX 2022

Across Europe

5. Get Home, Hit the Ground Running

Monday 21 March 2022, Spring Equinox, Budapest

On the way to my flat from Budapest's Ferenc Liszt International Airport, I was lucky to have a very nice cabbie. This was a treat, since there were always so many negative possibilities. We chatted a bit as an introduction, and then he let me daydream out the window. A perceptive, relaxed fellow with good priorities, he focused on the road, a moderate speed and unusually calm driving manners for this part of the world. The sunny clear day made it impossible not to smile. We zipped along the boulevard, past the city's beautiful, beloved, classically crumbling old buildings with their charming, frilly ornamentation from the days of the Austro-Hungarian Empire, those elegant hand-kissers. Some Soviets hated this about the Hungarians: too much charm and hand-kissing, too much strudel, too many pretty cafés. Not enough grey for them. Not enough khaki.

I was elated to be back, recalling how I came here five years ago, researched my ancestral history, intended to stay a month, but found cousins and friends and stayed several years. Budapest and I were pals – newish ones, but pals. I'd grown warmly fond of the place, and now I could say I had roots here.

My ancestors – what would they say? Some might be puzzled, others sceptical. I'd like to think someone might see the humour, but Dad's people were not the smiling, laughing sort, but more to the dour side. It was ironic in any case that they firmly ran away from this city, and I was running just as firmly towards it.

My Hungarian grandparents had two very different stories. Grandma Anna emigrated to New York for the usual reasons: to escape relative poverty – in her case, on a small obscure farm – and to seek a more comfortable life, as so many millions did. And she succeeded. Of my grandparents, Anna and Eugene, she was the true potato in the Big Apple. The family called them City Mouse and Country Mouse, after the children's story. She was the country bumpkin, a muscular farmgirl with an eighth-grade education. He was middle class, better-educated, with more money and from the big city. In the story, the country mouse visits the city but flees back home to comfort and rural safety. Grandma, on the other hand, sailed away to New York City and never looked back. There, in her case, she met her city mouse, Eugene, and married him, and the rest is our US branch – including myself.

As for Eugene, that was another story altogether. He was certainly not referenced in the noble offer of the Statue of Liberty, that welcoming Mother of All Exiles, who proclaimed via poet Emma Lazarus in "The New Colossus" (1883): [1]

"Give me your tired, your poor,

Your huddled masses yearning to breathe free,

The wretched refuse of your teeming shore.

Send these, the homeless, tempest-tossed to me,

I lift my lamp beside the golden door!"

Isn't that grand? That was not Granddad in the least. He was no potato. There was nothing poor, huddled or wretched about him. Family said he held up a bourgeois little finger when drinking tea, English style with milk, never lemon. He was not homeless but upper-middle class and trying to escape fraud charges due to his own dumb, youthful mistakes. That story was told in *Noodle Trails 2.*

Thus began the US branch of our tree back in 1906. It was not reunited with – or even much aware of – our Hungarian branch until after 2016, when my research and tenacious digging began.

In the 1940s, by the time the Second World War was underway, our US branch was safely ensconced in the New York City of the New World, unaware that dozens of our cousins in Europe had perished at the hands of the Nazis or their Hungarian fascist collaborators like the Arrow Cross or simply unrestrained thugs needing any excuse. Only a few escaped, like Cousin Andreas in Vienna.

Nowadays I thought of them all, and hoped they might approve of my attempts to find a way to assist people fleeing war, as so many of us had fled, as well. I wasn't joining many discussions of this or any particular war, or its politics or economics. I was wanting to take a humanitarian focus, where possible.

So, under these bizarre circumstances, returning to the city while millions were arriving to flee yet another of the wars on offer on this planet, it was like heading towards a flood, and then a series of more floods that were going in various directions. This would be one of the biggest human migrations this century, and I'd never witnessed anything this huge, historically.

I tipped the driver well, and he was surprised. He deserved it, he was so considerate. I buzzed myself inside, yet again asking myself if, in the event of an electrical problem, would we be trapped inside, with this sort of electrical buzz-gate? I have never had an adequate answer to that question, only evasiveness, which is worse. In an attempt at emergency thinking, I do have heavy rope near my balcony, knotted at intervals, but I doubt I'd have the strength to shimmy down it, to the street below. But that was the plan.

Yet again putting all this out of my mind, it was quietly thrilling and comforting to be back in this building. I knew it was probably a temporary home but it was home for now, and it was lovely.

It was a classic old beauty, built before 1900, later renovated in a Bauhaus style, and well looked after to this day. It felt like a fort. It had sheltered people from the Nazis, just like a similar building down the road hid our cousin Jolán. It had history and style and a courtyard with nice big trees and a picnic table. It had pretty mosaic floor tiles, cool stone steps and an old lift of rich dark wood and a fold-down seat that ought to be in a classic 1940s black and white movie.

The nice landlady had locked every silly lock there was, and there were five, which was funny because, other than my computer which was usually on my body, there was disappointingly little to steal, unless the thieves were truly in bad straits, in which case they were welcome to the sheets, the plates, the tinned corn.

In that moment of stepping back in, what was my first thought? I loved this place. The honey-coloured parquet floor cast a warm glow. What good fortune to live here! What a fine win-win situation this was: I was a conscientious, deserving, great tenant, and they were responsible, deserving, great landlords. We'd shaken hands and we both really meant it. Trust! An honest mutual agreement is a beautiful thing, especially here where the city was teeming with enraged, arguing tenants and landlords. We were agreed and fine.

Although not usually a gushy sort, I had to confess that I truly loved being here, in this place, in this city, in our ancestral homeland, where this people's history of suffering and cynicism gave them a special brand of black humour, deadpan irony and eternally deep sarcasm. I was developing a taste for it. My own grandparents may have over-emphasised darker points of view, but I hope to keep alive the absurdist humour embedded in our historical legacy.

And surely too, in general, there must be hope and the seeds of daisies underground, anywhere. Hope grows like daisies, even through concrete.

***

First steps first: I had to get my own house in order, get the groceries in, then make a list of whatever might be next. Those lists would probably soon generate more lists, and so be it. Once my house was sorted, I could face the outside world.

The flat was surprisingly tidy. That's not what I remembered.

I'd left in a hurry, and assumed that slovenly sights would greet me on return. It was suspiciously presentable, as if for guests. Then I remembered, it *was* for guests. The Vienna Cousins were invited to visit while I was away. Vera and Andi were tier 2 cousins i.e. twice removed - her dad and I shared a great-grandmother. They were my first guests when I was new here, a few years ago. That visit was a joy. I thoroughly enjoyed buying the extra sheets, blankets, pillows, in anticipation of that inaugural visit. A home is not a home until you're ready for guests.

As it happened, this time the cousins had no chance to use my cool pad as a weekend bolthole. There would be other chances, but not forever. I was a guest in Budapest, ultimately, too – a resident but not a citizen. Before, I'd been dreaming about perhaps retiring there, and was in the middle of exploring that territory. Still, it wasn't a fervent search, especially since learning their eccentric language was, at present for me, a slow and annoying process. That was language number nine for me and I was not enthusiastic. Other priorities called more. I felt less a resident and more a regular visitor.

The lady who lived here before in this flat was elderly, and had been there a long time. She'd been there since "The War", as many call the Second World War although nowadays, "The War" probably refers to Ukraine. She retired as a widow here and died at an advanced age. I nicknamed her Rose.

I often thought of her when I sat at the kitchen window, which was by far the best seat in the house. There's no way she didn't sit there by the window where the branches of the walnut tree were almost within reach and sometimes held sleeping mourning doves. How could she not sit right there? I once asked a neighbour about her but they protectively said she was private, so I did not pry further. Instead, I made an imaginary vow to her that I'd look after the place carefully and sweetly, especially in the kitchen.

Then I fell into some fake news. I found a stack of children's books, all in Hungarian, all looking charming. I imagined they must have been for her grandchildren. I was quite happy embroidering upon that hypothetical scenario when my landlady informed me that just before I lived there, there was a divorced guy whose kids visited on the weekends, and those books were for them. She took them away for her kids' school and I reminded myself to remember that sometimes a theory is just a theory and nothing more. Beware of possibly fake news and possibly wrong assumptions. This was the message.

In the meantime, the courtyard garden looked promising, walnut tree included. It was fairly naked but with lots of little green spring buds, knotted tight. Today was the Spring Equinox. A new season stated today! Next door's garden was stripped down to its pure brown base, with no cover for the big pink flamingo statue. That thing was unexplainable, which is what I liked. I hoped it was controversial too. It was a pink prank in a grey climate. The social climate could feel grey too, around here and, some say, across Eastern Europe. It's often said there's a tendency toward melancholy here. The cadence of the language is based on emphasising the first syllable of every word and then things trail away, over and over. To an outsider it can give the impression of moaning, groaning, sighing, pleading, imploring, yearning, or just a bit miserable.

Practicality is a good answer to anything, I find, so I unpacked, separated things into categories and left them there, splayed all over the room, waiting their turn to go to their cubbyholes. One step at a time.

Life was all about textiles for a while: one load of laundry was done, another waiting to go in.

The slow toilet drip was still there, like last time – slow but tolerably slow. The bucket was nearly full but not overflowing, so that was under control.

As for food, another surprise greeted me in the kitchen. I'd left a ton of groceries. The cupboards, shelves and freezer were packed full. I didn't remember doing that, but apparently I'd gone overboard at the thought of guests. Today's huge grocery list could be shaved down to fresh fruit and vegetables, which I'd go get in person, plus a reward slice of pizza. I contentedly trotted down the road to my usual places, and that was always a pleasure – to feel like a regular. I was also an outsider, a foreigner and a stranger, but a regular and known to be well-behaved.

Otherwise, in terms of refugee support, I started at home, where most people started, in my own cupboards. A strict clear-out produced several bags of things to be donated: clothing, food, toiletries – according to the requirements I'd read. This was not above and beyond the call of duty, as I needed to declutter anyway. This bag was placed by the door, and would soon head to Nyugati station where somewhere, nearby, someone was bound to be collecting such donations.

I had rules about these sorts of bags. Once it was by the door, it had to go, and as soon as possible. In the past, they had a way of sneaking back in, but not now. The new policy was firm and well-established. Onwards and outwards and never to return, that was the motto and I stuck to it.

In the meantime, outdoors was bright, sunny and crisply cold. I had a lovely invigorating stroll through the neighbourhood, and walked a favourite route, got a bagful of fruit and vegetables from the nice older lady near the tram, then bought a treat at the best pizza place nearby There were four pizza places that tempted me daily, all close to home.

These guys were always friendly and didn't mind switching to English for me. The long-haired one was cleverly juggling spatulas. We joked about upping his game, the way bartenders do ultimate juggling with bottles and other things that break.

It's nice to be a regular, where they smile when you walk in, and you all know you can joke around.

That entire stroll, I was grinning contentedly and could not stop. I was so happy to be back. I struck up a few neighbourly conversations, all cheerful, all sweet, all simple. It was a delight to be accepted as a good neighbour, and to feel like one. Everybody was up for friendly, sunny chit-chat. I did my beloved riverside stroll, said "Hi" to the Danube, and sailed home on a flood of gratitude, ready for the next proper full Day 1, where I'd plunge blindly into this refugee aid scene and see where the currents would take me.

***

In some ways the ensuing week was a total blur. My various newly joined internet groups were awash with messages, which appeared by the hundreds if not thousands, every day:

Help, family of 8 (2 old, 2 parents, 2 kids, 2 dogs). Needs a room for a week. Who can help?

Hello, I drive to Vienna every day, who needs help?

I took the donations to Nyugati station. Bizarrely enough, the station was quiet, both inside and out. Maybe there was a lull in the train timetable. By all accounts, this area was either a mad, frantic beehive or empty as a desert. It depended when trains arrived from Ukraine.

I'd been following these activities, so I knew the Red Cross was there, as was Migration Aid. I'd read all kinds of accounts of people showing up with home-baked food, sandwiches, cookies, coffee and tea (the weather was still very cold in March).

There was one role I was delighted to take on. Refugees arrived with mobile phones but no way to connect. There was no free WiFi inside the station. They couldn't text loved ones to say they were safe, and they also had to wait a long time in line to get a place to stay. They needed local maps, a thousand bits of info – they needed to be online, especially during all that initial waiting.

Therefore, local people volunteered to be human WiFi hotspot providers. They met an arriving train with their phone charged up and a big sign displaying the code, and all the arrivals would gather around and phone home. I could do that! I was all ready, had a folding chair, and even imagined a sign in several languages. But fate intervened the next day. My fantasy of acting as a human internet hub was not to be realised.

The next time I went to the station, ready to ask how to set that up, everything was gone. The Red Cross, Migration Aid, all the helpers and their tables, the women with sandwiches, water bottles, everything I expected to be there, had disappeared. This was more than puzzling. It was disturbing. Where was everybody?

As of that lovely crisp early spring morning, Budapest was a changed city. No more totally clogged train stations, only moderately clogged in the usual way. Many trains from Ukraine were no longer arriving at Nyugati station, but were sidelined, and everyone was taken to a sports stadium called the BOK centre. This was one of Mr O's many stadiums (he collects them, it's a controversial hobby). It was converted into an emergency accommodation and transit centre. Some used the phrase "detention centre". It would have been very useful several weeks ago and that's a darkly deep understatement.

This new use of BOK Hall B had been announced by the Prime Minister's Office on Friday 18 March and it was opened officially the following Monday,[2] which explained why I found very few people at a train station which until recently, had been swamped. This was 21 March, Spring Equinox, and my arrival day.

There had been reports of many snags when NGOs' help points were removed from train stations. There were problems for refugees arriving in the following days by normally scheduled trains rather than extra trains laid on exclusively for refugees – those trains went straight to the BOK processing centre. These were arriving to no help at all, no clues about processing or anything.

It was reported that at the train stations, there was a lack of well-thought-out assistance. The help desk was not near the arriving train but on the other side of the station, the police officers on duty did not provide assistance (only answering if they were asked), and there was a shortage of official translators (only one person). They also closed the mobile toilets, which were previously free of charge at the railway stations.

Nevertheless, the good Hungarian people kept finding

places to hand out sandwiches and drinks, spare rooms and spare couches.

Plenty of people noticed that when most of the refugees disappeared from the train stations, it gave the impression that the problem was solved, just swept away. This was a convenient impression to give people just a few weeks away from an election. There was no proven connection, of course, but it was accepted widely as obvious.

The BOK centre was getting mixed reviews, to say the least. One volunteer repeatedly witnessed white Ukrainians at the train station being immediately escorted to the ticket counter and encouraged to move as soon as they could, while Africans had their passports inspected and then were left standing there with no direction. But, in the weeks to come, what most people were disturbed by was the secrecy and lack of information about the place, and what was going on in there. This led some to call it a detention centre, in the darkest sense of that phrase. There was simply no way to know.

GASH, the student group, went from strength to strength, but the Amen Church was losing other volunteers and some of their credibility. On the one hand, there would later be suggestions and allegations that donated money did not go where it was promised. On the other hand, I cannot offer hard evidence. I can say that overall, unlike charities who also escape taxation, religious institutions are not known for their financial transparency – quite the opposite. I wish they were. In this case, some aid volunteers may have come to similar conclusions. There were basic differences of opinion about such fundamental things as who must obey whom, who must ask permission to do this or that with their own money, on their own websites, with their own fundraising activities. Some volunteers felt bullied, mistreated and used. Some left.

GASH struggled on as best they could. But many other volunteers fled that venue and contributed to other similar projects in the city. Many chose to do their own individual private fundraising, among friends – along the same lines as I'd be doing in a few months' time. I'd never have guessed that, earlier on. At first, I was only following other people's initiatives, pitching in with bits of time and bits of money, where I could. If a kitchen needed a few sacks of rice and lentils, I'd throw a tenner their way. There was a massive maze of things like that, in those early, whirly-swirly days.

In the meantime, back at Nyugati station with my pathetic little bags of clothing, shoes and soap, I could see there was only one tent left, not in or near the station itself, but across the main road and the tram tracks, near the shopping plaza and the underground entrance.

They had basics to hand out. They were happy to take donations. They looked quite organised. Their tent had a logo with a funny little cartoon dog. He was cute. He had two tails. I made a note to find out who this 'MKKP' was. It rang a vague bell.

6. The Hungarian Two-Tailed Dog Party [1]

MKKP (Magyar Kétfarkú Kutya Párt) started in the early 2000s as pranksters, doing political satire and surrealism via street art, graffiti, posters, and also public protests, with Gergely Kovács as leader.

A quick disclaimer: the name of this party is nothing to do with the English saying, "as happy as a dog with two tails". I think they'd like the idea of a dog so happy and excited, his wagging tail looks like two. But, I was told by linguistic experts that Hungarians don't measure happy excitement in dog tails, but in monkey tails, as in "happy as a monkey with his tail" (örül, mint majom a farkának)

It's over twenty years since the early days of the Dogs, as many people fondly call them. Nowadays they also take serious action with small community projects on a local level. Their slogan is "The only sensible choice". They take a strong liberal, almost libertarian, position on most issues. They still joke around too. And sometimes it's difficult to tell the difference. But here are some of the best examples from their website, translation here thoughtfully provided:

- Let's say we (allegedly, in theory) put graffiti on the walls of the János Hospital (we totally did not do that, I swear!): the wall gets properly painted for the first time in decades.
- We redecorate piles of trash left on the streets, they are moved immediately.
- We paint the broken sidewalk, it gets mended.
- We also build really nice bus stops. So far only one has been demolished.

(Now they do not sign their names any more on bus shelters. When they did that before, their political opponents often vandalised the shelters. Now unmarked ones are safer.)

They were officially registered as a political party in 2014, but began their political mischief back in 2006, when they participated unofficially in their first election as what was then called a joke party. It's still sometimes called a joke party today, by detractors, like the ones now allegedly vandalising the bus shelters that the Dogs sponsor.

They promised eternal life, world peace, a one-day work week and two sunsets per day. Well, why not? If politicians make meaningless promises, why can't we all? How about absurd joking all round? How about making promises as lovely, absurd and fantastical as possible, since it's all fiction anyway? The leap from fact to fiction is huge: leaping from fiction to satire is not a big step by comparison.

Their humour is often surrealistic. For example, all of their many candidates that year were identically named István Nagy (like a Hungarian John Smith). One particular István Nagy was shown on a poster as a cartoon two-tailed dog, with the caption "He's so cute, surely he isn't going to steal".

They staged silly things in a grey nation. Many Hungarians have called them refreshing, in a place that's increasingly depressed and has lost its sense of humour."

I think all satire is not just light entertainment but is desperately needed, so I liked the idea of a political party with a sense of humour. In fact, it was more than just liking humourists; rather, one's sanity started to need them. When we stop laughing, this is an unhealthy sign. It's a warning signal – personally, socially, culturally.

Here's a twist to Hungarian elections that I did not know: the government gives their citizens money if they run for public office. The snag is that there have been completely bogus parties that took that money and disappeared. At least fourteen fake parties attempted to register in 2018 according to Euronews. Some of these were the Party for the Poor, the Party for All the Poor, the Hungarian Party of Poor People, the Hungarian Party for People Who Want to Do.

What do they want to do? That's the question. Satirist John Oliver thought it might be a no-nonsense Eastern European orgy, where they're all shouting that they want to do! They want to do, right now!

In the meantime, it's well worth a skip through some highlights of MKKP's history.

A History [2]

Since 2006

Founding members met as students in a provincial university town in southern Hungary called Szeged. Later, one of their joke campaign promises, along with eternal life, lower taxes, etc., was the construction of a mountain in Szeged, which is as flat as flat can be.

They made a series of mock ads for the Hungarian railways with slogans like "Our trains are deliberately delayed" and "We go out of our way not to clean the trains". Their targets were not amused and sued them, but the charges were dismissed by the court.

In another instance, police caught Kovács spray-painting "For Sale" on a public rubbish bin. The officers agreed not to report him so long as he allowed them to spray-paint "For Sale" on his stomach. "It seemed like a good deal to me," Kovács said.

2009

Three hundred people protested at the Hungarian Central Statistical Office to demand: "Tomorrow should be yesterday!"; "Look stupid!"; "Disband!"; "What do we want? Nothing! When do we want it? Never!"

2010

In the 2010 elections, when Mr O. finally got his super-majority, the Two-Tailed Dog logo appeared with a necktie on a series of unconventional campaign posters. The title of their so-called party programme was "Let everything be better!" One of their candidates ran for mayor of Budapest.

Their main promises were summed up in the slogan "Eternal life, free beer, tax deduction!"

Other offers were "We'll introduce the Euro in 2005!" (this was in 2010); "More everything, less nothing!"; "Are you tired of people? Give another species a chance. Vote for the Two-Tailed Dog."

They also promised to introduce new express metro lines that don't stop anywhere.

Another popular slogan was "We promise anything!" That might sum it all up.

In Erzsébetváros (district VII, Budapest), the mayoral candidate of the party was stand-up comedian Dániel Mogács. In the end, he could not run because the party could not collect enough "knocking tickets" (voter recommendations) for him to run in the election. But it's a reminder that Ukraine elected a former comic actor, the USA elected a TV host who plays the clown, and democracy is unpredictable.

2014

In July, they applied to register as a political party, for real. This was initially rejected by a municipal court for being "frivolous" but that court decision was overturned. MKKP, the Two-Tailed Dog Party, was registered as an official Hungarian political party.

"We joke around much more seriously now," said co-founder Suzi Dada (pen-name of Zsuzsanna Döme).

Kovács added it was time to get serious, but not to become serious, convinced that they're much more effective as "passivists" rather than activists.

Political satire is saving our sanity and it always has done. If I listen to or read too much serious news or anything in the usual style of political or economic debate, afterwards I feel the need for a very thorough shower. I certainly do not feel better, revved and ready for another day. After being poisoned, polluted and spewed at with word-rubbish, manipulations, lies and spin, one can only take so much of it.

But on the other hand, if a comedian follows bad news with

a punchline, I'm listening, I'm there waiting for more and I cannot thank them enough.

Where were Hungary's social and political humourists? Had the opposition gone underground? Were there right-wing, racist, fascist comedians out there, and did I even want to open such a file? Was I asking a load of vague, rhetorical questions because I had no idea who Hungary's comedians were? And, was I rightly suspecting there were not many stand-up comedians at all, even fewer political satirists, and almost no one would arrive with subtitles?

In the meantime, back in 2022 and on a more serious note, how did this so-called joke party become serious contributors to the refugee aid crisis? What was that cute little dog doing on that crucially important tent? MKKP was organising volunteers, donation collection, distribution. They were not joking about that.

In 2022, Hungary's "joke party" was serious about getting into parliament. However, they were also well-known for their ridiculously silly campaign pledges, so would they be taken seriously enough?

Overall, more and more people see where this party is actually deeply serious. Their bid for parliament is serious, and they have serious political goals. They also happen to be funny, and they use humour in their politics.

For opposition voters, the government's words and actions are so contradictory and weird that the line has been blurred between political jokes and reality. This is generally the source of so much surreal, absurd comedy.

And tragedy too, of course.

7. Meanwhile, Forgotten in Erd

March, Week 3, Erd

Focused

We were completely without food when we first arrived, and nothing was provided. The only possibility nearby was KFC or Burger King, which was costing us all we had saved up. We ate KFC once a day for over a month.

But then, different people on Facebook reached out, sent us food, and also came over.

There was confusion about whether we could cook there or not. Hotplates were donated, and ingredients to cook with, sent by anonymous people. But we weren't allowed to cook or use the hotplate. It was considered a fire hazard.

During that time, we repeatedly requested ways to cook, but this did not work out. This is when one of us contacted the church again. They provided cooked food every Saturday and Sunday. Other anonymous people reached out and sent things or delivered them.

Altogether, we were in Erd almost two months – all of March, some of April. Most of the time, we got to know each other, attended classes online or slept. We were all trying to rest and recover.

We were not able to focus and study all the time. Some people were unable to study, due to personal upset – including me. Some were able to cope surprisingly well, although some people were not really showing their real emotions.

We went out for food and exercise, but I stayed indoors a lot. It was cold.

Speaker

During this time, we only ate once a day. Later, it was a collection of different people that helped solve this food shortage.

In the nursing home, we sometimes saw the elderly residents. Most of them were in the same building with us. They didn't speak English. We sometimes had contact with the staff who took care of them. We asked the staff for soap, and we asked questions about the place.

Everyone was trying to study, attend online classes and prepare for their exams. But most of us were down emotionally.

We went out for walks and exercise. We went out a lot just to get our mind off the situation and to also buy some personal things.

It was not possible to apply for a stipend to stay in Hungary. We searched for other medical schools where perhaps we could transfer, but none were willing to accept us. We were constantly searching online for information to help us, in this time.

Devotion

I didn't meet the others right away. We were at the same location for a while but we were not in the same building so it took time before we met – even after I had moved to the building where they were located. I think it was on 28 March we all met.

I'd not met them yet. That was ahead. But, coincidentally, the day they met each other, 28 March, was also my birthday, in fact it was a big birthday – it was the day I officially turned senior, age 65.

Meanwhile, the students, as refugees, had been officially processed and could stay a month. Their education and life plans had been literally bombed out of existence and they needed a new path forward, but first they needed the basics. They had rooms, beds and showers, but they did not have much on the kitchen table. For them, the grocery issue was next.

I didn't yet know anything about that or about them. That was still ahead. We would soon connect.

8. Bag-Ladies of the Resistance, Madeleine's Sexual Warfare

Monday 21 March 2022

Migration Aid did tremendous good during this time, earning only grudging praise from the government – who had opposed and criticised them strongly in 2015.[1] Recently, a representative of the Hungarian prime minister said, in response to a question from a journalist, that he admitted that the activities of Migration Aid were something that the government supported to a large extent and thanked. Not totally, but to a large extent. Previously, they labelled this NGO as a political front, a puppet of George Soros, an outfit for organising immigrants to invade the country and impose a violent take over. [2]

For the uninitiated: Soros is a Hungarian-born billionaire and educational philanthropist, now in his nineties, who founded CEU (Central European University). This university had the aim of fostering free speech, which probably explains why it was forced to close by the government and had to move to Vienna.

Soros was accused of having a secret plot to flood the country with migrants, his alleged motive being that he was Jewish and therefore trying to subvert a Christian nation by flooding it with Muslims. There were many people who believed this. I heard from some of them directly on the Budapest Metro.

At the time, I distinctly recall Budapest being plastered with posters in a startlingly disproportionate way. The reigning leader's materials were mostly what you saw, by far, everywhere. Opposition party posters were small, few and only on street posts. Escalators to the underground were flanked by dozens of reigning party posters. It was bizarrely one-sided.

There were also streams of posters of a face I did not know. It was not a politician. When I asked for translations, I was told this was George Soros. Hungarians gave me two very different interpretations of Mr O's posters of Soros, and what this had to do with the election. Some people said this was a smear campaign, promoting racial fear, creating a rumour that Soros as a villain trying to destroy white Hungary. Others said they really did have racial fear, that Soros was a villain, and that they were afraid that most dark and/or Muslim foreigners probably were terrorists. Solution? Big Mr O will protect them – from the fiction he created. Provoking hate and paranoia could be a classic vote-grabber. It worked for Adolf and others, after all.

That was the government's narrative, back then in 2015 with the Syrians, when they hated Migration Aid who helped anyone running from bombs, regardless of religion or race. At that time, Hungary built fences and refused to let any refugees stay or even pass through.[3] Another common comment from government supporters was that this was not racially motivated. Instead, they said there were cultural differences. Another example of a so-called cultural issue was that Slovakia only took in Christian Syrians, saying the reason was that they had no mosques. Did it not occur to them that they could build a mosque? I suspect that was not the issue. One can build anything. One can build a totalitarian fascist state, if one can instil enough fear into people.

Then suddenly in 2022, just a few years later, the government grudgingly deemed the charity to be OK. It was a quick and total turnaround, a game, a dance – a policy cha-cha. Or, more bullshit-tennis. This time, the war victims they were supporting were not from another culture. They were pale-skinned church-goers with nice suitcases. They did not need as much help, so therefore they got more – this was the so-called logic.

Tuesday 22 March 2022

I had a list of places to visit, and it was probably an arbitrary decision to start with this one. As long as I went down the list over the course of this week, I'd reached that goal. Today, I went to the Migration Aid Shelter on Madrid street, on a somewhat long and winding bus ride.

Since 2015, the mission of Migration Aid (or Mig-aid) has been to help anyone trying to escape from a war, any war – and they have dealt with a few. Their website, which is in Hungarian, English and German, states:

> *Since the Hungarian government did not provide any assistance to normalise the situation, local civilians spontaneously organised assistance in support of*

those who had to leave their home. The coordination was typically conducted through Facebook groups, one of which was named Migration Aid by Sándor Ujhelyi, the founder of the group. Later they became a non-profit company, Migration Aid International ... We are typically on the front lines of helping, we come into contact with the escapees when they are still on their way. We build bridges between strangers and recipients.

I'd prepared ahead by checking their wish list. It was clear and lengthy. I proceeded to one of the best cheap markets for bargain hunting near me, and a personal favourite, Lehel market, home of aggressive shoppers in sensible shoes and kerchiefs under their chins. Yes, those women … you know the ones. Cheaper by the dozen that day were men's boxer shorts, women's socks and underpants, female hygiene items, nappies and the constantly requested fresh fruit. I trimmed my weekly pizza and treats-for-the-week budget accordingly.

Then came the hunt for a bus I didn't know, to an edge of the city I'd not heard of. Did Angyalföld really mean Angel Land? Here it was bleak and grey, partly industrial and partly unidentifiable.

Even at my advanced and experienced age, I can feel apprehensive approaching a place for the first time on my own. I went slowly up the path toward the building. It was simple and modern, narrow, about four stories high. It might house a few hundred people, at a guess. I'd read this was mainly Ukrainian mothers with children.

Outside, halfway along the path was a covered storage area

occupied by a gang of young people. At the moment, they were not doing much, just chatting to one another. Their job was clearly not that of receptionist, let alone a welcome party. At the sight of me, all smiles dropped, all chatter stopped, and obviously all joking and flirting fell to total silence until I entered the building. I can only hope it resumed immediately after that. I was not trying to block anyone's fun. They were young teens, and nervous with it.

Inside, the large reception area was clean and organised, but also quiet and tense. Around the edges of the room and down a corridor were young women, each seated separately, half of them on their phones. The others were either filling in papers or simply sitting and waiting. Most looked worried or depressed. No one was talking to anyone else. I didn't see any kids. But I'd read that this place made an effort to provide a variety of child support, play areas and activities – if there were enough volunteers. There were notices all around to that effect. The kids were playing or resting somewhere, together, one hoped, with some kindly souls gently looking over them. One hoped.

Straight ahead in an L-shape were two tables and five volunteers, all smart, attentive and speaking many languages. They were all white, female, middle class and middle aged. I went to the information table and found English speakers – all of them. I said I had some donations.

Their reactions were striking and familiar, and might seem odd if you hadn't been in their shoes before. It was the Unwanted Gift issue, yet again. I'd seen this dozens of times before in a variety of volunteer organisations, with great sympathy but mostly practicality. At the sound of the word "donation" they flinched, and then asked what exactly had I brought? I said I'd followed their online list, and they were visibly relieved.

"Wonderful," sighed the lady who rose to join me. "Our storage area is – well, you'll see."

I have been there so many times. I have volunteered for charities that were routinely used as a dumping ground for people's unwanted miscellany or rubbish, and, lots of time, backache and occasionally money was spent getting rid of it.

I was led up the stairs. I saw what she meant. It was like a Rubik's cube in there. The shelves were stuffed tightly all the way to the ceiling, and ruled over with military precision by a tall grey-haired woman who was especially glad to see small women's socks. I said I'd chosen from the Today Please List, and she approved. She inspected my bag, smiled at my choices and began putting them away. She was not talkative. She had a lot to do and she was busy doing it. Then people came with requests and I was in the way, so I went back down the stairs.

This place did look well-staffed and well-organised, which is more than one can say about many such efforts. I was truly impressed by them and by what I learned on their website. They had loads of volunteers. I found myself wandering out the door before even thinking of donating time. Maybe there was somewhere closer to me? I could still send this place socks, or fruit, by remote.

***

My intention that week was to visit a few of these places, with the hope that eventually I'd discover where to zoom in and focus on one job – one role to play, one project where I could follow through, at least somewhat.

I left the grounds feeling lighter and better in some ways, but frustration was part of everything these days, including my wrecking the social lives of those same teenagers in the forecourt, for the damned second time that afternoon. How inconsiderate am I? I scooted through the flirtation station and headed for the bus stop, bumping my empty roller-bag behind me.

Walking past a large window, I caught sight of myself and noticed that I was only a few garments and props away from the look of a homeless bag-lady, which made me laugh. This was not the first time I've spotted this potential. If I needed to complete such a disguise, it would not take much. Then, especially if I were horribly fragrant, I could be carrying anything in the mad shopping cart – guns, fake passports, foreign currencies, anything. If it were wartime, I could join the Resistance properly. What a pleasing daydream.

Even now, showered and in OK dull clothes, I was still mostly invisible, just another boring grey old lady trying to do boring grey shopping, and who cares about that? These could be my first easy disguises, should I segue into a new career as spy or revolutionary. I could play a mad homeless woman, a boring librarian or a boring old lady shopper. Lately, I'd been reading plenty of biographies of women working in the Resistance during the Second World War. Their stories added further proof that all clothes are a drag costume; it's always a disguise, so you may as well put it to good use.

I also thought of Madeleine, my dear neighbour and first friend in London, back in the early 1980s. Madeleine was French, bosomy and shapely, heavily accented, lively, saucy and smart, and full of life and opinions. She was much older and much more worldly than I was, and she played my wise adviser. She was exactly my mother's age but a world away from my proper, thin, prudish and inflexible biological mother.

During the war, Mom dutifully worked in a defence plant in New York, lived with her mother and waited for her husband to return and start telling her what to do. It was an extremely old-fashioned arrangement. By contrast, in those same years, Madeleine was a teenager in Paris who worked with the French Resistance along with her mother and sister. None of the three had a husband, but plenty of boyfriends, and they took both their independence and their Resistance work very seriously, even passionately.

On her girlish bicycle, she pedalled messages and contraband all over the city. She was never caught once. She was young, blonde and beautiful. She was also, if she chose, very bold and sexually suggestive in her manner. A bit of targeted flirting at every checkpoint worked every single time, without fail.

Her home life was a very liberated scene. They all had lovers when they felt like it, and there was a top-floor loft with a spare bed, where they took turns bringing men. They called it the Bais-o-drome. The French word *baiser* means to kiss, and in street slang, it also meant to have sex, so the translation she offered me was that they called their attic the Fuck-o-drome.

Madeleine was gutsy, wild and funny, and I loved and admired her. It was a different sort of war and a different sort of Resistance. But, whatever the application, I wanted some of her gutsiness to rub off on me.

***

Meanwhile, back in the present day, a dozen acquaintances and friends from the USA and Europe wrote to me to say that they could donate to the Ukrainian refugee cause, but did not know where. They didn't know who to trust. Most of them wanted their donations to go entirely to the beneficiaries, via a volunteer force, however inefficient and unprofessional those volunteers might be. They didn't want donations going to salaries.

All of them wanted to know what I'd seen with my own eyes. They wanted eyewitness recommendations. I was collecting them. Migration Aid was my eyewitness visit number one, as far as it went, and now I could offer another good strong candidate for consideration.

Wednesday 23 March 2022

The next day was a visit to the Mandák Mária Evangelical Church [4] in Budapest's district of Mixed Reviews, meaning district VIII. Views ranged from "It's perfectly safe" to "Be careful!" On another note, I will admit that the word "evangelical" has never been an inviting one for me. Where I grew up, that meant they were diabolically keen, if not forceful and coercive, about you joining and swearing to obey their every command. This is not so in Hungary where for some reason, it's their translation for Lutheran. This particular church served as a hub where several organisations jointly fundraised and provided aid and services for about eighty families.

I was impressed by their web pages, which were thorough and practical, plus very respectful, not coercive or manipulative at all – in fact they had rather a sweet and humble sense of humour. I am paraphrasing below, but this was the sort of kindly spirit I saw:

- Really, please, you are wonderful, but we have no more room for big furniture!
- Women need shoes appropriate for the season, which is winter: no high heels [smiley face]. [Ironically, some weeks later, many of these young mothers were seeking office work, so calls went out for office shoes and professional clothes. But, at the moment, open-toed stilettos were not required.]
- After a long text: "If you have managed to read so far, contact me and we'll have a coffee [another smiley face]."

Unlike many well-meaning groups, here was a good list of phone numbers and email addresses, and they actually answered. This is where religious organisations have an advantage over a newly formed group. Any congregation of any faith already has some kind of group system already in place. As the saying goes, they've formed, stormed, normed and now perform. A community like that is ready to act quickly when a crisis hits.

Their team included two social workers who were experienced in the areas of asylum, care, administration, legal assistance, healthcare, kindergarten and school enrolment. They arranged accommodation in spare spaces at nursing homes and created a childcare playroom. Placing the kids in schools was done with volunteer teachers and two psychologists.

There was a poignant turning point for these eighty Ukrainian families – meaning mostly mothers with kids who'd left their men behind. At the start of the month, everyone thought this was a temporary shelter until they could go home. Now it looked certain that this war would drag on. The mothers now had to make a decision about whether or not to enrol their kids in Hungarian schools, whatever the language barriers might be. Most of them did, reluctantly, not liking what this meant. It was too long term for comfort but there wasn't much option for most of them.

That's when this church made an appeal for donations of school bags and supplies. That one, I dove into. I worked for about fifteen years as a private tutor in people's homes. I have worked with hundreds of families. I will not speak against schools but I'd rather not work in one. Home is where most real learning happens, there and in real life. But, the overall cause of learning and education was close to my heart. A good education saved my life, without question. May everyone have that who is seeking it.

I went back to Lehel market with its grumpies in their headscarves, and procured a small mountain of small backpacks, suitable for primary schoolkids. Although perhaps it's petty under these wartime circumstances, I was dismayed at the clichéd, gender heavy implications of the imagery. There was no escape from either one extreme or the other. On the pink and lavender side were unicorns, ponies and cartoon bimbos. On the black, blue and blood-red side was Spider-Man or Superman, or computer-generated iconography such as Minecraft, or military khaki camouflage. Absolutely no other choices.

I filled each rucksack with lined notebooks plus a pencil case holding all the basics, a plain-paged art notebook with coloured pencils, and a couple of chocolates.

I also added a note of encouragement and support, in Ukrainian, Hungarian and English.

Hello young student, and hello to you, Mom,

I made this translation on Google, so apologies if it is not 100 per cent correct in grammar.

My name is Eileen, I am a retired English teacher. I am giving you this schoolbag because I hope you will enjoy learning – inside and outside of school. I hope you try your best – with everything, not only school. I hope that when you find new friends, you will be the best friend you can be.

Maybe someday you can find ways to help other people too, like I am writing this to you, a little old lady and a total stranger, who got you this bag at my local market, and put the little things in there too – to wish you good luck.

Of course, you don't need to buy things to help! Smiles help. Kindness and sympathy help! Being a friend helps! This is what the world needs.

We are wishing you good luck! We are your friends. You have many, many friends that you cannot see, but we are all wishing you good luck!

I squashed everything into a big rolling suitcase and a backpack, and rolled us onto the tram and then a bus ride to a part of the city I did not know well: district VIII of Mixed Reviews. The bus delivered me to an area full of people who may have been homeless, drunk or high, or in other ways troubled or desperate. If I'd been mugged en route, they'd only have got a disappointing heap of schoolbags, although the suitcase might have come in handy. Nevertheless, I got there in one piece.

It was a classic old-style square of buildings set around a large central courtyard with too much garden to be tidy. It was huge, like a whole city block, and at first it was unclear where I should go. Soon, though, other people appeared with bags, so I followed them to the reception area which had a couple of busy and efficient-looking women.

They gave me tea, as the smiley-faced website promised. They were sweet and smart, and their English was excellent. The entire time I was there, people kept arriving, steadily, one by one, each with a bag in each hand. It was like a long, gradually moving chain of ants, and every bit as orderly. They clearly had a big strong support base and everyone knew what went where. They'd built walls of supplies. The office had each nicely labelled department piled to the ceiling: nappies, food, clothes, and so on. This group or, rather, this community was performing very well indeed.

One of the women volunteers offered to show me the basement, but I just laughed and said I could imagine something extreme, which she said was indeed the case.

When I heard about them supporting eighty families, my heart sank a bit. I'd only made a small dent into this total, but she reminded me that these things add up. They took my email address, and later I got the news that they had indeed provided each and every kid with school supplies, thanks to a few schools plus some individuals, and I could count myself as part of that, even if it was only once.

By the way, they never again pestered me for more. They simply thanked me. That's respect.

Would I go back? Did they really need another set of hands? Maybe not. Despite one good day and generally good intentions, at the moment I was yet another dog chasing its tail. But, one could always search on, so that's what I did, trotting around and sniffing for a lead.

9. Vienna, Vitae, Vouchers

Sunday 27 March 2022

I left Budapest, but I did not totally leave Budapest. Physically I went to Vienna and spent the entire week with the cousins. At the same time, I was on the internet nearly as much as before, if not more, and Budapest activities simply continued. I was still on that search to find something which I hoped I'd know when I saw it. It was that worst of searches, when you don't even know exactly what you're searching for. You don't even know which search words to search with. It was like looking for your glasses but you can't because you've lost your glasses. But still, I hoped to bump into something useful.

There was a distinct advantage to the online work life of digital nomadism. It could be liberating, if occasionally weird, and distancing too. I wanted to keep an eye on things, whichever way I could, even from afar, and I could feel like that Budapest file was still open, on the edge of the desk.

I could see what a whirlwind it had been. I'd only been back there a week. In that week, I'd plunged into activities all over town, met a few groups, met a lot of individuals, read and learned a ton, folded sheets and made beds, delivered groceries, and generally started to see how a small city could take in and host millions of unexpected guests. I heard lots of stories – mountains of stories. I saw a great deal to admire in people, everywhere I went. I saw way more good than bad. The situation was bad, but not the people concerned. I saw people rising to the occasion, as the saying goes. I saw how a crisis can bring out the best in some people.

On the weekend I went to the Vienna Cousins because that Monday was a big day for me. It was my sixty-fifth birthday, I was officially welcomed as a senior, and my third book was published that same day as well. We were having a special lunch party. I hadn't seen them since last year. It's only a couple of hours by train and I used to go once a month until Covid time. Now I planned to spend a whole week there, as I was not sure when the chance would come by again. The Oldies were in their nineties, so the time was now. I liked the Budapest–Vienna trip. I knew it well. Going to Vienna was one of my favourite treats, and this trip had extra special treats – once in a lifetime treats. Senior Day treats.

My next area of reading material was about the newly created Vitae Shelter,[1] which I was hearing more and more about. I thought they sounded like an excellent project. The following quotes come from their web pages:

> *Vitae Hostel, part of the (sadly former) Budapest Party Hostels, has been welcoming guests from all around the world for the last 12 years. Having only just reopened this summer after Covid, in light of the war in Ukraine, they have now also opened a shelter to*

house up to 60 refugees a night, and have already helped well over 200 people.

The owner negotiated free rent on another floor of the building, had the help of armies of volunteers to assemble beds and gather supplies, and has been almost entirely full since opening on March 1st. He managed to secure three free meals a day, toiletries and bed linens, as well as translation/ psychological/general assistance working together with local restaurants and NGOs.

Unfortunately, the Hungarian government isn't currently offering any monetary assistance for shelters and so that's where we need your help.

First, they used up $5,000 of $10,000 raised in startup costs. Photos showed completely empty rooms slowly filling with furniture, etc. They made estimates to cover bills that had not yet arrived from the authorities, and that would make a scary difference later. Fortunately, local officialdom's inefficiency was on the side of the shelter, for a little while.

They wanted to try to keep going for at least another month or two. Most of the volunteers were from the USA or Europe, and flew in for the project. Some left, just as quickly, going on to whatever was their next adventure.

Here was a fine example of the kind of folks helping out:

LAPO from Germany was only planning to be in Budapest for a few nights in the beginning of a 3+ year trip around the world, when he heard of plans to build Vitae Shelter. He jumped at the chance to volunteer. He's been meaning to continue his travels but just hasn't been able to stop helping out. He's still in touch with many of the now 300+ refugees who have made their way through Vitae and is hoping to compile a list of everyone who's come through.

Everyone here helping does it completely unpaid. Donations are needed for electricity, heat, and boiler maintenance.

Zero governmental support was demoralising, but this project was inspiring. It was a great group effort and achievement, plus it looked like a blast of fun for the construction team.

The Vitae site continued, "Lots of local changes to the refugee crisis here, with the government opening a new transit centre [the BOK centre]. Vitae Shelter still hosts its share every night." I could find very little information about this BOK centre and what they were doing there. There seemed to be mostly rumours and secrecy. But the BOK centre sent Vitae their overflow, somehow.

As a linguistic side note. I was hoping that BOK was pronounced Boke, which is Scottish slang meaning to vomit or gag – to heave with nausea. But alas, BOK is pronounced like Bock, and I had to stand corrected. One hates to lose a gag, meaning a joke, and I promise I'll stop soon. It does allow a brief detour to the English slang for vomiting – to honk – which is wonderful when you see US bumper stickers saying "Honk If You're Horny" or better yet "Honk If You Love Jesus".

Meanwhile in Budapest, I was generally impressed with the Vitae project and their spirit. They turned what sounded like a wildly fun party circuit into a cool bit of humanitarian aid connected with a wildly fun party circuit. That was an excellent and effective combination I was happy to support – from afar. I went to their online wish list.

There were photos of their modest but large kitchen. They needed various smallish things, not just food. An IKEA voucher sounded like a great idea. That jumped out at me from their list: it instantly made me smile which usually clinches a gift choice. I'd send them a credit voucher and they could choose what they liked. I sent them a message.

I'd done enough work. It was time to rest my eyes, which ached frequently because I was in front of a screen and reading way more than any two eyeballs could take. The last thing I saw, before sleep, having a random flick through my hand-written pocket-journal, was one of the many random things I jotted in there, some accompanied by translations. The theme seems to be independence and self-determination:

Svobodu dlya Ukrayiny, svoboda dlya Shotlandiyi.
My druzi!

Свободу для України, свобода для Шотландії.
Ми друзі!

Freedom for Ukraine, freedom for Scotland.
We are friends!

By the way, the Scottish national motto is "Nemo me impune lacessit" which is sometimes translated from the Latin as "You will not strike me with impunity". It might be "Mess with me and it's right back atcha" in cleaned-up New Jersey slang." I believe the Ukrainians can relate to that.

It was gorgeous and sweet, sunny and warm, without a cloud in the clear blue sky. The cousins went all out and assembled a spectacular delicious lunch outside on the patio, starting with cool white wine and ending with warm spicy rum, with many courses in between. There were vegan desserts in my honour. This is testimony to their open-mindedness about things they think are stupid. (Don't even ask them about the sugar-free bakery near me in Budapest. To them, that is a complete contradiction in terms and a ridiculous waste of time.)

The gifts were so thoughtful, it was touching. We only met about five years ago, and yet we're cousins to the point where I could invite myself to their place for my birthday and they accepted. Both family and Chosen Family. I found them because my mission of ancestor-hunting actually succeeded. Usually they don't, not to this degree. So, even though our two branches lost touch for over a hundred years, we're friends now, and they were all sharply observant about my particular likes and dislikes. They are beautifully practiced the art of gift-giving.

From Andreas and Agi was the classic book, Stefan Zweig's wonderful *The World of Yesterday*. From Vera, there was a bag of some of my favourite foods – she really understands what a foodie I am. Andi the hiker-and-biker contributed an excellent, strong, high grade traveller's thermos. I always whinge about cold weather, so Ruth and Sara gave me a cuddly wool shawl, elegant black with tiny golden specks.

I also got an answer from Budapest's Vitae Shelter. I'd written to them about wanting to donate an IKEA voucher. A very nice Mr K answered.

K *Hello Eileen, this is so great, thank you very much! How does it work, should we first say what we would need? All the best.*

E *I will find out. I think they send you a credit voucher and you choose what you want. I will check and get back to you.*

K *Oh OK, that sounds great as well, thanks!*

Tuesday 29 March 2022. Vienna

I met up with a new friend for the afternoon. She'd only just recently moved to Vienna. I'd only met her once in Budapest, in a symmetrically cute way. She was moving out as I was moving in. She was chucking out things from her flat, and I took them in to my new, empty place. My new place was so totally empty that I sent an appeal to the Women of Budapest Facebook group to help me furnish it with their leftovers. "Please let me clear your clutter" was what I broadcast, which inspired lots of replies. This resulted in an elegant, even visionary project in which I went out each evening with large empty luggage to a nice woman suffering from clutter. She would fill my suitcase and backpack and I made her life cleaner. It was one double-favour after the next. It was a city-wide win-win with an international cast that, overall, furnished a whole flat in one month.

We met up and discussed hundreds of things, including how her mother was in Belarus and she was worried, since that nation was now aligned with Russia. This war was all too close for comfort. We both admitted to having a small suitcase ready to go at short notice. Mine wasn't 100 per cent ready but it could be in five or ten minutes. This is the first time in my sixty-five years that I have ever felt the need for this kind of preparation.

However, "Be prepared" is the international Girl Scout motto, isn't it? Once a Girl Scout, always a Girl Scout, I have been told. So, as a lifelong Girl Scout, I'd have to try my best, make some effort and go for another badge – one of the wartime badges, this time.

Meanwhile, we agreed to meet up at the Freud Museum, followed by lunch and food for thought.

A Detour to The Freud Museum and Migrations to Escape Nazis and Death

This had been on my radar for a while. It is a must for anyone interested in Sigmund Freud and his world, although its counterpart in London would be an equally magnetic must. Of all the thought-provoking matters discussed in the Freud Museum, of all the intellectual gymnastics, for me there was an additional bonus, a hidden gem and a dramatic takeaway. It was a tiny room that initially I walked right past, until I spotted the small explanatory plaque and I backed up. My friend didn't notice it at all. It was a tiny alcove so small that even I could not stretch out, lying diagonally. It was the sleeping area of a loyal servant who lived in but had no bed. In that area she spread out her bedding every night on a bench; she "didn't have the gumption" to ask for her own room.

Did they have any idea where she slept? Shall we analyse this, Dr Freud?

Paula Fichtel (Oh! She had a name!) worked for the Freuds

as a chambermaid since 1929. She went with them when they fled to London in 1939, to escape Nazi persecution.

The museum showed a film of the Freud group in London, in exile from the Nazis. The faithful Paula was there. In one memorable scene, Freud had finished his lunch and still had the big white linen napkin across his chest, tucked into his collar, while he read a book. She removed the napkin and brushed him down, and he never even noticed, just kept reading. She was utterly invisible to him.

Do great minds always need slaves? Is an invisible underclass always necessary? How little did she register in this family's minds?

This is what happened to her after Siggy's death in 1939: "Neither politically nor ethnically at risk in Austria, she was considered an 'enemy alien' in Great Britain and detained in 1940–1941 at an internment camp on the Isle of Man."

This gig was not exactly brimming with good luck for sweet devoted Paula, was it?

Over a post-Freudian lunch, we I talked about how I'd got involved with the aid scene in Budapest. I described how whatever I witnessed or did, I recorded as much as I could in daily journals. This story was different to those in my first three books. They were personal travel memoirs. One had some history in the background of our family history. But here, live history was unfolding. I was observing the aftermath of a major historical event, a global turning point, where I and millions of others found ourselves in the flood of migration that resulted. In this story, I had to include more current affairs, more journalism. She thought some would say that what I was doing was in itself journalism. This took me aback. Allegedly, I was practicing what was now called Citizen Journalism or Witness

Journalism. These were new terms to me.

I did not and do not think of myself as a journalist, in deference to those who actually do this for a living, especially those in hard news reporting. I wrote autobiography, as far as I was concerned – non-fiction with probably more listed sources and references than usual, but all with one eye on seriousness and the other towards entertainment.

I hadn't done anything other than university journalism before, which I'd loved. I'd been glad to be schooled in the basics of it. I recall being told it was easy to learn and hard to perfect. That was from our editor-in-chief, Tom Rosenstiel. He is now a distinguished journalist, author and academic.[2] I am only one of those four things. So by contrast, I'd be reading the work of journalists, possibly writing to them, and at no point would I think of myself as one.

Even on my college newspaper, I started in news and was soon transferred to arts and features. Still, considering what one reads on social media, I was – and am – a more reliable narrator than most of what's out there. My friend had made a good point. This opened a door. I made a mental note to read up on these things. Maybe this was accidentally what I'd been doing blindly, in between wisecracks and simply trying to record what the hell was going on around me, and then share it. I wanted to be a reliable witness: writing a credible account of a missing part of the puzzle, and place it in the world library, to share. This potential wanted some exploration.

***

Back home with the cousins, and our mutually-compiled

entertainment and tourist attraction list, we were sad to miss the *Third Man* Sewer Tour. That iconic film told another tragic tale of post-war chaos and migrants, but in this case it was post-WWII starving Vienna made stylish by Orson Welles, stunning black and white cinematography and a guy playing a zither. We agreed to pursue this next time. There was also a hankering to go to Salzburg for one of the award-winning *Sound of Music* tours. We were dreaming of possible future treats. Treats was the theme. No one likes giving up their treats, be they movies or yachts or acquiring the land of a large neighbouring nation.

The rest of that birthday week was much like all of our visits, in that most of it happened around a kitchen table. If we went out, it was often to another kitchen table. Chat that is food-centred is the best kind. As a rule, the more kitchen tables that fill a visit, the happier I am.

Wednesday 30 March 2022

I'd promised the Vitae Shelter an IKEA voucher for their kitchen, but this was easier said than done.

I launched an excursion into the Hungarian IKEA website. For me it was like a jungle. Some of it was in English, but not all, and not all the time. I pretended to know enough of the Hungarian language to navigate, and devoted substantial time to cut-and-pasting things to a translation page.

It took time and persistence. But with the voucher in the shopping cart, I went to pay, only to learn IKEA did not take cards from outside Eastern Europe.

I did not see that coming. This was a large waste of that day. I texted Mr K at the shelter to tell him what had happened and that I would sort it in person once I was back in Budapest.

Now on the return train, I put aside my phone and all things with screens, and went into the movie screen in my mind. I replayed favourite scenes from this beautiful week in Vienna: reunited with the cousins after Covid had kept us apart, loads of talk, loads of food, news, gossip and silly things to make each other laugh. Plenty of nice memories to take away. Now I had a couple of hours to daydream and drift.

In that internal cinema of the mind, I also commissioned an imaginary film set among Resistance fighters in the Second World War, featuring sexy young messenger girls like Madeleine and myself on our bicycles, flirting our way through checkpoints and delivering a stream of essential messages, guns, money, passports and other forbidden things. Then, on second thoughts, I did a rewrite so my colleague specialised in the flirting and bicycling while I gathered intel and masterminded ingenious plans back at HQ.

Then I probably had a short snooze.

Later, I noticed an intriguing lady in the train carriage, a few rows away, facing me, her table activities fascinatingly visible. I could not take my eyes off her and I was not the only one. Most of us were observing her covertly or blatantly. She did not care. She was focused and involved with her task, in a straightforward, well-paced manner.

She was ripping up a large document. It sat in front of her on her table, at least 400 pages, in loose sheets, manuscript style. She was checking each page, quickly but carefully. Author? Editor? Corporate worker with a big report? Unwilling and bored committee member? No idea. I couldn't even guess. But it was big and heavy, and she was intelligent, experienced, probably educated, authoritative and professional, with a task in front of her. Soon, we all heard the sound of ripping paper.

About twenty pages in, she selected a chunk and ripped it into small squares, then placed them in the rubbish bin. She did this again and again, each time ripping them smaller and smaller. That document was shrinking and shrinking. All 400 pages, about twenty at a time. It took some time, and she fit it all in the bin, too, ingeniously. Like a Rubik's cube.

She did it like it was routine, only slightly annoyed and mostly tired. Was she tired of her day, her month, her whole career? She was not young. Her career had decades on the clock. She did not look unhappy. It was just routine.

She saw us all watching and listening and she almost smiled, shrugged, and kept ripping and ripping – quietly but thoroughly, explaining nothing.

That paper-ripping lady set me to thinking about my latest writing project, and this was where a certain turning point happened. My third book had just come out, and I'd already started the fourth one – Continued Adventures in Thailand, that was the idea. I'd already written about adventures in Thailand, so this would carry on from there, with more memories of lizards, snakes and tourists. But maybe now was not the time for this kind of lightweight divertissement. Maybe a silly amusement about an old white lady in a jungle was not top priority right now. It didn't feel urgent. It felt far away. Maybe it could wait. Maybe it was time for a different project. Maybe it was right in front of my face, happening in real time.

There was no need to rip the Thai book to pieces, like the lady editor on the train. It could simply go on the back shelf for a while and wait its turn. The refugee trail was going right by my front door, right now. My writing and other activities in Budapest would need to take a different turn – not a detour, but a new direction. I would record whatever I witnessed, whatever happened, whatever fell into my path, even if all I did for the next few months was donate oranges and help make soup, but otherwise act like a dog chasing its tail.

The irony was that the title of the third book was *Nothing Went to Plan and Other Silver Linings*. So I really should have expected a big change in plans, and yet somehow I seldom do.

I was dwelling on that old proverb: it takes a village to raise a child. I take that further. I say it takes a village to do anything. Some kind of group support was key. So, the new question was, where was my group? Would I know it when I saw it? I had no idea, but I just kept reading and reading and reading when somehow, I stopped when I saw the following, and I jumped.

> *There are fourteen medical students who were studying in Ukraine, and now housed in Erd, outside of Budapest. They need hotplates, rice cookers, pots and pans, dishes and utensils, rice, tomatoes, peppers, chicken, oil, spices, salt, spaghetti, eggs. Can anyone order from a supermarket and send it to them? They need help. They don't have enough food. They're waiting to be accepted into university programmes here. Many are already in their fourth or fifth year when they had to leave Ukraine.*

Stranded medical students? Without food? This was it. This was my group. Whatever support group was forming to help them, I was joining. Our village would help their village. I sent back a message, and that's where it all started.

APRIL 2022
Hungary

10. A Detour to Kozma Cemetery

Wednesday 6 April 2022

I was back in Budapest, having spent a week with the Vienna Cousins. In the meantime, I'd been given a phone number in connection with the housed-but-hungry medical student refugees, whose representative was someone nicknamed Devotion. I didn't exactly know how to address this man or woman, or was that relevant? It was not. I was not sure of their various nationalities either. I stayed generally evasive and gender neutral and messaged them.

> *Hello, I got your name from the church. I can help. What do you need? Food? Cooking pans? Maybe you got some donations already, but I can arrange a delivery, when I know what's needed, and when you are there to receive. Can be the day after I hear your reply.*
>
> *From Eileen*

I assumed he or she would answer quickly enough. It was much later that I learned Devotion was a Nigerian medical student. In the great migration, he'd been slung into a collection of fellow students from his own country, and also Ghana and Zimbabwe. He was a smart, sweet, quiet, studious church-going fellow, who at the time was perhaps not familiar with the name Eileen. Therefore in his early texts, he addressed me as Sir, which I liked.

There are precious few cultures around the world with one word for everybody, a version of sir for us all, every single one of us, in the spirit of that old saying that all God's children get to sing in the choir. In Thailand, everyone is Kun. There must be other cultures too. I like this.

While we're on a short detour through Thailand, let me add that the twist with the Thai language is how they import our English into what you might call English-Thai-style. No one calls it Tenglish, but it's neither one language nor the other. It's their own special adaptation or perhaps even dialect. They streamline it, for example, using sir for everybody. In Thailand many a foreign woman is addressed seriously, sincerely and politely as sir, which I find funny and endearing every time, especially when Mrs White is uncomfortable, because that's funniest of all.

The present he-or-she question about Devotion was also a bit funny, but it could wait. As for serious matters like food, I awaited their answer, however they addressed it. Under the circumstances, I thought it might be soon, so I made frequent checks for new messages. Otherwise I got on with my day as planned, keeping the phone at the ready, checking it regularly. In between that monitoring, the main activity of that day out was an enjoyable treat.

For months, I'd been looking forward to this research trip, yet another genealogy excursion with expert Karesz Vándor to the Kozma Street Jewish Cemetery. It's a beautiful place I've grown fond of, and it's become a mini-hobby to hike through it. I've lost count of how many visits I've made there over the last six years. There were discoveries of dozens of ancestors and lots of information about the history of a massive family tree – which started out as a very small, unpromising twig! That project was life-changing. I was now friends with this land and nation when before I was a total stranger.

However, now I was starting to run low on new cousins. I still wanted one last tromp in stout boots around that overgrown, eerie, woodsy, poignant place, where over fifty of our people were laid to rest, and probably more. A short list of rather distant cousins was the excuse to return for what my mom would have called the umpteenth time – meaning you'd lost count and it didn't matter anymore.

It was a dramatic moment, the first time I saw this huge place. I saw it from a plane at dawn, after waiting all my life to visit this place – my grandparents' homeland. Like many others who flew away to find their roots, I was far too sentimental about it all. I'd been obsessively studying photos and more, in preparation.

We landed at sunrise, when the river and the city were shiningly gorgeous. It was known for being a very photogenic place, and this view was breathtaking. Then, as we veered towards the outskirts of the city, something looked familiar: a big white U-shaped building which I remembered from photos. It was the big entrance gate to the Kozma cemetery, where I'd soon go with my list of over fifty ancestors, who were all in there. I realised suddenly, looking down from the plane, that those fifty graves directly below had been waiting to simply be acknowledged, and at that point, I had to face the window abruptly and closely because I'd started crying and couldn't stop. I probably leaked non-stop until an emotional and cathartic arrival.

Today's genealogical searching was straightforward and undramatic, yet not without a surprise or two. At this point, in terms of our tree, I was crawling onto faraway branches, fifth and sixth cousins and beyond, plus their descendants, in-laws – anybody, really, I do admit that. There was a whiff of a last chance about it. How many more years would I have to visit this part of the world? How many more distant cousins could I conjure up? It's been an excellent project that may have run its course. I strongly suspected there wasn't much more family info to find.

I was wrong about that.

I booked a half day with Karesz. These were fun, easy gigs, always interesting and enjoyable. As always, I had my printed list of plots (in the relevant block-row-grave format) in impeccably numerical order. This was the running order for navigating the forest – or jungle, as the case may be. The older the stone, the more likely it was to be buried in thick woods and vines, but you never knew what you'd find.

Where possible, we'd clear overgrowth as needed. He'd translate engravings as I wrote and photographed. There was always information to discover – someone had a kid or ex-wife or a religion or something else you never knew. It was never a wasted trip, not once.

Most of this day we dealt with, or rather arm-wrestled with, our Deutsch branch, which was enormous, far-flung and needing some context:

My great-great-grandma Johanna Nathan (1828–1900) was one of several sisters.

The eldest sister was Fani Nathan (1819–1907), aka Mrs Sam Deutsch. He was a general storekeeper and they had more kids than you have toes.

Second oldest was Magdalena (c.1825–after 1900), who had neither kids nor husband, and we don't know exactly when she was born or when she died. But she attended her sister Johanna's funeral, as did the other sister Fani: they were listed in the obituary. So, Magdalena appears to have existed, or just about, perhaps not in the most robust or noticeable way.

Karesz more recently discovered a fourth sister, one Katalin Nathan, born 1835 in Budapest and we don't know when she died. Age twenty-four, she married Bernard Breitner, in 1859. He was six years older than she was, and we don't know when he died either. We couldn't find any trace of children, which was disappointing, because possible links to living relations is always on the hope-list. These ones are a few generations removed from me, so it was a bit of a trek down that trail.

Her death record confirmed she was divorced when she died of alcoholism at the Pesti Jewish Hospital age sixty-four, in 1899. That last date is significant because when I saw her sister Johanna's obituary in 1900, it only listed the other two surviving sisters, Fani and Magdalena. I had concluded wrongly that there were only three sisters in total. This fourth one had died just the year before that obituary of Johanna. I never knew she existed. Now I knew.

It was a strong reminder not to assume things and to double-check all your theories.

Great-great-grandmother Johanna, by the way, gave her

daughter Sarolta (my great-grandmother) an apartment building on Sziv (Heart) street. Up to this point, I did not personally know anyone on earth who owned a whole building. Owning an apartment or a house was thought a substantial achievement, once almost unheard of, in our branch. Owning whole buildings was not a dimension I was accustomed to.

Did Sarolta get most as the oldest? Were there treats for the other seven siblings? It's true that some died young, but not Sarolta's brother Miksa, or her sisters Jeanetta and the youngest, Fani. Was Sarolta the only one to get a whole building? This is gossip we will never know. Sarolta's husband's last will and testament is on the internet for all to see, if you can read both German and Hungarian. But her dad's will, if any, had not yet presented itself.

Great-grandmother Sarolta's closest sibling who died was her immediately young brother Armin, whom I thought of as Tragic Armin. He was second in that line-up of eight siblings. Armin died age thirty, exactly one day after their younger brother Miksa got married – and the two brothers were living together, as well. That would always be a sad double anniversary. Armin died of chronic stomach ailments – at home, at 10 Dob street, the family home at that time. Miksa's marriage document says he lived there too. So, the day after Miksa married Szidonia, his older brother Armin died in the same flat they all shared together.

There was something horribly tragic about Armin. I thought that every time I walked down Dob street.

These people were high drama and moving pathos in some moments, average soap opera material in others. For now, we will zoom in on the Deutsch branch because it's huge and unwieldy.

Great-Uncle Lipót/Leopold Deutsch (1860–1928), was an upholsterer. He was the eleventh of twelve children produced by the busy Sam Deutsch and my great-great-aunt Fani Nathan. Lipót seems to have had two wives but not at the same time, so that's very poor quality gossip. Karolin Klein was Mrs Lipót Deutsch number one (1889–1918). She was almost thirty years younger than he was and probably died of Spanish flu, because in 1918 it was probably either that or being a soldier in the First World War that got you, sometimes both.

Ilona Illés was Mrs Lipót Deutsch number two (1878–1958). She was almost twenty years his junior, but lived a long life and died a year after I was born, which was a bit shocking, like someone from history reaching out of a book and tapping you on the arm.

Let's turn to the least relevant, least successful enquiries, as proof that I am clutching at straws as justification, when really, I simply like walking around in cemeteries. They are thoughtful places unlike any other.

In my notes were senseless questions like "Was György Szekács the brother of Edit?" There were a few people by this name, at that time. My notes from then said, "Same guy? No documents. Died after 1940. Could be. Wild guess." These were not what you'd call conclusive results. "Were his parents Karoly Szekács and Julianna Pollak?" This was the question. And, every so often, answers appeared on gravestones, but not this time. This time, so far, was just a nice walk on a sunny day.

Other enquiries, i.e. Who the heck are these people?

- Who was Julia Grosz, Mrs Geza Schwarz? I don't know, but she was not one of ours. What was she even doing in here? I wish I had taken better notes sometimes. When I began this activity over six years ago, I was not exactly systematic about it, and that fact has come back to thumb its nose at me.

- Jenő (Klein) Kálmán. No idea – wait! He was Great-Uncle Elemér's brother-in-law, of course! He married Elemér's only sibling, his sister Iren. Elemér landed in a right soap opera, and he was one of my favourite legendary characters. There's more on him later.
- Stefánia Deutsch/Mrs József Wertheimer (1885–1954) and her husband (1893–1944), were not buried together, which was often the case, so that fact has no gossip value whatsoever. Moving on.

Let's veer back to the root of all our Deutschs, Fani and Sam. When I say they had loads of kids, I mean there were twelve of them, spanning twenty-three years. That data didn't quite sink in dramatically and realistically enough, until I saw it laid out like this:

1841 – Mor

1844 – József

1847 – Emmanuel

1848 – Heinrich

1849 – Ludwig

1850 – Hermine

1851 – Charlotte

1852 – Anna

1853 – Karoline

1855 – Katalin

1860 – Leopold (A bit of a gap, there, what happened? Did we lose a few wee ones, as often happened back then?)

1864 – Rosa Rachel

Back then, in the glory days of the Austro-Hungarian Empire, Hungarians registered their kids with German names, and, at the time, people mostly spoke German in Budapest even if it was all Hungarian at home. Gradually they'd have switched over to using Hungarian versions of German names for everyday use. Charlotte became Sarolta, Leopold was Lipót and so on.

The above list produced twenty-one children, but not distributed evenly across the twelve of them. Most of them had spouses but no children that we can find, while a couple of them had two or three offspring. Then there were two main producers who had eight kids each, and those eight in turn produced sixteen grandchildren.

One of those main producers of eight kids was Anna Deutsch – a first cousin, three generations removed. Her production line ran as follows:

1875 – Antal: a doctor and a mysterious figure.

1876 – Josef: had one wife, one daughter, the story stopped there.

1877 – Olga: had one husband and probably no kids.

1880 – Béla: of whom we'll hear more soon.

1882 – Aranka: one husband, one daughter, end of

story as we know it.

1883 – Gabriella ("Ella"): one husband, three kids, and grandkids no longer alive today.

1886 – Geza, another mystery man with a long life and very few facts.

1890 – Jenő, died young in the First World War, aged about eighteen.

This lot produced only five kids and hardly any grandkids, and almost all of these were on Béla's line. He was the only one who did not keep his surname. He changed Bleier to Bánó. He married the beautifully named Piroska Bakonyi, which sounds like the name of an infamous spy or femme fatale, or at least someone who raises eyebrows when she makes an entrance.

They had one precious son, Endre, later to be known as Teddy. His grave was a work of art, perfectly manicured, pristine. On the headstone, in swirling script, was engraved "Draga Teddyke", which translates as something like Dearest Little Teddy. There was a stone bowl filled with tiny round stones and some candles. It looked like admirers and loved ones came here regularly. I stood in admiration as Karesz scrolled through his phone and discovered that this man was a famous graphic artist.

A Short Detour to a Famous Graphic Artist in 1960s' Socialism [1]

Later, I learned that there had just been an exhibition of Endre's work that very week! Classic retro posters were shown in the Endre Bánó 100 exhibition. WeLoveBudapest.com described him as one of the most renowned graphic artists of the Socialist era. He created cinema and advertising posters from the mid-1940s until the change of regime in 1990. He died soon after that, age seventy-one.

Posters from the 1960s and 1970s promoted products and events of those years, offering a curious insight into marketing under Socialism. My personal favourite was a poster depicting Sophia Loren wearing a big hat featuring a small mountain of spaghetti on top.

Hungarians might enjoy knowing that Bánó also designed posters for the popular 1970s TV series *Abigél* (Abigail), the 1964 film *Hattyúdal* (Swan Song) and Zoltán Fábri's *Körhinta* (Carousel).

The promotional materials for this exhibition promised me that if I stood in the middle of this room surrounded by advertising posters, they'd exert over me a magnetic, naïve charm and the warm embrace of nostalgia. I can't say if that's what would have happened. I was sorry to miss this exhibition – as a cousin, that is, not as a fan of the world of advertising, which I am not.

Bánó was known for creating the classic masthead of the main daily paper *Népszabadság* (Freedom of the People). His career included graphic design for journalism, commercial logos and publicity, posters for exhibitions and sports events. He also did illustrations for educational books.

So, Socialist advertising's nostalgic naïve charming magnetism or not, it was annoying to miss this opportunity to see his work. It was even right down the road from me. I could have walked there. But I'd arrived in the city a few days too late. There would be no rubbing shoulders with arty people this time around, no snooty chance to drawl that, oh yes, this was a cousin, a rather distant cousin but still a cousin. No such bragging, and just as well.

Still, in the meantime, back at the cemetery, the question was, did this Teddy Bánó have any kids? This was often the next question. Karesz investigated, searching on his phone, until his eyebrows jumped. Teddy had a son, András, a news man. "This guy is famous. He's been on Hungarian TV for years. Look at this."

A Short Detour to Visit a News Man [2]

András Bánó is a journalist who once won the Hungarian equivalent of the Pulitzer Prize.

He earned a doctorate in law, was a sports reporter from 1969-1978, worked for Hungarian State TV and then at ATV News, the first private TV channel in Hungary, where he was a presenter, editor and then deputy editor-in-chief, leaving eventually in 2016.

Since then, he's done community TV, hosted a classical music programme, is an art collector and has also written six books.

It looks to me like, in spirit, he was the Walter Cronkite of his generation. Or perhaps David Dimbleby, for the Brits.

I was reminded of meeting one of our American cousins, another retired teacher. We spoke of all the Hungarian ancestors and family over there who were so successful – property owners, lawyers and doctors, professionals. We, humbly, on the other hand, were mostly teachers, nurses and other modest earners. She laughed while crying out, "What happened to us?!" The Second World War is what happened. We survived it and may just need another generation or three to climb up the economic, professional and social ladder again, where possible.

Our Legendary Great-Uncle Elemér

The final treat of the day was to do with Great-Uncle Elemér Szente (born Stern). Iren was his only sibling, that we know of, and she married a man named Jenő Kálmán (born Klein). Their one and only daughter (probably) was named Lili Magdolna Kálmán, who in turn married a guy called Gyula Erdelyi. So far there's been no sign of offspring, so probably or possibly that's the end of that line. Again, one never knows, and one must never assume anything. This was continually challenging, in the face of hopefulness and also a love of gossip.

To me, Elemér was a poignant figure in our family history, and I feel a lot of his story remains untold. He married our Great-Aunt Frida, one of Granddad's four sisters. He was Frida's second husband. She was a teenager of eighteen when she married her first husband, the upholsterer and furniture-maker Sándor Gömöri (born Goldstein). He was much older than she was, fathered their three children in quick succession, and died soon after that, age thirty-seven.

When the widowed Frida married Elemér, he took on her three small kids, in full. He took them on in a very strict sense of that phrase. Elemér was a clerk who worked for Frida's brother Markus the Successful, who ran a company of electrical engineers that was then busy constructing the foundations of the future electrical infrastructure for all of north Budapest, Obuda and beyond.

Shrewd businessman Marcus's capable and possibly intimidating lawyers took care of his sister Frida's pre-nuptial agreement. That very protective document was a whopper that left no stone unturned.

A year after Elemér married Frida, when her three kids were in primary school, they had a daughter of their own, Angyalka – Little Angel. Their pre-nup stated the terms in case they divorced, which later they did when Angyalka was ten and the other children were teens. A generous amount of alimony and child support times four would be taken directly out of Elemér's salary, by his boss and brother-in-law Marcus. What's more, if Elemér went to work somewhere else, the amounts he was expected to pay Frida and the four kids would go up.

Marcus meant business. Frida was safe under his iron wing. Poor old Elemér, his people would have hated our tough old Kardos line – and their even tougher lawyers, as I imagined them.

In the end, Frida nearly survived the Second World War, but not quite, dying in early 1945 of gangrene and heart failure, age sixty-seven. She'd suffered the ghetto, that nightmare of a detention area that whole harsh winter, but only lived a few days into the liberation in the new year.

Elemér made a different choice. When he was taken to be imprisoned in that hideous, infamous ghetto of wartime Budapest for the crime of being born Jewish, he died by suicide that very first day. The specific cause was gas inhalation.

I thought of him every time I passed by that building on Wesselényi street, the big boxy red-brick school with the plaque commemorating those who served in that infirmary during the war. Poor old Elemér, I thought, every single time. Poor old guy.

His niece Lili Magdolna was born in 1903 to his sister Iren, and therefore would have been a close cousin of his daughter Angyalka, only two years younger. They'd have known each other, without question. Lili married her dentist Gyula in 1931. Gyula Erdelyi was younger than she was, came from Debrecen and was Greek Catholic. He was a master dental technician, living in Budapest's district VIII. She was a neighbour. The witness was her mother's brother, good old Great-Uncle Elemér.

We don't know when they died and we don't know if they had any kids. As usual, you never know – however much you want to believe your guesswork.

Angyalka married an artist, József Suto, the very next year. Nothing was heard from either of them, once fascists and Nazis starting dominating Hungary in the 1940s. Lots of that branch of the family disappeared without trace around that time.

***

And so, for today, we'd run out of documents, gravestones and gossip – either ancient or contemporary. By the end of that morning, we both declared it a very good day at the cemetery. The weather had been perfect – clear and warm and pleasant – during all the tromping through the forest, and we found everyone on the list, plus a few surprises.

Over lunch I asked about how we might go to Erd afterwards. He knew it, said it'd take half an hour to drive there, maybe more. It'd be easy, he said, but why did I want to go to Erd?

I explained about the students. If he was free, I wanted to go to a supermarket near there and deliver groceries to them.

He agreed instantly. As a translator fluent in Russian, Hungarian and English, he'd been going to train stations to help. He was sympathetic to this cause. We only needed an address. We were poised to head for Erd as soon as we knew where to go. I was waiting for that message.

I was ready to change our plans and head straight over there. If that did not work out, I'd send them something via a delivery. Then we got a message from Devotion, which sounds poetically like getting the answer to one's prayers. In a way, that's what happened, thanks to some strangers who were quicker than I was.

D *We already got some sir. Just now. And others have also replied. Thanks so much sir [four sets of prayer hands]*

E *I am happy to hear this. Please message here later, someday, when things are needed.*

D *OK sir, thanks so much sir.*

So, there was no need to think about Erd today. I'd keep an eye open for the next round, whenever that was. With a group, this was doable. It just needed a small village. Then our village would fill the emergency larders of their village.

This was a good plan.

For now.

11. Medical Students Stranded, a Gender Reveal

I was glad I told Devotion to message me again if anything was needed. I had an inkling this might come to pass and it did. I had no idea who else was in this mystery group and support-village, but my turn was probably due. The last message I'd had was on 6 April. Ten days later came a new text.

Saturday 16 April 2022

D *Good evening sir. We were unable to receive some of the donations because we weren't allowed to bring a hotplate to Erd sir. We were just recently moved to Budapest [to the northern suburb of Obuda, to student digs at Obuda University]. There's now a kitchen sir. I don't know how, but we would really appreciate if you could help us with a few foodstuffs now sir. Thanks so much sir.*

E *Yes – please send your full address. Is there a*

fridge, cooker, oven? They can only deliver on Tuesday. [It was the long Easter/Passover weekend – no delivery slots, no shops open.] If you need things before Tuesday, please say, I will bring what I have.

D *Tuesday is OK sir. Thanks so much sir.*

I got the address for delivery after the long weekend, and was reassured there was no need to do an emergency delivery from my larder and fridge by bus or more likely several buses, or perhaps no buses at all because it was that kind of holiday. About the grocery delivery, I later nervously double-checked some details.

E *OK! It will arrive Tuesday 10am. One last question and sorry for my confusion: do you have a kitchen for real cooking? If yes, I will send chicken, rice, vegetables, etc.*

D *Yes sir, there's a kitchen and hotplate sir.*

E *Is pork OK or not?*

D *Not, sir.*

E *Thanks. Arrival time is between 10 and 11am. Please text me to say it arrived OK.*

D *OK sir. Thanks so much sir.*

E *Also, you can call me Eileen, that's what everyone calls me.*

D *OK Eileen [smiley face] thanks so much [prayer hands]*

Continuing the mystery gender theme, there was no reason to mention I was a woman/lady/ma'am, not a man/sir/whatever. By the same token it was irrelevant who Devotion was. But this was now becoming a mini-comedy where the punchline had not yet arrived.

Before, with no kitchen, I'd sent what I could: nuts, dried fruit, cereals and long-life milk, tins, breads and spreads, some fresh fruit but not much. Now I could change the whole order for the better. This was a much more pleasing project. They could cook. This was progress. This was a relief.

Wednesday 20 April 2022

There was some confusion re logistics, and this resulted in a double-gender reveal, that later we both found quite funny. I'd written to see if the delivery went OK, and they said it hadn't arrived yet. I panicked – it could so easily be stolen, after all. There was more desperation about the city than usual. The company said it had arrived! I did an email panic-cancellation of the order, and later had to cancel the cancellation. How stupid! I think this company was used to such panics and misunderstandings. It must have been like watching a dog chase its tail until it finally stops and sits down, none the wiser but tired out.

There had been a lot of that lately, in all the chaos and confusion. This era, in this very city, was the hub of one of the biggest human migrations in history. Lots of us were chasing our tails in circles, not sure where to go.

In the meantime, on the trail of the groceries, I phoned Devotion. Unfortunately, with my hearing aids, that was often a challenge. I wished I'd sorted that. I couldn't hear everything, but I could hear that Devotion was a young man with a particularly quiet voice, closer to a whisper. This, I saw later, was his usual telephone voice in most situations. It was a whispering, behind hand-cupped privacy, and hearing it was beyond me, even at the best of times.

Here, instead, all I could say over and over was that I couldn't hear him, sorry but I was old, please would he text? He did. And so, lo and behold, all details were clarified, with foodstuffs as well as genders. Texting is so convenient but a living voice tells you more. With a bit of actual spoken dialogue, many facts were now clear.

In short, the food arrived, and now it was confirmed that his correct full title was Mr Devotion, while he promoted me from sir to ma, which was customary politeness to your elders in his part of the world.

D *I've seen it ma. Thanks so much ma.*

E *OK now go have lunch.*

D *Thanks so much ma. We really appreciate ma.*

E *I can send more in about a week. You can send a list. Please eat well, and study seriously.*

D *OK ma. Thanks so much ma [four sets of prayer hands]*

About a week later came the new list, much the same as before, highlighting brown rice and pasta, chicken and eggs, potatoes and tomatoes, onions and carrots, bread and butter. I really liked their priorities. I added fruit, nuts, cereal and chocolate.

There were eleven of them. At first, there had been about fifteen, but wars have a way of scattering people, and now there were eleven. I sent a nice fat heap of groceries the next day, attempting to guess what eleven people might eat in a week, if they all ate together and erred on the careful side. I am no caterer or restaurateur, and I have not often cooked for that many people. So I wondered how one could stretch such a budget that far. I still have a nagging, persistent fear that overall, it was on the skimpy side.

With these students I was also getting used to someone being polite enough to call people sir and ma – like the ultra-polite Yes Sir, Yes Ma'am of my childhood. It was difficult for me to imagine being that young and inexperienced, staying cool and polite when terrified from warfare, feeling hungry and abandoned, geographically displaced, and all the while trying to be students preparing for exams. There was too much to think about, and sometimes it was best not to. The least we could do was get them fed.

Focused later wrote, "I remember the first set of groceries you sent to us. We were so happy and surprised that someone cared so much. Most people at that period were already tired of the war and just stopped helping, but you kept going and always checking if we got them. Most people in the group then didn't even know you, they just knew food was coming and they were happy."

E *OK, it will arrive tomorrow morning, between 9–10am. Please text me afterwards?*

D *OK ma. Thanks [two sets of prayer hands]*

E *Are you all medical students?*

D *No ma, but most of us are medical students.*
[It was all but one.]

E Well, good luck to you all.

D Yes ma.

E We need medical professionals, please keep going.

D OK ma [two hearts]

He continued the next morning.

D We have received it ma. Thanks so much ma [two sets of prayer hands]

E Excellent. You can send another list next week.

D OK ma.

E Are your classes in session? Busy with studies?

D Yes, online ma. [They were able to finish that semester online with their universities in Ukraine.] Although we are still looking for scholarship opportunities to continue here ma.

E I heard you can get help with tuition fees here, but not living expenses, is that correct?

D I have only heard about the Stipendium Hungaricum. I am applying, still awaiting ma.

There would follow various conversations on this theme of what opportunities were available to them and the tens of thousands of others pouring out of Ukraine and clamouring for the same opportunities. These students knew they might not be able to continue their education in Ukraine, and they knew they had to begin thinking about the possibility of transferring elsewhere, if it came to that. They applied wherever they could in Hungary. So did many others. Many, many others. And Ukrainians were prioritised.

As far as local options for financial support or work permits were concerned, I suspected it was a typical case of the time-honoured tradition of not telling you the answer is No, but not saying anything at all, ever. They let you apply, they let you wait a long time, and they don't mention that an answer will never arrive. Ever. This way you can't accuse them saying "No". That's a popular administrative pastime around here, reportedly – or rather, allegedly. They just sort of slowly starve you, knowing there's nothing in the larder but never admitting that.

The renowned medical school Semmelweis did not like taking transfer students but preferred people to start from the beginning in a six-year programme that most people could not afford anyway.

A Detour to Visit a Medical Genius and a Typically Tragic Hungarian Hero [1]

Dr Ignac Semmelweis (1818–1865) has been called the saviour of mothers, and helped change medical history. It was this Hungarian doctor who got health workers to wash their hands, and thus he has probably saved more lives than we can count. It's sad that he was vilified and punished for his ideas and died alone and rejected.

Many of the deaths he saw were due to puerperal fever or childbed fever – basically a blood infection of the reproductive system, after giving birth. At times in those years, one in ten birthing mothers died because of this.

He noticed that the obstetric ward served by medical

students had far more such deaths than the ward served by midwives. He was also puzzled that puerperal fever was rare among women giving birth on the street. What was the difference between the two clinics? The medical students also performed autopsies but the midwives did not. And no one was washing their hands going directly from an autopsy to a birthing mother. This was the heart of the problem that no one had worked out, until he did.

When a colleague and good friend was accidentally and fatally stabbed with a student's scalpel during a post-mortem exam, the autopsy was similar to those of the dead mothers. That's when he saw the link between handling cadavers and directly contaminating birthing mothers.

He instituted the practice of washing hands with chlorinated lime solutions in 1847 while he was working in Vienna General Hospital's First Obstetrical Clinic. As a result, the mortality rate went down by 90 per cent after hand washing was instituted. Rates then fell further. For the first time, the death rate was zero the year after this discovery.

Despite these and other dramatic results, Semmelweis's ideas were vehemently rejected by the medical community. Some doctors were offended to be told to wash their hands. They were gentlemen, after all, so how could their hands be dirty? In general, Semmelweis's ideas were ignored, spurned or ridiculed.

Also, he had not published enough theoretical writing about his observations. Later, Louis Pasteur became known for developing a germ theory, in the 1860s and 1870s, and this persuaded doctors to more widely institute antiseptic procedures, like simply washing one's hands.

Semmelweis was dismissed from the hospital and harassed

by Vienna's medical community, eventually being forced to move to Budapest. In 1851 he took unpaid work as head physician of the obstetric ward in a small hospital, Szent Rókus. He stayed there six years. When he started, childbed fever was rampant there. After taking over, he nearly eliminated the disease. Still, his ideas were not accepted by other obstetricians or fellow doctors. He was an outcast, subjected to contempt and mockery.

He was outraged, and began writing angry, public letters to well-known European obstetricians, expressing his bitterness and desperation, furiously calling them irresponsible murderers.

He became increasingly aggressive, isolated, erratic and alcoholic. Some speculate it was the madness of syphilis, others that it was the pressure of stress and overwork that caused his deterioration. It was probably also due to the frustration of being able to prevent many senseless deaths but not being heard.

In 1865, his public behaviour had become so difficult for family and colleagues that he was taken to a mental institution by a colleague, without his knowledge. He guessed what was happening and tried to escape, but was badly beaten by guards. They put him into a straitjacket and left him in a dark cell. He was also doused with cold water, and administered castor oil, a laxative. He died two weeks later.

As for the cause of death, his hand had been wounded and had become gangrenous. Some say this may have been caused by the struggle with the guards. Others say the infection was the result of an operation he performed just before the incarceration. Another version is that he purposely stabbed himself with the infected needle, just before the incarceration, knowing that the result would be fatal, as it was with his dear friend and colleague.

In any case, the autopsy gave the cause of death as pyemia or septicaemia, meaning blood poisoning. In other words, he died the same way as many of his patients.

He was buried in Vienna in 1865. He was 47. Only a few people attended the service.

The rules of the Hungarian Association of Physicians and Natural Scientists stated that a commemorative address be delivered in honour of any member who had died in the preceding year. There was nothing for Semmelweis; his death was never even mentioned.

His ideas earned widespread acceptance only many years after his death, when Louis Pasteur offered a theoretical explanation for Semmelweis's findings.

Today Semmelweis is considered a pioneer of antiseptic procedures. Many hospitals and clinics are named after him. There is now a new term named after him too, the Semmelweis reflex, which is a reflex-like rejection of new knowledge because it contradicts current practices, beliefs or habits. He seems like a clichéd typical academic Hungarian tragic hero – brilliant, arrogant, deeply humanitarian and a visionary but a bit crazy therefore ignored and forgotten by history.

A More Personal, Much More Gossipy Detour to Semmelweis Medical University

Long ago when it was known as Budapest Medical University, a distant cousin by marriage was head of the obstetrics department there. Dr Jenő Barsony (that surname means velvet) lived from 1894 to 1969 and was hospital head of department and a professor of obstetrics. His career was littered with honours but he did less well in the marriage stakes, at least first time around.

He married Olga Neufeld, my dad's first cousin. It was his first marriage of two, and Olga's second marriage of three. She was a bubbly and energetic, spirited divorcee. This I knew from cousins who'd known her. The marriage did not last long; that I knew from the Budapest City Archives. Two months after the wedding, she filed for divorce, stating on a notarised and witnessed document that the two of them lived separately, used separate entrances, kitchens, bedrooms, sitting rooms and everything else. They virtually never saw or spoke to each other. The witness who signed the document, asserting that she had observed all of this, was cousin Jolán, the piano teacher and book-lover and the one that I resemble.

The divorce followed efficiently. Later he'd have Olga sign the following statement – not written by her, but by his lawyer and sent to her to sign: "My former husband Dr. Jenő Barsony does not owe me anything, and never will. I will never start any claims against him or take him to court. I will not even bear his name as 'the former Mrs. Jenő Barsony'. If so, I pay 1000 pengos per break of agreement." [Pengos were an old currency.]

I don't know whether she paid that fine but I have seen documents where she signed her name exactly as he told her not to. Bravo, Olga.

Olga married a third time to complete her lawyer-doctor-lawyer trilogy. She had one son by her first husband, a civil rights lawyer. That son was also a lawyer, besides being an Olympic fencing champion.

As for Jenő the obstetrician, he lived to the age of seventy-five and was buried with his second wife Livia Of No Maiden Name. The obstetrician had no children with either wife.

These are only some of the reasons that Semmelweis University, as it was renamed in 1969, is one of those places in Budapest that I cannot just walk past. I have to stop, face an ancient wall, and let the histories wash over me one more time, like the warm stories of gutsy Olga in her fragrant kitchen with the constant guests including a hungry young cousin Andreas, fresh from the war. Sometimes I have to stand in certain locations and try to breathe in what I imagine her kitchen smelled like. This is one of the million reasons why I feel attached to this city.

***

Back in the present, I took a moment to wish that these medical students, when they pursue their medical careers, will not suffer such obstacles and impediments. Then I remembered they were already knee deep in obstacles and impediments to their education, including bombs and migration. It would be a longer road than usual to become doctors.

As for present-day Budapest, with the students stocked up with groceries, I could turn to other matters for a while – like not losing my day job, for example. It was easy to get caught up in volunteer emergency activities and fall behind with everything else. Still, I was glad that the students, who would be here another couple of months, were somehow managing the basics like eating, sleeping and studying.

Many a doctor, nurse and other healthcare professional has rescued and helped me in my long career of health catastrophes and accidents, so here was a chance to say thanks.

My evening internet trawl turned towards the online crowd-funding world. I'd only done it once before, when I turned 60 years old and wanted to do the big family tree project. It could happen again. If we want to fill their larder, and if the current village shrinks or disappears, then we would need to create a new village, one way or another.

I was thinking ahead to new villages. They were changing all the time. Just like everything else. It keeps you on your toes.

12. Detours to 2015, Dogs and Syria

During the height of the 2015 migrant crisis caused by the war in Syria, the Hungarian government was criticised by the EU and the UN for forcing back refugees and physically building fences to keep them out, along the southern border. The country's asylum system was dismantled and gutted altogether. Perhaps the most extreme of all their actions was that it was made a criminal offence to help migrants. [1]

What's more, this was not just about Hungarians not wanting migrants to stay and settle. Migrants weren't even allowed to pass through. The Hungarian government introduced a series of acts to repel both migrants and refugees passing through Hungary on their way to Germany, Denmark, Sweden and elsewhere.

MKKP/The Dogs' leader Gergely Kovács expressed anger that the government used public money for a campaign that told Hungarians who to hate.[2] He pointed out that in Hungary, they already hated each other enough. The government campaign was a questionnaire on the subject of immigration, couched in an inflammatory, racist, one-sided, manipulative and fear-mongering way – allegedly or evidently, depending on your values.

In response, The Dogs created their own mock questionnaire, which quickly went viral. Here are some of the highlights:

Who do you hate the most?

- People who are different from me in any way
- People who are the same as me
- Everyone

Who do you think is making your life suck?

- Because of others
- Because of people who I do not hate enough
- Trianon [the 1920 Treaty of Trianon limited Hungary's borders to the 1918 ceasefire lines, leaving it landlocked and greatly reduced in size. This is still a passionate issue.]

Some people blame the Freemasons, some blame the Jews or the UFOs, why do you think the Hungarian national debt is not decreasing?

- Because of the Jews
- Because of the UFOs
- Because of the bloody UFO-Jews! [There were other translations for "bloody".]

Some say refugees are driving up cost of rents, others say it's because of immigrants. Who do you think is responsible?

- The immigrants
- The refugees

- Trianon

If you hate someone other than those mentioned above, please write here! [They generously provided several lines of space for this.]

The government's national consultation was estimated to cost HUF1 billion (€2.6 million), about double what they spent on processing refugees. Most of the funding for refugees in Hungary came from the European Union.

An *HVG* magazine article reported that HUF18 million (€47,800) was raised in a couple of days by MKKP and the political blog *Vastagbőr* (meaning Thick Skin) from community donations to counter-balance government propaganda. This would be used to pay for the anti-government poster campaign. One example said, "Sorry about our prime minister, he is trying to distract us from seeing the money stolen." [3]

Sometimes new posters were not needed. People were inventive. The government's campaign also took the form of posters and billboards, and some graffiti commentators changed the meaning of the text by painting over just a few of the letters.

"You cannot take away the jobs of Hungarians!" became "You cannot eat the livers of the Hungarians!"

"If you come to Hungary, you must respect our culture!" became "Our tour is heading to Hungary" or "Hungary thwarts".

"If you come to Hungary, you must respect our laws!" became "Hungarian vortex!".

Meanwhile, the government passed a law that made vandalism of posters punishable by up to a year in prison. [4][5]

A Detour to Orbanistan

Hungary's authoritarian leader Mr O. was once said by comedian John Oliver to look like a henchman from a Steven Segal movie.[6] [7] Now sixty years old, his career has been chameleon-like in the extreme. [8]

On the one hand, in June 1989, several months before the fall of the Berlin Wall and the collapse of Communism, he gave a speech calling for Soviet troops to leave Hungary. This was even though, according to several sources, the withdrawal of the Soviet Southern Group of Forces was already underway. He wanted to look like he'd called for it. He was 26, ambitious, a football-loving village lad representing the common man, making a popular and impassioned speech to be free of a communist dictatorship.

In 1988, he had co-founded the reformist anti-Communist student movement, the Alliance of Young Democrats (Fiatal Demokraták Szövetsége). Just about anything sounded democratic and free in that much-hated tyrannical Communist era. He called for civil rights, a free press, and the rule of law. A lot of that is gone now.

It's hard to believe those Young Democrats were forerunners to the far-right Fidesz Party of today. The earlier version was pro-EU, centre-right, in favour of a classical liberal democracy with tolerance for all. Now it is quite the opposite, perhaps because that was more profitable.

He saw that to stay in office he needed to capture the uneducated votes in the countryside. He did this with scare tactics. He demonised intellectuals, the homeless, migrants, anyone not born and bred nearby, and don't forget the Jews. He stoked racist fears and then sold voters the solution. There were government handouts too. This all bought votes, power and plenty of treats. Nice expensive treats.

Later the NGOs would have their turn. Accused of helping migrants (potential terrorists), an evangelical (Lutheran) group that gave shelter to hundreds and served 800 meals a day, was suddenly cancelled and stripped of official status. The same happened with about 300 other religious groups. Later too, he'd build a tall imposing office which towers over the main cathedral of the city.

He transformed his party, eventually, into something alleged to be as corrupt as any of the worst Communist abusers, dishonest and greedy. The new Fidesz is right-wing, nationalistic, totalitarian and based on making white people afraid of People of Colour, as one example, or making Christians panic about anyone outside of that, and so on.

His modest home village of under 2,000 people suddenly became the richest district in the country. Its mayor – an old pal – suddenly owned a bank, TV stations, media firms and a nuclear engineering firm. His old small company suddenly had contracts to build a bridge over the Danube and also, of course, a football stadium. They also supervised the closing of the last major opposition newspaper.

It's been said these newer voters admire all this. They'd do exactly the same. To them hoarding and not sharing is the natural way of things, even the cheating and the stealing.

It's reminiscent of what comedian Richard Pryor said in 1967, that one of the human race's biggest problems was not light people verses dark people, who were set against each other – the problem was greedy people. [9]

That's why I agree with the conclusion of a Hungarian neighbour who said that the current government's policies were not political at all, and you may as well call them the Greedy Opportunist Party, meaning they did whatever lined their bank accounts and those of their families – allegedly.

Double-talk was at the heart of it. There were endless examples of Mr O. saying one thing here and the opposite there. Comedian Tibor Bödőcs is known for his parodies in which every sentence contradicts the one before, along the lines of "To your good health! Stick it into your mother!" "I'm so glad to speak with you! Up your arse!" All his material is worth a look. I wish I could quote him more. I urge you to find more of his videos. [10]

Bullshit-Tennis can be called Bullshit Ping-Pong for smaller examples. After a while, you wanted to stop listening – and what they wanted was for you to stop caring too. Another tactic was for one government minister to announce something, a second minister says the opposite, and so on throughout the news cycle, creating confusion that, first of all is a good smokescreen for what was really happening behind the scenes, and secondly people might give up on trying to see what's happening. The trouble is, there are a lot of Tomato-women and Radio Guys out there, who do not feel like giving up.

What's not on the news worries me more than what's actually on the news. For every story we see, there's a bigger hidden story, while distractions try to steer you away.

Meanwhile, there was a serious discrepancy. The EU voted to punish Hungary for erosion of democracy and its poor human rights record, and the UN also criticised the government's human rights record.[11] But Mr O. has often harshly criticised EU policy yet taken their money and allegedly funnelled it to his allies and family, and placed new sports stadiums coincidentally near his friends and family.

Several Hungarian friends, colleagues and neighbours explained, sarcastically. First of all, it's easier to steal from a big fund than a small one, so think big. Secondly, no one knows what a stadium costs, and each is unique, so they always cost more than you think. Of course there are tax breaks involved. And in the end, what's wrong with giving a 3,000 seat stadium to a town with fewer than 3,000 inhabitants?

Tibor Bödőcs suggested that any such projects should depend on the approval of the boss's mother, and he demonstrated how Mr O's mother would scold him for having too many stadiums, and to behave himself, while he slunk away like a kid complaining about wanting more toys.

On a serious note, in direct opposition to EU policy, he announced that he favoured "an illiberal democracy", meaning intolerant and not allowing minorities any rights. He cited ideal models such as Turkey, Russia and China, which are intolerant of anyone who disagrees with them, or is in any way different than the majority. As authoritarianism goes, Hungary has featured on lists of the ten worst places for civil rights violations, and that list has also included, besides the abovementioned, Venezuela and North Korea. The government's views here cost Fidesz its membership in the transnational European People's Party, the largest party in the European Parliament.

Mr O. is accused of destroying most independent press, excluding all political opposition, weakening the judiciary, and of being a dictator who silences all who do not serve him. His party changed the national election system in 2010, so that it rewards the strongest two parties with more than their share. In 2022, for example, they got 54% of the vote but 69% of the seats in parliament, thanks to the new system. That's how they grabbed power and kept it.

Those who have more, got more. Small parties were made even smaller.

Mr O. often stands accused of being more interested in hoarding wealth rather than doing anything for the general public. US Secretary of State Madeleine Albright called him a thin-skinned opportunist who likes to command.

How did Mr O. silence the media? Here's an answer from someone not yet silenced but heavily surveilled. Hungarian investigative journalist Szabolcs Panyi was interviewed by US comedian and political satirist Jordan Klepper. [12]

Panyi's explanation was that after Mr O. lost elections in 1994 and 2002, he blamed the media. So, in 2010 when he was re-elected as prime minister, he severely limited the freedom of the press and he changed the constitution. Panyi explained that new media laws were put in place, that limited any criticism of the state. State TV started to broadcast pure right-wing propaganda on state TV – something like Fox news in the US, but a cheaper Eastern European version.

Panyi started looking at business dealings between Mr O. and Russian premier Vladimir Putin. He was then put under surveillance and the state gained access to all his text messages and emails, every single one. It was an Israeli type of spyware called Pegasus. This can access encrypted things like WhatsApp or Telegram. They now know all his sources. Every one.

Meanwhile in 2022 public media received 130 billion forints (about 360 million USD), Mr O. addresses the nation

on radio for an hour every Friday morning, and a leading editor of public TV explained to the staff that public media is pro-government and the same is expected of the staff as well. That policy had been in effect since before 2018.
Mr O. has certainly been called a dictator more than once. I doubt many people have called him a dictator to his face, let alone smiling cheerfully with the world's press recording it. But this is exactly what happened in a deliciously funny and bold video clip that I urge you to check, for sheer bloody cheek, as the Brits would say, and this time the cheek-slapping was literal.

European Commission President Jean-Claude Juncker was in a row of dignitaries on stage, greeting world leaders at a summit in Riga, Latvia, on 23 May 2015. In the clip, Juncker says to the woman next to him, "Here comes the dictator," and she laughs. He greets Mr O. by raising his hand in a modified Hitler-style salute, looks him straight in the eye and calls him "Dictator!" With the Hitler-saluting hand he shakes Mr O.'s hand. With the other hand he playfully slaps Mr O.'s face. [13]

John Oliver rejoiced that Juncker got away with it, saying that his man from Luxembourg didn't give a Fuxembourg. [14]

There was a wide range of reactions, the most diplomatic and supportive of which called it friendly, cheeky and playful, which made me laugh. Perhaps the smile was cheeky, but the word "dictator" was clear, and there was, in fact, a slap in the face. Nothing got lost in translation.

And while we are on the topic of humour, here are a few more examples of counter-posters:

- We know you are stealing.
- Abandon all hope ye who enter here!

- Welcome to Mutyiwood. ["Mutyi" is Hungarian slang for corruption.]
- If you are the prime minister of Hungary, you can build stadiums out of public money.
- A space station will be built here soon.
- Felcsút, we have a problem! [Felcsút is Mr O.'s hometown.]

A Battle of Billboards

As 2015 and 2016 progressed, things got more serious and, in some ways, so did The Dogs of the MKKP. Real debate was mostly impossible, with most media outlets shut down. Most of the time, opposition spokespeople and spokes-chickens (more on that later) were barred from state media, and that had been the case since 2013.[15] The nation's billboards were one big advert for this top dog. The Big Man was getting bigger all the time, politically, financially and physically.

That's what made his nickname Kicsi so cute. It's pronounced like "keetchy" and means Little.

Another nickname was not so cute. The abbreviation "O1G" (which fits into a circular, nifty logo), stands for an obscene expression, so you should skip this paragraph if you don't want to see its translations which were variously bastard, dick, scum, cum and motherfucker. However, the meaning originated with cum, meaning a person who is not much more than semen. Unfortunately that reminds me of a joke. What do a politician and a single sperm have in common? They both have a one in a million chance of becoming a human being.

Let's get back to our story.

When the government put up racist billboards, some kind

of reaction was inevitable. In this case the government and the Dog Party had a national battle of billboards. Humour would be one of their weapons.

This was in anticipation of a referendum about redistributing asylum seekers more evenly across the EU. The question facing voters in early October 2016 was: "Do you want the EU to be able to mandate the obligatory resettlement of non-Hungarian citizens into Hungary even without the approval of the National Assembly?"

The Hungarian government launched a €10 million poster and billboard campaign that stoked racism and raised fearfulness. It was the "Did you know…?" campaign, criticised for offering paranoid, exaggerated, provocative, inflammatory suggestions, making unlikely events seem likely – fear-mongering.

Those fears were faked. One academic who lectures and talks to soldiers, future police, secret services and anti-terrorist departments said most of those guys have a very different point of view from what the propaganda says. A police officer summed this up when he mentioned the so-called immigration problem. He said it was propaganda, that there were no facts behind this, that there aren't terrorists coming in. They all knew it. The government knew it, and only said the opposite to create fear.

The budget for propaganda is higher than anything else, higher than social issues, anything. Education gets less than propaganda. And so, the government poured out a series of threatening billboards.

They did not expect billboard-sized replies from the friends of The Dogs, who had decided two could play at the billboard game. Joining forces with an alternative news blog, they raised €100,000 from 4,000 people, through crowd-funding, for their own major counter-campaign of rival posters and billboards. That amount was ten times what they expected to raise. Their billboards mocked the government's xenophobia and disproportionate claims – in both English and Hungarian. They bought space on 900 billboards for one month, which was the same number as the government had bought.

"We know it's a lot of money," they said, but "the Fidesz hate campaign has become so degenerate that we must do something extraordinary to counter it."

The government put up a billboard saying, "Did you know that the Paris terror attacks were carried out by immigrants?"

The Dogs put one up that said, "Did you know there's a war in Syria?"

Government: "Did you know that nearly one million immigrants want to come to Europe from Libya alone?"

Dogs: "Did you know one million Hungarians want to emigrate to Europe?"

The government's claims were so politically loaded, an MP took a complaint to the Constitutional Court, but that challenge failed.

There were twenty-seven versions of the Dogs' billboards; here are some more:

- Did you know a tree might fall on your head?
- Did you know that in the 16th century in Somogy county, 42 people were attacked by bears?
- Did you know during the Olympics the biggest danger to Hungarian participants came from foreign competitors?
- Did you know the perpetrators in most corruption cases are politicians? [16]

Overall, in terms of satire, a personal favourite was a custom-made sticker added to the government's "Stop Soros!" poster (this campaign was a plea to keep brown people out of their white land). The sticker added the phrase "Goebbels likes this" with a thumbs-up icon. The graphics were so cleverly done, it looked all too real.

Elections appeared to be profoundly distrusted, with many people not bothering to vote any more, believing the whole system to be rigged. Apathy hung as heavy as the grey weather. It's often said a third of the nation support the government, a third oppose it, and a third don't care or don't vote. But, as far as the ballot papers during Mr O.'s referendum were concerned, some people decided to have fun by posting ballots that were defaced or spoiled.

Newsweek wrongly reported that MKKP encouraged people to spoil ballots by drawing penises on them.[17] In fact, this was not officially encouraged by the Dogs, although they had suggestions for those who wished to do some defacing. They demonstrated how you could add a sticker to your ballot paper, glue a pamphlet to it, colour it red, spray-paint it, burn it (partially), cut pieces out of it or drill holes in it. There was no mention or demonstration of drawing a penis on it, and I watched this video faithfully to the end.

In total, 6.2 per cent of the total votes cast were invalid. It was not confirmed how many of these disqualifications were penis-related.

Seriously, I want to believe it's better to vote for real, come what may, which must seem naïve in a context like this one. If voting is truly not worth it, that's a level of despair I don't want to face. That level would need some seriously dark jokes and black humour. Fortunately, Hungarians have had plenty of practice.

13. Easter Surprises, Good and Bad Eggs

April, Week 1, 2022

Before I even got back to Budapest, I'd already started following a good project I wanted to visit and join or support somehow – the Vitae Shelter, which had started helping people by the hundreds with a spirited team, and I liked the sound of that.

We return to the beginning of April 2022, the second full month of the war, which would be an altogether different sort of challenge. For one thing, the international brigade of volunteers was beginning to disperse. In many cases, these young digital nomads had had their adventure, built their big team project, and were scattering to the four corners of the planet for new adventures of various kinds.

They weren't all gone yet, though.

Once I finally got back to Budapest, I personally went to IKEA and bought the vouchers I'd promised them. Despite all the magic of the internet, it was easier to physically go to IKEA, which was rather a trek. But there I could use my actual hands to pick up and literally pay for paper vouchers with cold hard cash while looking a real live human cashier right in the eye and even talking to her – now how primitive is that?

Tuesday 5 April 2022

E *Hi K, I got the vouchers. I can meet you Thursday. Or after.*

Thursday 7 April 2022

E *Hello? K? Did you get my message? Still need the IKEA vouchers?*

Later that day:

L *Hi Eileen, sorry, K stopped working with us, but yes, we would love those IKEA vouchers.*

E *Can I meet you tomorrow afternoon?*

L *Perfect, we will be there.*

Friday 8 April 2022

The shelter was in a central area of the city in a classic old building with a courtyard in the middle. There was an all-transparent lift that made me so nervous that I chose the athletic alternative and walked up those big long flights. The building had high ceilings and a sweeping, echoey circular stone staircase, which made me dizzy, so I went slowly.

The original hostel was on the top floor, and the month-old refugee shelter was one floor below. All around the quadrangular courtyard, drying laundry was slung over every conceivable surface. I dropped off the voucher and they were extremely happy. "They" were a dozen or so super-healthy-looking, nicely dressed young white folk clustered around the main desk. I asked if there was anything else I could do, and at that moment, there wasn't. The laundry was done, the beds were made, key areas had been cleaned. I was given a quick tour, and it was amazing what they set up in a short time.

They looked like an energetic, happy team. There were quite a few volunteers just milling around, chatting, hanging out and socialising. These guys were like a more grown-up version of the teenage crew at the Madrid street place.

They already knew each other fairly well. They had probably been right the way through the good old form-storm-norm-perform template of group dynamics. They'd seen the place go from empty to furnished and filled.

Today their work was done but no one was going home yet. They were busy talking to each other. Lots of guys, only three women, nice odds. I drifted into memories of being that age, going to Europe from America at age nineteen. Not everyone did that back then, far from it. Among young, intrepid women travellers, there were even better odds, like one woman for every twenty or thirty men, meaning plenty of choice. I probably got a bit lost daydreaming at that point. I'm not sure how much time went by. By the time I woke up, I saw no conversational space for me here. I told the happy crew that I'd come back another day, but in the meantime I'd send some groceries based on their published wish list, plus large reinforcements of fresh oranges. Later that day I contacted them.

E　*Hi, whoever is there today. A grocery delivery will come to you today, between 1–2pm. I hope it arrives OK.*

W *Hi, thank you so much! The fruit is very popular – most of it was taken within 5 minutes of me putting it out! And we're currently putting together an IKEA shopping list, so we are able to use the voucher.*

I returned about a week or so later with more oranges, but again, I happened to arrive when there was not much to do. I folded some sheets and made up bunk-beds. Another cool crowd of young white volunteers had clustered around the counter again, bless them, and they were entirely distracted with each other. I asked the young woman at the computer when was a good time for me to come back.

Missy at the computer was at one end of the desk; two quieter helpers were at the other end. Missy was slick at her keyboard, eager for me to come in on the Easter weekend. This was fine: they had plans, I did not, that was OK – except for one thing. I peered at the chart as she typed me in, and asked, "Is that me alone? Is anyone else coming in that day?"

Miss Helper pricked up her ears. She cautioned that I was new, had no training, and that I should join someone more experienced. I agreed. So did Miss Helper's Friend. But Missy said nothing and changed nothing, looking pleased at the allocation. We all backed off and exchanged puzzled looks. I wasn't sure about this. Then again, holidays were when they really needed people. They would all go out partying. They needed someone – anyone. Perhaps I was better than nothing? I wasn't sure. Now questions were flooding my brain.

What would I do in an emergency? (Let me check my

notes. Do I have any notes?)

Do I even know how to phone local police or rescue squad, intelligibly in their language? (Not very well.)

In this scenario, was I really better than nothing? (I was still seriously not sure.)

But, in the end, it was an emergency, a crisis. Everybody had to up their game.

Sunday 17 April 2022

This was the middle of the public holiday in Hungary, a four-day weekend for both Easter and Passover this year. Almost everything was shut, but I'd stocked up well. I'd been indulging in a quiet, hermit-like and well-fed rest, with lots of reading in bed.

I was not looking forward to my volunteer stint on Sunday, but decided it was time to be brave and step outside my comfort zone. I said I'd help and I'd keep my word. I'd get up and show up. But it still looked like no one would be there to tell me what to do. I texted ahead and heard nothing. None of it sat well with me but I went anyway. It was time to egg myself on, perhaps pretend I was Sarah Connor from *The Terminator*, or maybe Norma Rae, or just about anyone cooler and braver than I actually was. Then again, they both started off humbly enough, and that thought can spur someone on.

I went into the open lobby at street level, where a scruffy man was loitering. He immediately approached me, speaking angrily, demanding I know not what. I assumed his language was Hungarian but then thought not. It was slurred in any case, with a strong accent, maybe an obscure dialect. There was a long stream of it, from which I determined it was certainly not

Hungarian, Russian, Ukrainian or anything recognisable to my ear. I wondered if drugs and/or alcohol were involved. He seemed to be yelling questions, pointing upstairs. I had a strong instinct not to give him the door code.

I pointed to the intercom, where anyone could ring and speak to the receptionist, which perhaps was supposed to be me. Or, perhaps by now someone competent had showed up as a last moment save, giving up their precious partying weekend. I had no idea. But was this the procedure for anyone getting buzzed in, even an angry drunk speaking a mysterious, hostile dialect?

In truth, rightly or wrongly, I did not want this guy up there, with or without me. Yet perhaps he was desperate and in need. He became more agitated, shouting louder, and then he lunged at me. It was the lunge that did it. I left.

I stepped around him, crossed the lobby and ran from the building. I walked around a few blocks to calm down my panicked, pounding heart, and eventually walked off the adrenalin. But I did not want to go back into that building. Instead, I headed for home and messaged them.

E Apologies, I could not come in.

Unknown Volunteer: Not a problem!

E I can come another time but please not alone? I am too new for that.

UV Of course. Feel free to sign up for shifts which already have other staff members. Your first shifts will be cleaning shifts, so there should not be a lot of pressure to learn too much too soon.

I wish I hadn't scared so easily. A psychiatric nurse, a cop or any average mother or teacher could have dealt with him better. Would they have let him up there? Did they let absolutely anyone up there? How do you sift needy refugees from crazy screaming aggressive possibly drunk or drugged-up people who are not making sense? What does one do then?

I was too embarrassed to ever go back again. I'd leave drunk-wrangling to others, whatever wars people are running from.

14. Going to the Dogs in 2018, and a Joke Party Tour [1]

In the spring of 2018, MKKP were ready for the April parliamentary elections. This was even though Hungary's state media was almost completely controlled by the government. The opposition got a tiny fraction of the airtime that the prime minister got. It was, as the English saying goes, beyond a joke. What could one do? Some people replied with more jokes, jokes that were even more absurd.

According to *Newsweek*, "Ahead of April 8, [MKKP] has put forward a range of human, subhuman and animal candidates, including a gorilla-guerrilla gardener who is planting edible plants in Budapest playgrounds." [2]

Their finest moment was "chicken candidate" József Tichy-Rács, who ran in his native Győr-Moson-Sopron county's fourth electoral district, and showed up dressed head to toe as a chicken.[3] He clucked his way through the interview and his prepared statement. He emitted not one word of any human language. It was about as meaningful as any speech from a politician, and certainly more engaging. The message was funny, smart and clear. It was painfully accurate as criticism but also was entertaining. It got more press overseas than many "real" local stories.

He told *Newsweek* he was also campaigning to replace school buses with helicopters and to trade with other countries, continents and planets.

His choice to run was dictated by the obvious perks of the job, he admitted. "The world of politics has everything we want. Women love politicians, we also get invited for beers. It's not hard to do, and still, people get acknowledged. It's ideal, isn't it?" He said these things in human language, not the clucking he reserved for the state-run TV's precious five minutes. Over four years that worked out to one minute fifteen seconds per year.

It did not sound like joking when Tichy-Rács said he was working hard, in line with the party's principle of "promoting active citizenship, fostering civic attitudes" and, when necessary, taking over "activities neglected by local authorities with the intent of spurring them into action and enhancing their operation".

That didn't sound funny at all. That sounded just fine, as far as it went.

According to the MKKP website, "In the 2018 parliamentary elections with a budget of exactly zero, we got 1.73% of the total vote – that's about 100,000 votes." Unfortunately, they won no seats.

For all the opposition parties in general, the 2014 and 2018 national election results were disappointing, with much rivalry between many small parties. But there had already been a major obstacle to democratic elections, ever since the changes in 2010. The new electoral system was calibrated to deny small parties access to parliament, to keep the current rulers in power and to greatly reduce democratic representation.

In 2022, however, in reaction against that, a surprising coalition was formed by most of the opposition parties as the only way to replace this monopoly – or at least to make a statement against it. Anti-corruption was the key issue shared. But the coalition's main difficulty was easy to see. The group included left-wingers, liberals, moderate-right and former far-right elements. Their parties included youth, green, socialist, social democrat, liberal – and even the infamously extremist right-wing Jobbik party.

Jobbik are worth a mention here because they call themselves radically patriotic and Christian, and they were founded on principles of fascism, racism and a neo-Nazi reputation, but ever since 2015 they declared themselves centre-right with only some residual nationalistic tendencies. Perhaps they believed that last bit to be reassuring, but it received mixed reviews and scepticism.

The only thing these groups had in common was the view that the current regime was a greedy, corrupt autocratic system needing fundamental replacement. Many people thought it was good for a coalition to state their common goal. But other than making a public statement of shared values, it was hard to see such a coalition working as a practical alternative and a ruling party.

MKKP declined to join.

If the choice is between a bizarre coalition, a scary dictator or a candidate dressed as a chicken, it can be surprisingly hard to choose. [4]

In the meantime, the Dogs were busy with other matters. For example, according to their website, "In 2018 the amount of the campaign subsidy provided by the state was 190,000,000 HUF (roughly €600,000). We never thought this kind of money really existed, and we were so terrified of this amount that we launched a program [jokingly] called the Rózsa Sándor State Fund Wasting Public Program. The purpose is to redistribute most of the campaign funding among the people through tenders – we could have spent the money on the actual campaign, but we really wanted 'to waste it' on sensible and useful ideas."

By the way, here's another joke: Sándor Rózsa (1813–1878) was from Hungary's Great Plains and their best-known bandit and highwayman. His life inspired numerous writers. He was admired as a legend, like English highwayman Dick Turpin, with elements of Robin Hood thrown in.

Let's concentrate on Robin Hood's spirit of helping the poor, rather than public servants being iffy with public funds.

MKKP set up a ministry to resolve local municipal issues and carry out repairs and redecoration projects. They founded the People's Community College of MKKP. All the courses are completely free; foreign languages, sports and welding are all popular so far, and more teachers with new courses are joining.

"This year we had round 2, and received less money as party subsidy (about 60,000,000 HUF or €200,000), and we had more than 400 applicants. These included a pre-school renovation project, a public oven, a skate park, a success story generator and as much as 4 human teeth."

I really don't know what that last bit meant. There are often weird mistranslations. Or we can write it off as a joke, but sometimes that's exactly their dilemma. I'm not sure it's to their advantage to keep people guessing whether they are serious or not when it comes to spending public money. I prefer to know when a leader – when anyone – is joking or not. I have a feeling I was not the only one asking these questions. But after all, I could not understand much Hungarian, and was an outsider to their humour, their voting system, and their strange, strange history.

It was easy for me to seriously agree when MKKP's leader Gergely Kovács told BBC News, "What we can do is appeal to the millions in Hungary who are upset by the government campaign. We want them to know they are not alone." [5]

In the end, the majority voted No. They did not want the EU to resettle non-Hungarians in Hungary. Good old Slovakia said they'd take some but only Christians.

MKKP billboard: "Brussels, we still love your money!"

A Detour Through a History of Joke Parties [6]

As far as political parties with a sense of satire go, there have been a few in the history of Central Europe.

In 1911, popular Czech writer Jaroslav Hašek created "The Party of Moderate Progress Within the Bounds of the Law", a mockery of Austro-Hungarian Empire conservatism. Campaign promises: to reintroduce slavery, nationalise janitors and make alcoholism mandatory.

He has also been described as a journalist, a bohemian and an anarchist, best known for the novel *The Fate of the Good Soldier Švejk during the World War*, a collection of farcical incidents about a First World War soldier and a satire on inept authority figures. It's been translated into sixty languages, making it the most translated novel in Czech literature.

Here are some other contenders:

Rhinoceros Party

Canada's Rhinoceros Party's predecessor was founded in 1963, which makes it one of the oldest of all odd political parties. Campaign promises:

- Repeal the laws of physics!
- Award every Canadian citizen with a rhinoceros.
- Outlaw gluten-free products and Android devices.
- Move the capital city of Canada to a tiny town called Kapuskasing.
- Declare war on Belgium because Belgian comic book hero Tintin shot a rhinoceros in one of his cartoon booklets.

They receive very few votes during elections but they keep fielding candidates anyway.

Canadian Extreme Wrestling Party

It is what it sounds like. Their party leader is chosen by a wrestling match. Policies:

- They denounce the overfishing of Canadian lakes.
- Fishing is their key issue.
- They also wanted Canada to leave NATO, which was not a popular idea.

Die PARTEI

"The Party for Labour, Rule of Law, Animal Protection, Promotion of Elites and Grassroots Democratic Initiative" was founded by a German satirical magazine, but grew fast. In 2014, it became the first joke party to win a seat in the European Parliament. In 2019's EU election, they won two seats.

- Comedy policy: rebuild the Berlin Wall in order to divide

Germany.

- Serious policy: healthcare reform, introducing a new constitution.

Polish Beer-Lovers' Party

In 1991, two years after the fall of Communism, they won sixteen parliamentary seats in the country's first free election in decades. Their sole aim is promoting beer, and their chief policy was to introduce pubs to Poland so that people would drink more beer. Most Poles prefer vodka, so this did not work. The party soon split into smaller factions. One faction preferred pint glasses, the other did not.

There are/were Beer Parties in Ukraine, Belarus, Russia, Czech Republic, Austria and Australia as well. In 2020, in the Viennese state election, the Austrian Beer Party, formed in 2014, won 1.8 per cent of the vote.

In the miscellaneous category were an Anarchist Pogo Party of Germany, a Donkey Party in Iran, and an Imperial Party of New Zealand.

Some joke parties presented as enigmatic, hard to read:

Partia e Fortë

"The Strong Party" in English. Unlike most parties that want to change things, Kosovo's Partia e Fortë wants to keep everything the way it is. When a member was elected to the local assembly in Pristina, their political ideology was listed as "fantasy".

Others were clear in their vision:

Death, Dungeons and Taxes Party

The Death, Dungeons and Taxes Party, in Britain, want to introduce medieval-like measures to control the population. Their policies:

- Use boiling hot oil to scare immigrants away.
- Reintroduce the death penalty.
- Invade France.

They always receive fewer than a hundred votes.

Some of these parties come and go fairly quickly:

The Best Party

Founded by Icelandic actor, comedian and writer Jon Gnarr in 2009, in 2010 they won six out of fifteen seats on the Reykjavík City Council. Gnarr ran purely as a joke and was annoyed that he won.

- Original comedy platform: It will not honour any of its election promises. Free towels in all city swimming pools. A polar bear for the city zoo. Disneyland. A drug-free national parliament by 2020.
- Later serious platform: Helping families, those less fortunate, or disabled. Better social equality. More transparency from government. Pro-democracy. Taking to court those responsible for the country's economic collapse in 2008. Cancel debts.

It was dissolved in 2014.

Oddly enough, among all this oddness, there have been a few

parties that, accidentally or not, made a positive difference, and they may have had no intention of doing so:

Union of Conscientiously Work-Shy Elements

This is a Danish political party founded in 1979 by comedian Jacob Haugaard, who was elected to the Danish parliament in 1994. Campaign promises:

- Better weather. Import whales into a local lake. Tail winds on cycle paths. (He did not achieve these.)
- More bread for ducks in urban parks. Nutella in army rations. A public toilet in the park where he held a post-election celebration. (He did actually achieve these things!)

He served a whole term in the parliament. It was no joke that more than once, he was the deciding vote in a hung parliament, and this made a difference in Danish politics. It's said he took the rest of his term seriously after that, but he did not run again and left politics altogether in 1998.

Monster Raving Loony Party

This English one is very popular. It was founded in 1982 by a man known as "Screaming Lord Sutch". Policies.

- Make unicorns a protected species.
- Force terrorists to wear loud horns and bells so they can't surprise anyone.
- Give a knighthood to Ozzy Osbourne.

The party is said to be beloved by the political establishment, who apparently don't mind being made fun of in this harmless case. Surprisingly, several of the party's policies have actually been made into law by the British government. These include issuing passports for pets and scrapping certain exams.

A Detour to Visit Politicians, Actors and Other Jokers

This is in honour of the TV careers of both Volodymyr Zelensky and a certain former US Clown-in-Chief:

- US President Ronald Reagan was once a film actor.
- Arnold Schwarzenegger, the body-builder and action movie star who once played an assassin-robot called The Terminator, then became known as "The Governator" when he was elected governor of California, which was how Ronnie started too.
- Clint Eastwood became mayor of his hometown of Carmel, California in 1986. Previously, the local planning board had rejected his attempt to remodel an office building next to a restaurant he owned. This prompted him to run for mayor and he won the election by a few hundred votes, and then sacked the planning board members who'd turned down his application.
- Stage and screen actor Glenda Jackson became a British MP for the Labour Party.
- Child film star Shirley Temple Black served as US ambassador to Ghana and also to Czechoslovakia.
- Harry Belafonte was US ambassador to the Bahamas.
- Eva Peron was in a few B-movies before becoming First Lady of Argentina.
- (These are obviously in random order.)
- Comedian and writer Al Franken became a US senator until some of his old jokes came back to haunt him, meaning multiple allegations of sexual misconduct.
- Tabloid talk show host Jerry Springer was elected to

Cincinnati City Council, resigned when he was caught soliciting a prostitute, and was re-elected the following year.

- Sonny Bono of the singing duo Sonny and Cher became the mayor of Palm Springs and later served as their congressman.
- And finally last and probably least in the eyes of cruel showbusiness – TV actors:
- Fred Grandy played a character called Gopher on *The Love Boat*. He served in the US House of Representatives for the state of Iowa, from 1987 to 1995.
- Ben Jones played Cooter Davenport in *The Dukes of Hazzard*. He served from 1989 to 1993 in the House of Representatives, for the state of Georgia. He also runs the music festival Dukefest.

The Surprise Party

Please allow me to end with a personal favourite that combines the best elements of these examples.

In 1940, American comedian Gracie Allen, who performed in a duo with her husband George Burns, decided she'd run for president, and therefore created the Surprise Party. A kangaroo was party mascot, she went on tour with a rented train, and 42,000 people voted for her. She failed as a presidential candidate but was elected mayor in a small town in Michigan.

Gracie's project was perfection from a comedy point of view. But what happened when a political party started as a joke and a bit of entertainment, but later they saw ways to try to make real, positive change and not just joke around? How could they then persuade people that they could be trusted, that they would try to take positive action, that when asked questions they'd really answer and not just spew wisecracks?

MAY 2022

Obuda, North Budapest

15. Finally a Kitchen, and Back to School

May, Week 1, 2022

The last I'd heard from the medical students was in connection with the previous food parcel sent on 25 April. We had not yet met in person at this point. But we had a clear, easy routine, an agreement that they could send not just a minimalistic survival list, but a wish list to eat as well – as healthily – as possible.

I said I could not promise to get everything. It was a wish list, after all. But I'd get as much as the budget would allow. It was certainly smart of them to band together, pool their resources and cook together. It was better economically, nutritionally and socially. I know this sounds like a public service announcement or, worse yet, a boring teacher, which is enough to make anyone shudder and put their fork down in nausea.

I was so glad they finally had a kitchen. I also thought they had healthy habits. The usuals were:

- Carbs: rice, flour, noodles, spaghetti, bread
- Veg: onions, tinned and fresh tomatoes, peppers

- Fruit: they never asked at first, but I sent apples, bananas, oranges
- Protein: eggs, chicken, milk, nuts and nut spreads, seeds
- Miscellaneous: sugar, salt, spices, butter, cooking oil (their first choice was groundnut oil, but that had to wait)

Because the war was dragging on, I also noticed they now needed replacements in large, economy, longer-lasting family-sized quantities of toiletries, cleaning and laundry things. It was now a whole season we were looking at, not a month.

The students were given permission to stay in this student dormitory until the end of June. At least there was that.

Or so we all thought.

Tuesday 3 May 2022

The new wish list came in. It was much like the week before. I hoped their food-stress had abated for the week, anyway – maybe even for this and the following month, with luck. I couldn't believe they were studying online through all this. My distractions as a student were boys and parties. Theirs was a war.

Each wish list for groceries contained requests that did not make the cut.

- Evil colas of any kind.
- Bottled water. Nearly everyone drank the tap water in Budapest, although there were accusations of lead-pipe poisoning and worse, which were all too plausible. Most people could certainly drink it for a few months or even all the time, although I personally might not commit to a lifetime's consumption.

On the other side of the cookie, I always added chocolate-covered oat-and-nut bars, or some kind of half-healthy treat with a sugar buzz for fun. I was teased by friends who thought this was as pathetic as comedy in a sermon, but I saw it as a nice middle way and the best of both worlds.

***

Back on the internet, cruising the usual local refugee support groups, I checked the latest wish lists for donations and deliveries. No one had large-scale storage. I didn't know who could offer wholesale. Everything was being done in tiny parcels, on bikes and motorbikes. Budapest, ever since Covid times, had become a city of gliding bicycle delivery people, criss-crossing all over the place. Also, there were individuals like me with their wheely-carts, roller-cases and scruffy backpacks – the bag-ladies of the Resistance.

People chose what to donate, of course, which is why it was truly stupid for so many trolls to be posting criticisms of what was on the list. Give or don't – why all the whining and barking? Some of these time-wasting idiots were worse than a room full of yapping chihuahuas.

One explosive issue in troll-town was the request for body lotions, shea butter or similar. There were extraordinarily petty yet lengthy debates about whether or not this was a luxury and how dare refugees even ask for such luxuries. An outcry puked forth. It was explained that dry cracks in the skin can lead to infections, so moisturising was medically advised. Wading through the internet can be like wading through a swamp and an extra stinky swamp at that.

A guest asked for beer and of course, wasn't given any, but online time-wasters went on for hours about it. These were all red herrings, distractions, detours. It felt like swimming upstream at times, and it was a stream full of rubbish. The challenge was to be practical yet positive, which was both difficult and uncool.

It was time to get seriously practical in a small, manageable, doable way. It was becoming obvious I needed a new sponsorship group. There were local people taking turns with me to send food to our group, but they disappeared, and now it was just me. Crowd-funding became my reading theme. I reviewed the crowd-funder I'd done about five years ago. This was in aid of my sixtieth birthday project, to research our family tree. As I've mentioned, that research revealed such a dramatic history combined with happy meetings in the present with real, new-found cousins that the story became my second book. It was life-changing – a fantastically good investment.

For this current project, I returned to the same crowd-funding website, being lazy. It was familiar and easy but their cut was higher now, and there were more snags and hidden rules. Still, I was already registered in their system and the banking was already set up, which had been time-consuming to arrange the first time. This was not an overwhelming amount of homework. It was doable. "Doable" was becoming my favourite word and concept. I wasn't reaching for the sky and I was not thinking big beyond the usual scope. I was thinking realistically and practically, and ideally with some connection to food. These were the "filters", the checklist, the imagined coordinates.

It was a huge relief for these students to finally have a

kitchen. The difficulty was that this kitchen came with no equipment. Everything in there from pots to spoons were the private belongings of the other students there. So, this group had to ask to borrow things when others weren't eating. It was a very awkward challenge to constantly work and cook and eat around everyone else, and there were a lot of them.

These others were the "real students", the paying students, many from around the world. For the most part, they kept to themselves and did not much mix with or talk to our group of students who had just been bombed out of their medical education. I was sorry to hear this. There were even some "Go back where you came from" comments. But, empathetic or not, speaking to each other or not, there were about forty people sharing that one kitchen.

Therefore, our students' wish list sprouted kitchen basics like plates, cutlery, a cooking pot. There was nothing like that at the online supermarket which would deliver straight to them, a system that had worked well up to now.

This was also true of mild painkillers like paracetamol and ibuprofen, and I was sympathetic to that request. I needed to procure these things elsewhere and deliver them myself. The students didn't want to trouble me but there was no other way. Really, of course, it was my opportunity to meet some of them, if they felt like it. And it turned out, sweetly enough, that some of them did.

Wednesday 4 May 2022

First, we got our order in order. I needed to clarify a few things with Devotion. Our communication skills were widening all the time.

E *I need to clarify a few things, please. When you say pads ... you mean paper to write on, or female hygiene pads or tampons?*

D *Yes ma, female pads.*

E *Which spices do you like?*

D *Maggi or Knorr Meat spices ma.*

E *Do you eat Beef?*

D *Yes ma.*

(We were splurging out a bit, but pork was out.)

As for the other things, it meant a neighbourhood trawl of the cheapest places on offer. When conditions were right, I was ingenious at this sort of thing, morphing into a fearsome and determined bag-lady, a skinny cousin of market women here who reign by sheer fierceness. I could play cousin to Tomato Woman. For kitchen things, I did a sweep: the 1-Euro shop, all of Lehel market where I met those formidable cousins in spirit. I had the attitude, if not the kerchief.

I also went to every place with plastic things where the shop was run by an Asian family. There were three of those nearby. Two remembered me as a regular, always smiled and welcomed the chance to drop speaking Hungarian and practise their English. The third Asian place was the biggest and busiest of all. They never remembered or spoke to anyone, except to spew out a number at you, grab that amount off you and abruptly shunt you towards the door. They were on a busy road and they were always busy.

Even despite that, I especially love gift shopping when it's practical.

I was particularly happy with the dozen matching super-cheap coffee mugs, all in one pattern but many colours. It gave them a look as a group, which may seem silly, but if you've had any experience with the pilfering of student accommodation, you'll understand why they wanted to keep track of what little they had.

Procuring mild painkillers in Hungary is weirdly limited, compared to what I know from elsewhere. Hungarian supermarkets cannot, by law, stock much to do with health or first aid. Pharmacies have a strong monopoly. Elsewhere in the world, supermarkets have whole aisles with everything from paracetamol to first aid bandages. Here, you can only find these in a pharmacy. Also, most of it is behind a counter which in turn, is behind a screen. If you are bleeding and in agony on a Sunday, and haven't hoarded properly, you must beg from a neighbour or wait until Monday.

All my hunting and gathering was completed, assembled and arranged for delivery – both from the supermarket and from me.

E   Grocery delivery will be tomorrow between 9–10am. I will come too, with plates, etc.

D   OK ma. Thanks so much ma.

E   I will arrive a bit after 10am. Please look for a white lady, grey hair, black suitcase.

D   OK ma.

I took care and pleasure in preparing what to drag there. Another modest talent of mine was pulling impressive loads on wheels with my tiny frame, very much ant-inspired. I constructed a bag-lady's dream contraption. Only building it on top of a rusty abandoned baby carriage could have been more iconic. The small roller-bag had a second lumpy cloth bag strapped on top, with a tangle of garishly coloured bungee cords. It was heavy but draggable. I also wore a backpack, sensible shoes and probably non-descript dark, practical simple clothes. In transit this helps me be invisible, uninteresting and unimpeded.

It was Devotion who came to the bus station. He took the parcels and led the way to their rooms in the residence halls of the University of Obuda in north Budapest. I recall that walk as pleasant, perhaps a little nervous, probably accompanied by some polite introductory chit-chat. He was always polite and a man of few words with a fine-tuned radar for others around him.

The student residence hall was a large, modern, shabby, cheap, simple brick building in a 1970's style that reminded me of my own undergraduate years. He let us in with his security key, and showed the way down a long corridor. A lady poked her head out of an open office door, so I waved and said I was visiting friends, but not for long. "I'm with him," I said and pointed. She stared without expression and quietly went back in. We did not break stride but Devotion glanced back with some hesitation.

D Should we go back and talk to her?

E No. She didn't ask. Let her find us, if she needs to. She knows where we are.

No one came to ask. It was a case of Don't Fix It If It Ain't Broke. Later, the others agreed with me. Don't draw attention if you can avoid it. That seemed to be their attitude, whereas Devotion was just trying to do the right thing. But they were nervous about everything these days. One could see that at every turn.

What I didn't know – and perhaps he'd never had visitors here before – was that there was a strict policy that all visitors must report to reception and surrender their ID before entering, which you collected upon leaving. On later visits, I did that, and the guy on reception remembered me, and I produced proper greetings in Hungarian as well as my ID. Unfortunately, one time he went for a long bike ride and I waited nearly an hour to get my ID card back. Still, I was compliant. I did not resist. I brought my resident's card and he liked that. In his eyes, I was a higher class of alien.

By contrast, it was a different matter when one of the African students allowed inside a friend who was staying elsewhere. He only wanted to use the toilet quickly, but he did not sign in properly or show his ID. As a result, that student was asked to leave his residence and had to move out immediately. It did seem too sudden and too harsh, but I do not know any other details. Policies can always be "flexible", "subject to discretion", or similar.

Devotion led me to Speaker's room, where we knocked and knocked again. It seemed like she was not expecting us yet. When she finally cracked open the door, she shrieked and hilariously leapt back against the wall in a comic attempt to hide her slightly unkempt hair.

I started laughing, and Devotion was quiet and patient. We gave her a little time and she soon answered the door, looking tidier. It was a tiny student's room for two with perfect symmetry: two narrow beds, two small desks, two shoddy chairs and barely enough shelving – but there was a fridge. I'd have given a lot for one of those, back when I was a student. This was so much better than their last place.

Soon others joined us. This was when I met Focused and Princess too, and there were others who drifted in and out. Focused was also a man of few words who watched and listened carefully and sharply, taking everything in, storing it, thinking about it.

I opened my bags, and the mugs were received with approval. Speaker took stock of the other kitchenware, sighed to have storage containers at last and smiled at chopping knives, stirring spoons and spatulas. The grocery delivery had already arrived and was piled up in the corner, partly unpacked. It looked like a lot, but then again, there were eleven of them. Things got divided up. A few people arrived with chopped-down drinks bottles to take away some laundry detergent from the big family-sized drum. Same with shampoo. Some kind of system was making this work, somehow.

Speaker was organiser and chairperson, Devotion explained to me. He was a sort of deputy, her number two, quiet and capable in the background. She was the talker, a natural, efficient group leader and spokesperson.

We all talked about many things – how they needed work, but that it took too long to get a work permit unless you were Ukrainian, in which case you got one instantaneously. Many of them were applying to continue their studies here, but living expenses would be a challenge. They'd all applied for financial assistance. I hated to inform them how unlikely that would be.

One student was offered free tuition at Debrecen University, and the authorities accepted that he needed work to pay for living expenses. So, they found him a job in Budapest, which is several hours away from the university, and none of us could see how a six-hour daily commute could ever be feasible.

They just wanted to continue with their studies, somehow, somewhere. Back in Ukraine? Only online at the moment. Here in Hungary? It wasn't looking hopeful. If not here or there, where? They were trawling the info-network. Everything was up in the air for now. Everything.

Then, of course, it was time to explain myself. The six-hour commuter candidate boldly tried to pose a question, paused to rephrase it, hesitated in choosing his words and stammered a little so I made a suggestion.

"Are you all wondering who the heck I am? (Laughter.) Like, who is this strange person?" This got more laughter and broke the ice. Mr Bold took the lead.

"Are you representing a group?"

"No."

"You're part of an organisation?"

"No."

"You're…?"

"I'm just one individual. Please let me explain."

I did my best to describe our point of view, us residents of Budapest, when that tidal wave of people crashed over us, wave after wave of people needing help, when the war started. It was overwhelming for so small a city. We all felt it. A hundred thousand people arrived every week, at the start. The government didn't do much at all. But we all felt we had to do something. It was chaotic, frustrating and upsetting. Everyone was asking, how can we help? What can we do? We had to do something – anything, big or small, we just had to do something.

I was the same, I explained. I was looking out for one project, one role, one niche, maybe one small group. I could not offer a room. Then I saw the post saying that a group of medical students had rooms but no food. Future doctors are out of *food*? I snapped my fingers: "This is it. This is my group. You guys are now my group," I told them.

They understood instantly.

They were stuck with me now.

What occurred to me later were thoughts of my own student days, when I was searching for a future. I wanted work in a career that contributed to society and was helpful, something like education, or an NGO, or maybe healthcare. Healthcare was impossible but I tried. I volunteered in hospitals and hospices, but could not cope with people in pain and distress. I just got upset, and I'd do my best and then go home and cry and cry. If I saw bloody, gory things, I either felt faint or nauseated or both and had to quickly find a chair. Clearly, I was not suitable for that work. I admire those who work in healthcare. They've saved me countless times.

The atmosphere loosened up. We talked on and even laughed a little. The group chat turned into lots of little chats, so I found I had a chance to have a quiet word with Devotion. His words were few, serious, cautious, polite, thoughtful, diplomatic. I really hated thinking about him in an air raid bunker.

I discreetly remarked to him that I'd had ups and downs in my long life, certainly, and a couple of times I might have died, but nothing like what they'd experienced. I'd been almost near a war but never in one. No bomb ever fell near me or my house. I was always a safe distance away. Their terror was hard for me to imagine. Their whole ordeal was hard for me to imagine, in fact, but I could feel some of the fear. If I were in their shoes and had to ask a total stranger for food, that would be horribly painful and difficult for me. So, to me it was impressive that he'd faced such a terrifying thing and succeeded, despite shyness and fear, and he benefited his whole group. He'd succeeded in doing a brave, needed service on behalf of them all.

A smile slowly crossed his face and grew warm, a spark of light in a dark time. Then I could easily picture that, in any healthcare situation, if this young man was helping you, you'd relax and trust him to help you.

Later, Focused said to me, "The first time you came, we were all surprised. We never expected someone to actually come and see us. You were, and still are, lively and happy. If we were depressed, you would have lifted up our mood.

"Another thing, the fact you spoke English and were living in Hungary was a surprise at first, and then it was a relief. We finally found someone that can fully understand what we say."

They spoke about Nigeria, and I told them about my Nigerian friends back in the UK. They told me that the country had three main languages and way too many local dialects, so there were over 200 ways for people to not understand each other, and this has not been helping matters.

Closer to home, we talked about what they needed most at that moment, which was groceries and information. They needed to keep studying, keep eating, and try to see their next best step.

Speaker announced that it was her birthday that Friday, just two days away. I said our custom involved cake – what about theirs? Oh yes, cake was central to birthdays in their homeland too. That settled that. I'd return on Friday and I'd bring a cake.

I'd even bring her favourite evil cola, may I be forgiven. Texts came later.

D *Thanks so much for today ma [two sets of prayer hands]. We really appreciate. [two hearts]*

E *Yes, we are friends now.*

16. Birthday Cake

Thursday 5 May 2022

"Close to Speaker's birthday, she requested a cake, and you actually did bring the cake. We were all surprised and grateful and stated you were sent by God." And that, dear readers, was a first and it was fabulously ironic.

It all started much more humbly than that. I started the messaging of that morning. We had agreed that now they had housing and food, the next thing they needed was information and communication, meaning phone and internet access.

E *I can come to you Friday between 12 and 1.*

D *OK ma, We'll be expecting you ma.*

E *Also – I just learned that if you have student or other ID from Ukraine, you can get a free SIM card, at Gobuda shopping centre. Near you.*

D *OK. Thanks so much ma.*

E *Document attached: This has general info you'll find useful, about Budapest, also links to medical schools if you want to transfer. It's from a shelter in Budapest.*

D OK ma.

Friday 6 May 2022

Speaker had been so excited earlier that week, talking about her upcoming birthday, it was touching. It could not be a worse time to have a birthday, in the middle of war, migration and nearly total uncertainty. It was a good excuse for something nice. They needed a boost. And new plates. And something chocolate.

In preparation, there ensued much cake research online, mostly with the Women of Budapest group. Many nice ladies had extensive thoughts on this. In fact, most of them had intense passions hinting at hysterical yet enjoyable, beloved addictions. I'd opened a floodgate.

These women clearly indulged in expensive bakery treats on a regular basis, and imparted details enthusiastically. Sugar buzz and chocoholism made for fascinating reading. In the end, I went with an old traditional cake shop, and selected a dark chocolate layer cake, allegedly Mexican style (with a hint of chilli), with very rich fillings, accompanied by a charming manager of a certain age who spoke elegant English from the hand-kissing days of old. He enquired about my surname and Hungarian connections. Both the dark Mexican number and the dark-eyed manager had a subtle hint of suave, so they got the order and I collected it on Speaker's birthday.

D Good afternoon ma. How are you doing ma?

E Lots of traffic, bus is slow, maybe arrive 1.30.

D OK ma.

E Maybe you can come to the bus stop? The bags are heavy.

D OK ma.

I brought the hateful cola she loved so much, which I'd never bought before, ever, although she asked every single time. But this was a special occasion. I dragged two massive bottles in the rolling suitcase, with pretzels around the edges to hold them snug, and more kitchenware on the other half. The cake (for fourteen) was in a large carrier bag, and there was more paraphernalia in the backpack.

It was my bag-lady disguise again, overladen and determined, providing a funny dance and juggling spectacle getting on and off the bus. The number 9 crossed the Danube and went north; it didn't take long, just long enough for one substantial daydream about working with Madeleine and the Resistance in the Second World War. In this episode, she was her usual honey-trap, while I played nutty bag-lady, running passports, money, cake.

A delegation met me. Speaker, Focused and Devotion carried everything for me, and conducted me inside. There was great pleasure at unwrapping the various goodies. The cake was a big hit. Speaker poured drinks as people gathered. She was giddy with high-energy chatter, took centre stage and poured a bubbly river of funny stories, hopes, beliefs and some energetic free association. I saw a natural-born charismatic speaker. It was her day, and she handed out the sweet drinks and the cake, which was super rich and overwhelming, and we were soon in a peaceful sugary stupor – or certainly some of us were. It was a sweet afternoon.

I hid the fact that I hate consuming that much sugar, but on her day I did as I was directed. I even put a glass of Despicable Cola to my lips and that's a disgusting, loathsome fact. Let me quickly add that those few sips I took were immediately slid back into the cup. Nothing was spat, nothing was swallowed.

I was hunting for signs they were seriously hungry, but they looked healthy enough. Still, there was so much I did not want to ask about. I'd certainly listen to whatever they wanted to say, but I wasn't going to pry. It was a volunteer no-no to pry. I also knew that they seldom admitted problems or difficulties to elders in order to spare them the worry. It was customary to say you were fine, regardless of how you really were. But the snag with that system was that I really wanted to know how they were. I wanted to be nosy, and of course I hate it when people are too nosy about me, so that shut me up and made me wait for them to open such doors.

At this point, moving into the third month of the war, a different fear had developed. They were not going back soon, this much was sure. It wouldn't be weeks or even months – it might even be years. Their option to be tolerated in Hungary was only on a monthly basis. They'd heard nothing from the various places they'd applied, and it wasn't possible to hurry that along or, in fact, get any kind of update.

In the meantime, they were still in classes and studying every day, some of them with nothing but a phone, while preparing for exams. At least they were not worried about food. At least that was taken care of.

Probably my fondest memory of that afternoon was the food talk. We agreed that when life was stressful, people needed their comfort foods, whatever those happened to be.

Often they were things from home, things from childhood, old favourites.

I asked specifically what they missed the most. They hesitated a bit at first, not wanting to complain, but I encouraged them. I reminded them that I'd been adding chilli sauce to their usual orders, but I suspected I did not send nearly enough, which made them laugh, until they confessed and agreed. Their part of the world is top class when it comes to peppery eating. By contrast, I was a one-chilli eater, not an extremist. I should have double-checked on quantities for them.

Still, they hesitated to ask for particular types of imported African spices because they thought it seemed like a luxury. I didn't think it was a luxury. I thought it was a good idea, a small investment for a great outcome, a very healthy and happy idea, a sure boost for morale. I asked them to get on their smartphones, right then and there, to find the African food shop of Budapest, because surely there was one. I was betting it was in district VIII – which it was, I'm pleased to report, feeling like a good native granddaughter who could sniff her way around here like a local hunter's hound.

I suggested we go on a shopping excursion. I'd sponsor a load of foodstuffs from wherever in this city Africa had landed. This proposal was accepted unanimously.

Speaker leapt into action as I handed her my notebook. I still have this list, in her handwriting, to this day. There was plenty of group input into our new, pleasing project. There was talk of Egusi (melon seed) soup, Eba – a sort of mash from Garri, which I learned was a flour made from cassava (manioc). They wanted groundnuts (peanuts) and groundnut oil. Dried crayfish. Thyme, chilli, pepper soup spices. Nigerian Indomie (instant noodles) and Ugu (an African vegetable).

At several points during the fevered and happy compilation of this list, Mr Bold burst out laughing, saying derisively, "You'll never find that! Here? Never! Impossible!" Speaker looked at him with defiance. She'd find these things. The challenge was on, and I stood loyally by her side.

It was decided. We had a date, a shopping list and a mission. We would make an excursion to African Budapest on Monday, and the idea was beautifully cheering.

17. A Tasty Grocery

Saturday 7 May 2022

After the birthday visit, it was time to organise our African food shopping outing. They said they knew where to go. This was partially true.

E *Monday, I can meet you 14.00 or later. I have 2 big pots and the bath things and will bring them.*

A few hours later:

D *OK ma. Thanks [prayer hands]*

E *Please, tomorrow, tell me where to meet, wherever you found the African shop. I am bringing one heavy bag to give you. And I need to leave before 16.30.*

D *OK ma.*

E *I think you'll need two people to carry things. And, whoever comes, please be ready for a photo, which we need for the fundraising app I am now setting up.*

This was true. As a result of lots of factors, I was setting up a crowd-funding account to link directly to their grocery bills.

Monday 9 May 2022

The weather was cold and rainy and windy and grey, but our third meeting was a fun one.

The first adventure was finding the African shop. This was not straightforward. This place, according to the internet (ha!), was near Blaha Lujza square. Not surprisingly, it was on what I call The Diagonal Street of Many Old Trams, better known as Népszínház utca (People's Theatre street). The rain was becoming steadily colder, stronger and windier. I was much too early and poorly dressed for the unexpectedly chilly storm. I could not find this place. I found an open doorway and shielded from the lively, icy elements.

D *We will be there by 3.30 ma. Speaker and I are coming together.*

E *I am at number 34, but it looks like an apartment building. I'm inside the courtyard. Not sure where to go. I will wait for you.*

They were late. I was bored and cold and thought I'd make another stab at navigation by walking up the road until I passed two black guys waiting in front of a shop. I asked them for help, showed them the ad on the phone, but they had no idea. I went back to my shelter. Speaker and Devotion showed up. We checked everything again online, and we were all confused. How could the internet be wrong? (Ha!)

We walked up and down and numbers did not make sense. Nothing looked African at all, especially not in cold rain. My friends also disliked the cold weather and we all agreed heartily about that. Speaker had an excellent coat, which she lent me, bless her. We sheltered again.

I said they must have been shocked when they arrived in Ukraine in winter, from Africa, and they burst out laughing in recognition. I did some comedy stomping and shaking. A dislike of the cold united us.

Speaker's eagle eyes darted up and down the street, and quickly she went to those same two guys. This time, the conversation went on for longer. They were happy to talk to this good-looking young black woman. Eventually their chat ended. Speaker returned and said to follow her. She sprung ahead like a gazelle, a very competitive athlete. Devotion and I sauntered behind, as he held the umbrella over us both.

E Does she always run ahead like that?

D (laughing) Yes, always.

She found it. On the outside, it looked Indian, but inside it was international food heaven, a tiny, overstuffed warehouse filled with fragrant foodstuffs from all four quarters of the planet. It smelled spicy, musty, dusty and wonderful, even heady and a bit dizzying. Devotion got a big rolling basket. Speaker wielded a hand-basket in one hand, her precious list in the other, and an attitude of authority.

She found the dried crayfish but I found the ground version, which I encouraged her to add as well. I encouraged other things not on the list too, like extra fresh plantain or anything made from it. I got them to add extra things, bigger quantities, take three not two – just fill the baskets, I said, needing to sit down. I located and perched on a crate in a corner. The staff in saris sweeping around me did not seem to mind. On the contrary, they seemed amused.

We got every single thing on that list. It was a triumph. I was hoping she'd joyously announce this to Mr Bold, that doubter, the guy who said she'd never succeed. That would be delicious in more ways than one.

Before dragging it all to the counter, we stood together for a photo that would soon accompany the crowd-funding appeal. Speaker did it for me. The photo is cute, warm, friendly. We three stood in a narrow, cluttered grocery aisle, looking up into a flatteringly high angle. The pitch would be simple: These refugees from the war are medical students taking exams – this fund is for their food budget, for two months, to get them to the end of term.

Small, fairly simple, doable.

I was presented with a comically long receipt (lots of little things!), which came to about €100 and worth every cent. I foresaw many good meals and uplifted spirits ahead. It was almost elating; however, we were not exactly efficient about packing and there were some impatient people behind us.

Satisfied but heavily laden, we heaved ourselves onto a crowded, good old 4–6 tram, and clattered off it before the Margit bridge, where I steered them to the number 9 bus stop, pointing across the Danube and going north to Obuda. Poor Devotion was looking more bookish than athletic, and sagging a bit, but he cheered up when I showed him he was not far from home.

I pointed to the chart on the sign. "We are here. Number 9 bus goes there, see? That's your stop, at the end. Easy."

And of course, he said, "Yes ma. Thank you ma."

***

Later that evening, there were lots of texts with a high proportion of iconography, including hearts, happy faces with hearts, smiles in different colours, assorted food products, prayer hands and imagery of jubilation. Ordinary groceries were also on their way.

E *The other things will be delivered tomorrow, between 10–11.*

D *OK ma. Thanks so much for today ma.*

E *Please be ready tomorrow. I told them to phone you, but sometimes they don't. Last time they thought you were not coming. They are in a hurry. Now go eat well!*

D *OK ma. I will. Thanks so much ma. I read the document and it's OK ma.*

The document he referred to was a statement for the crowd-funding campaign, which could now be launched very soon.

HELP ME FEED 11 REFUGEES FROM THE RECENT WAR

Imagine you're in medical school preparing for exams, but bombs fall on the city, so you flee.

This is a group of mostly medical students now temporarily stranded in Budapest with little support and no food. In March, a few of us volunteers took turns sending them groceries, but now there's only one volunteer (me) and still eleven of them. A college dorm gave them rooms to the end of June, but that's all. Our goal is that they don't worry about food or hygiene products until then.

My name is Eileen Kardos, and I can be found on Facebook under my pen-name Eileen Kay.

Most of these people fled with next to nothing – no bag, no passport, no money. They were total strangers who met on arrival, but they have banded together to make a support group who cook and share together. In all this chaos and fear, I admire how they united for common purpose.

They now await word from various authorities about where and what they do next. Their next steps will be decided by the end of June. Despite living in a nervous limbo, they manage to keep each other's spirits up.

This budget of $1,500 doesn't stretch to any luxuries, just food and essential toiletries.

On the non-financial side of my efforts, they all got free SIM cards, and I continue to research needed information and to network where I can.

But, for May and June, I want them to be worry-free about food and essentials. Based on costs so far, this $1,500 will cover most of that, and I'll cover the rest if needed. If we raise more, then the next priority is tee shirts, underwear, socks and shoes.

Thank you for reading this. If you can donate even $10–$20, it will add up: 100% of the money raised will go straight to the recipients in the form of the aforementioned goods, and it will be hugely appreciated.

Ironically, the first version of the above had the word "Ukraine" in the headline, which sparked complications. Automatically, the crowd-funder's anti-fraud people stopped my application cold, and warned me that scams galore were being perpetrated on their platform, so they had to ask for a lot more information. I was a suspect.

It was true about the scams. They were everywhere. Recently a British man was caught raising money for wheelchairs and crutches for refugees. This was soon found to be a total scam.

This crowd-funder therefore insisted that before I could proceed, I had to provide names and contact details for all the people who would benefit, and arrange for this to be verified one by one. There was also a long list of other requirements to prove I was not one of the scammers of the month. It could take days or even weeks to assemble all this information.

I tried removing "Ukraine War" from my headline, and substituted the phrase "The Recent War". I resubmitted this and everything proceeded immediately. If I could figure that out in a matter of minutes, I think proper scammers could too. The trust factor was becoming increasingly challenging – and, at times, alarming.

I do not want to criticise any crowd-funding website. They perform a function, and it's not easy to do what they do. Many of us need what they offer. But, in dealing with them, one may experience moments of frustration now and then. It was perhaps in one of those moments when I abbreviated that folder's name to GoFMe. That was both untrue and inappropriate, but funny, so I kept it.

Speaker asked if I was free on Saturday for lunch. She was going to cook that special favourite Egusi soup with Eba, that treat from home that they all missed the most. I was very much looking forward to it.

18. Egusi Soup with Chilies and Joking

Saturday 14 May 2022

D *Good morning ma. What time are you coming today ma?*

E *Is 2 OK? You don't have to come meet me. There's nothing to carry. I'll phone when I'm downstairs.*

D *OK ma.*

I managed to get only slightly lost on the way there, wandering past worrying-looking industrial wrecks, but was easily rescued by two nice guys who checked on their phones and pointed me into the right direction.

Devotion met me at the lobby, where the security guy already recognised me, although I guess not many old ladies show up at a university dorm. He took my ID card and waved me in. There was a bit of a wait in the lobby. Devotion had been sent to stall me. I was not early, as I feared, but the food preparation was taking longer than expected. I insisted this was no problem for me. I enjoyed seeing a meal prepared.

I love being in a kitchen when food is coming together, especially with a team effort. It's the best place to get to know people. I'm good at either staying out of the cook's way or doing whatever they say. Perhaps this was their version of treating guests right, in the formal sense, when the food is done and ready to present. I put my case to them, and was allowed into this student dorm kitchen, which forty people shared.

It was very sweet that they'd invited me and it smelled very good.

I saw the challenge in scheduling and the need for two big cooking pots and one frying pan. It was hard enough to work around that many stomachs three times a day, but to borrow plates and everything else in between other people's mealtimes? Especially with forty people? This was absurdly challenging and easily remedied with a few basics thrown their way. A practical solution is a beautiful thing.

It was a very studenty kitchen, plain and cheap as can be, with signs saying "Clean Up Your Mess BEFORE You Eat", probably in more than one language, but maybe memory is exaggerating. There looked to be students from all around the world. I was surprised the kitchen was as tidy as it was, and this group certainly left it in good shape as well. This is not how I remember my student days. I was impressed.

Speaker cooked, Devotion cleaned, Focused sat and talked with me, and Princess wandered around like a butterfly, while chatting. We certainly talked about food, and chillies, and how spicy we liked things. Princess liked the most. She said that with chillies, you must eat enough to make you cry. You always feel better after a good cry, she said, which made us all laugh.

I told them stories of Thai levels of chilli. Whereas I can stand one chilli per dish, they often have about ten. The students nodded with approval. Speaker assured me my low chilli levels had been taken into account today. There was additional hot sauce on the side for anyone who might need a good cry.

Speaker offered me a spoonful for a sample taste. It was zesty, flavourful, peppery, but not aggressive. I could taste the crayfish and many new seasonings. It was lovely. And another thing – she was beautiful, smart enough to be in med school, bold enough to study abroad, and she could cook like this? I was envious.

She served up, Devotion finished the last of the cleaning, and we all walked carefully with steaming, soupy plates, back down the corridor to her room, where I used a chair as a table and the others ate on their laps or on the floor. I wished I'd brought bowls as well as plates. I made a mental note to look around in the local plastic emporiums. I could bring them next time.

They said that, before, they were a bit worried if I'd be able to handle the pepper or even like the food, but that my reaction after eating was priceless. I liked it so much, I licked the plate. They'd made a big pot of it, more for others to have later. "Receiving this African food made us so happy, we didn't want the food to finish. It brought memories from home, a nostalgic feeling." A small investment for excellent results and far more than just the sum of those ingredients. So, there were multiple layers of deliciousness that afternoon.

A group of the students walked me back to the bus station and waited with me on the benches. This was my third time there, so now we had a pleasant pattern, a custom. Speaker and Focused would later say how they "remember the long walks we took to the bus stop with you. It was always fun". I remembered them too. We tried to keep the joking going. We exchanged stories, funny and serious alike. One told me about Russian planes following their trains out of Ukraine, flying low and sometimes shooting. They all had scary stories. But also we gossiped and tried to make each other laugh. That's what I remembered overall about this new partnership, looking back later. It was a dark and scary time, and we were trying to spark light off each other. We were trying to laugh our way out of fear.

In the meantime, that evening, I requested the new grocery list, and thanked them again for that very tasty lunch. I even spoke their dialect by adding a yummy emoji: happy face licks lips, smiles and winks.

They sent the new list, now a simple routine and another pleasant pattern. Lots of good healthy foods and also a request for sweet icky cola from hell, which once again I did not send. That was a boycott I needed to stick with. Instead, I added chocolatey snacks. That was fair enough.

Monday 16 May 2022

E *Groceries are coming between 10 and 11 am. Please confirm that you got this message?*

D *OK ma.*

E *And please text OK, after it arrives?*

D *OK ma.*

Hurrah, later I saw all had gone to plan.

D *I have seen it ma. Thanks so much ma.*

E *OK.*

That evening:

D *Thanks so much for today ma [heart]*

E *[smiley face with hearts for eyes]*

MAY 2022

Budapest

19. Journalists, Artists, Allies

Sunday 15 May 2022, Budapest

There was another delivery of basic foodstuffs – or what I'd usually call groceries, but I liked their word better. I texted them, but now knew that it may not be read for a while. They'd never take a voice call in class. I phoned directly and got through. I could not catch everything said by Devotion's nice low, gentle voice, thanks to my bad hearing. This is finally what shoved me to make an appointment to repair or upgrade my hearing aids, and also maybe learn how to use Bluetooth earbuds or whatever they'll be called next week. I think I'm trainable and now admit I must try to up my senior game.

By now it was clear that Speaker was an excellent communicator, networker and talkaholic, whereas Devotion was minimalist in conversation, all action or patience and mostly wordless. It was helpful to have them both at hand when another delivery was due. She played quick to his laconic, and it was good teamwork.

E Hi. Groceries will arrive tomorrow, Monday, between 10 and 11. They will phone Devotion's number.

S Hello ma. Good morning ma. OK ma.

The delivery went fine, but I'd made an error. This was an African politeness lesson I had been taught many times in Zimbabwe and failed many of those times. It was bad manners to skip the "How Are You?" ritual, however time-consuming it might be. This was a bad, crude, uncivilised, barbaric and much too direct American habit of getting down to business immediately. The following type of elegant chastisement befell me in Zimbabwe more than once:

> *"Excuse me, can you direct me to this address…?"*
>
> *"I'm fine thank you, and you?"*

A charming slap. You're supposed to send blessings on their good health and perhaps also that of their entire extended family, and only after respect has been paid may you ask your petty, selfish and childish tiny little question. The bigger your question, the longer you spend on respect-paying rituals. There is a proper tone of asking, a proper style. But if you were never taught this, you might be schooled with a light verbal slap.

Later that morning, I'd heard nothing from Devotion, who was supposed to confirm the grocery foodstuffs had arrived. He wasn't answering, but Speaker was.

E Did the groceries arrive? They said they rang 4 times and no one answered. I am afraid someone else took these things. Please talk to reception?

S *OK ma. We have taken it. Thank you so much ma. We are grateful.*

Soon after that, I sent the following to Speaker as their rep. I'd met a journalist covering the story about international students trying to escape the war but suffering from discrimination. Would anyone from Speaker's group do an interview? Most of them recoiled instantly from anything connected to The Media, but a few volunteered. As for mainstream media, most didn't cover this at all. Some did, once, but dropped this story completely, after a few initial reports. But these students wanted to speak up. They and I and others wanted some follow-up on this story.

E *Please forward this message to all the others. A reporter from Szabad Európa news company will contact you this week, hoping to set up a video interview.*

S *OK ma. What about me ma?*

E *Of course you too! The reporter will call, they said. But they're super busy.*

S *OK ma. Thank you so much ma.*

In the end, Speaker would be the main interviewee. She had already told me about all the troubles back home, how she'd left one war for another, how she was a prime target for kidnapping and impossible ransom demands, how her family urged her to stay away because she was safer. She was not the only one. There were many like her. This was apart from the fact that medical schools at home were few, competitive, expensive, and mainly for children of the ultra-privileged. Now she wanted to share her story and theirs, and I imagined she'd do a good job as spokesperson. She once said that besides wanting to be a doctor, she'd once wanted to be a news broadcaster. I could easily picture it.

Then I realised it might be wise to find out a bit more about these journalists, and thank goodness it appeared to be good news. *Szabad Európa* is a modern update of RFE/RL (Radio Free Europe/Radio Liberty) and their Hungarian Service. It closed in 1993 but was relaunched in 2020 because of the downturn in real news coverage and upturn in tightly controlled, exclusively pro-government propaganda.

Their aim is to offer independent news and an arena for responsible social debate and free speech. They provide this in twenty-four countries and in twenty-eight languages, wherever the free press is weak or limited by the government. They work digitally via their website, social media platforms, podcasts and newsletter. They're committed to freedom of the press, public service information and democratic principles. They aim to reveal human rights abuses, among many other issues.[1]

And I thought Radio Free Europe was a thing of the past, no longer needed, once the Commies were ousted and there were free elections in 1990. Maybe a lot of people thought this was no longer needed. Not so, not now. Now they are needed, very much so. There's no question about this.

Wednesday 18 May 2022

We were planning a cash-distribution day for Friday. Mark, one of my kindly donors, wasn't 100 per cent happy about the high percentages that crowd-funding takes. I don't blame him for feeling that way. But he was a fellow Budapester and not a distant neighbour, so the plan was to meet for a coffee and discreetly hand over cash literally under the table. We'd already hit our target for the basic grocery budget, so this was above and beyond that.

Thursday 19 May 2022

E *Did Devotion send everyone the message about the cash gifts from Mark? When can we organise everyone to be together, to receive them? And, does anyone want to accept his invitation to visit his home, with the great art collection?*

S *Yes, and Yes, ma. Ma can you come Friday, 5pm?*

E *OK.*

The aforementioned Mark Rimmell was one of many donors to their cause, a friend and neighbour. Artist and art collector and more, he retired to Budapest many years ago, but he is not at all retiring. He's well-known and well-liked in the expat world, that city within the city. We met at one of his favourite cafés for a snack, a catch-up chat and a gift, bless him. What's more, I'd trust him in exactly the same way. Trust. That theme. There it is again. It does not grow on every tree.

The agreement was to split Mark's donation ten ways between the students. The group had been fourteen, then eleven, and was ten at last count. At this point, they were all fed and housed, so Mark's addition was overspill. They all needed different things, such as phone data, shoes, toiletries – and, at this point, it was not our business, so cash would be handed over as pocket money, as unanimously agreed.

The number 9 bus went over the Danube from Pest to Buda, and turned north to Obuda toward the end of the line. I knew the way well now, and the short-cut. I went to see them again, partly to deliver the cash gifts, partly to deliver some more miscellaneous kitchen implements, and also to settle our plans for visiting Mark that weekend, to visit his amazing home and art collection.

It was good to see them more settled in the kitchen department, which was now financed to the end of June; a very nice relief. Things were feeling a bit more stable. This visit was more relaxed and there was more joking and teasing flowing between them.

We followed the directive of many crowd-funding sites in asking cash recipients to sign for the receipt of their money. I had the list printed out, and in no time, Speaker attached it to her clipboard and sprang into action, helping me with the distribution. We were gathered in her room. There were a few people who could not attend that day, and she signed for their share and promised to pass it on a bit later.

This woman could easily run a hospital, I have no doubt.

The scene led to some comedy grumpiness from Mr Bold, who started joking in a way that didn't sound entirely like joking. It may not have been joking at all, I am not sure, but it was extremely funny to everyone else, including me. He announced firmly that he did not understand why Speaker was in charge of the money. Instant laughter from most of the group. She'd been designated as group leader for quite some time now, by what looked to me like a consensus, but here perhaps was a dissenting vote, still disgruntled. I think he knew he was beaten but he was going to launch a fun rebellion anyway by proposing a round of Argument-Tennis.

"I mean it," he continued. "Why is she in charge of the money?" More laughter.

"Why not?" I asked. Even more laughter.

"I do not trust women with money". A burst of cascading laughs that took some time to fade, framed by face-palms and eventually falling into a long silence with awkward squirming that I tried to prolong, as much as possible, with my best big fat smile, leaning into him.

I asked, "You trust me, don't you?"

The best explosion of laughter so far, and even some applause made that round mine.

The comedy door now wide open, Speaker retaliated with accusations of who was the laziest student of them all. It was either Mr Bold or his friend, or maybe both of them tied for last place. She was on a roll, in full finger-shaking mode. Both men went quiet, not with chastisement, but with an elevated dignity, a self-righteous display of tolerance for her over-done indiscretions, her lack of cool control. They took the moral high ground, but not for long.

This was fun.

I remarked, "Oh, you went quiet. That's diplomatic. That's dignified."

They nodded. They liked this. They felt vindicated and approved, and took on a kingly posture and walked right towards a comedy trap.

"Or maybe," I continued, "you say nothing because … what she said … is true?"

A very nice explosion of laughter met that one. Bright spots, how we need them. When you can joke with and tease people, when you can make each other laugh, you've arrived at a good place. We laughed about a few other things that day. They needed it. They deserved some cheering up. And most of all, I was glad to see how skilful they were at several comedy sports like Argument-Tennis, Insult-Tennis and Shade Ping-Pong. They were champions, very imaginative.

To finish the distribution of the last few portions of cash, a posse of us went upstairs. Speaker bounded ahead like a gazelle, knocked on door after door and supervised everything with her clipboard, pen and commanding authority. I stood at her side. Recipients took the surprise rather well.

One young man had been awakened from a nap. His thanks were sleepy and incredulous, in that "Am I dreaming?" kind of way. We've all wished and dreamed someone would simply show up at the door and hand over cash without complications, I'm sure.

One of their group was a big-chested man who entered the corridor wearing a tee shirt that said "Fuck Off". I laughed hard at this and said I liked it. The others did not laugh at all and said nothing. He stared them down. "If you don't like it," he said, "then you can Fuck Off!" I laughed even louder and even longer at that, but it was just me. Maybe Devotion was not the only churchy one. Maybe we cussers were in the minority there.

I leaned over to Devotion and asked, "You never talk like that, do you?"

"No," he said.

"Normally, I don't, but sometimes I do," I admitted.

He looked at me patiently.

We finished our task. They still had a few more weeks of exams but now there was a smallish window to a few weeks of stability – a place to sleep, a food budget and even some pocket money. That smallish window of stability would change sooner than we thought. Today though we made our plans with Mark for a nice, social, pleasant Sunday afternoon. He'd asked how many people to expect.

Mr Bold truculently asked if they had to go. Had to? Of course they didn't have to. It was entirely their choice. But also, there was not room for twelve. It was a tiny place with room for six or seven people maximum, including myself and Mark.

This was an understatement. Mark's flat was unbelievably full of artefacts from floor to ceiling, so full you had to crab-walk sideways up narrow paths. It was a beautiful and fascinating place, but I'm not sure I've ever seen anywhere to sit.

Perhaps I imagined a few subtle scowls, but I expected divergent reactions to this offer to meet a sponsor. On the one hand, I knew that both Mark and his offer were sweet, and some might love it. But some didn't want to go, and I understood perfectly well. As difficult as it was to imagine being in their shoes, I think I'd probably not want to go. I'd be grateful for the help, but going there might make me feel like a performing poodle. I'd have stayed home and given those seats to the eager ones.

What I didn't know or see at the time was that all sorts of turbulence and confused decision-making were going on behind the scenes with this group, about which I'd only learn a bit later.

What I knew was that Mark's flat was a beautiful and unusual place, and he was a sweetie, so a special visit was in store for someone wanting to see the magic of the museum-like home of an art collector. The ones who accepted happily were

Focused, Devotion, Speaker and Princess.

***

Later, when plans were settled, several of them walked with me to the bus, the good old number 9. It was a Friday evening and we were all heading towards the city centre. I hoped they might do something pleasant, a short break from all the suspense and uncertainty. The weather was so much warmer than when they first arrived. Lots of people walked along the Danube in the evening. There were many beautiful walks along that river, by all those pretty bridges and the wooded hills. Budapest was known for this and its spectacular riverside sunsets.

I asked how often they spoke with their families. They did it as often as they could. The mere mention of family brightened their faces.

We joked again about the Ma title. I was reassured that it was more like Ma'am than Mom. That was best. I did not feel like family or even Chosen Family. I felt like their teacher. Sometimes a teacher can become neighbourly, an older friend and perhaps part-time mentor, and this is a pleasure – when you care about their life and not just their schooling. I also explained that everybody calls me Eileen – whether they're old or young, no matter what the connection. Speaker listened to my little speech, and she absolutely never accepted any of it. She smiled and said I was Ma and that was that.

This started us giggling. I asked about her mother and Speaker said she'd like to meet me. I'd like to meet her too. I'd like to think that, in a few years' time, we'll all be celebrating her graduation. Then the dream would be to make money rain from the sky in order to fly her parents first class to wherever she graduates from her studies. It was a very nice dream which I didn't say out loud.

Hope drives you on.

20. An Artistic Treat, A Sudden Departure

Sunday 22 May 2022

Budapest used to be two cities on opposite banks of the Danube, and it still feels that way. Whenever on a foray to The Other Side (i.e. the Buda side), I never quite have my bearings. I'd been to Mark's place before but only following others like a blind, trusting spaniel dog. I studied the students' route extra carefully and sent detailed directions. I was hoping for an enjoyable visit.

We were coming from different parts of the city and arranged to meet at Mark's. Speaker had many fine skills and I loved her, but navigation wasn't a strong point. Somehow, she misread the directions. I arrived at Mark's a bit early and promptly got tangled in texts and phone calls with her from an unexpected location. There were also so many photos my phone would need an hour to download them. There always seemed to be tangles, detours, delays and melodramas when it came to her getting from A to B, as brilliant as she was at so many other things. Still, we worked out the new route and they relaunched their onwards journey. Mark was relaxed and delightful. He was with his little doggie companion, a curly white-haired creature named Anton. He said with a gracious wave that he'd be ready, whenever they came. I went to meet them at the nearest tram stop to walk them to Mark's place.

On the way, they dropped a conversational bombshell. Speaker explained to me quietly and bluntly that in three days' time, they were leaving the country to go to the Netherlands.

That gave my stomach quite a lurch. "In three days?" I asked.

She took a very deep breath and answered with some tension but certainty, "Yes."

Their situation had become much more unstable, suddenly. They'd had letters from both the university accommodation and the immigration department. Immigration did not contact them directly, but via the university. Terms seemed to be changing. First they were told to present ID to the office that same day, or they'd be thrown out of the dorm that same day. Then they were told that, even if immigration let them stay in the country beyond next month, the university accommodation they were currently in, would not let them stay. In theory, they had two weeks to get accepted into some university or other, arrange for a new visa, find new accommodation, also keep up with their online studies in Ukraine, and probably look for work even though no one was going to hand over a work permit because they were not Ukrainian.

There was also the underlying issue of distrust. They were already used to the idea that some governments are unpredictable and inconsistent. They were used to double-speak and bullshit-tennis. They had not overstayed, but authorities kept visiting to check on them. It became scary because they couldn't see what the government's next move would be. They did not trust them, and they certainly did not feel like reporting in to a police station. They felt dramatically less safe being deported back home. That was going from one war to another. It didn't even occur to them to consider it.

So, they all decided they were leaving, quietly, by train, in another direction altogether. Germany, the Netherlands and maybe other places, said the grapevine, were still able to accept people straggling in from Ukraine – one might even get a visa to stay for a year, possibly. Friends had gone ahead and suggested they hurry. Europe's window could not stay open forever.

There were quite a few grapevines, or that's what it felt like. One was never sure who had up-to-date and accurate information. This was a whole issue in itself. But they were leaving, that much they had decided. It may have started sinking into my brain when we were nearly at Mark's door. They agreed to talk further, right after the visit. There were plans to make, ways I might help, things to organise. I held money raised for them which needed to get to them. Meanwhile, we rang the bell, climbed upstairs and entered the magical Aladdin's treasure trove that is the home of artist and collector Mark Rimmell.

It was very much a fantasy dream world. They forgot their troubles for a while. When they first walked in it was with trepidation that they might brush by or disturb something. They were nervous so close to that much art. They thought it must be alarmed somehow, and they were afraid to accidentally jump with a shock. But it's not that kind of place. Mark opens his doors often. If you can get in past all the clutter, that is.

***

Londoner Mark Rimmell first came to Budapest in 2005, working on the film *Eragon*. He was a set decorating buyer. At the end of that five-month contract, he'd bought a flat and declared the city his home. Lots of people fall in love with this place and its particular magic. At the time, people thought he was crazy, but he's been here happily for almost twenty years.

His place has been compared to a museum, an art and antique gallery, a work of art in itself. There are layers of things, floor to ceiling, on every possible surface. He's worked on many kinds of films, so there's a bit of everything:

- Drapes, curtains, beautiful textiles and costumes, kimono ties turned into neckties.
- Ornate mirrors which trick you into seeing double the real size of the place.
- Statues, bronzes, sculptures, gilded art.
- Sketches, paintings, prints, photography, fashion drawings.
- News articles, memorabilia.
- Stage props, mementos from the film world.
- Wooden and other masks.
- Custom-made, hand-painted wallpapers.
- Vases, ceramics – and there's a large green Chinese dragon in there somewhere too.
- A possibly controversial number of baby dolls' heads, fascinating or disturbing, depending on your view.
- Antique furniture everywhere, velvet chairs.
- Quite a lot of skull imagery.

The central area of one room is devoted to his own artwork. He was dubbed "The Crownmaker of Budapest" after he created a unique jewel-encrusted crown for the winner of the World Top Model competition. This is what started this passion for making multimedia art-crowns, and now he has a room full of them. [1]

You can wander around his apartment for hours and there is still a lot to discover and be amazed at. This is exactly what we did, wandered about wide-eyed. After a while, it feels as if your eyes are drunk on fine wine. We admired beautiful things and heard his stories while we stood staring, smiling, charmed. It was an art and sweetness picnic.

He didn't go in for celebrity name-dropping that day, but he could have. He's worked with some of the finest art directors in the film business. Paul McCartney was a gallery visitor. Charlie Chaplin commissioned a bust of Sophia Loren, and Mark met him alongside Marlon Brando.

There are many more but please just savour this last one: in 1986, in New York's Radio City Music Hall, at an MTV awards ceremony hosted by Eddie Murphy, he linked arms at the finale with Tina Turner and Joan Baez as they all sang together. Mark is modest about all this.

***

We gathered around a table where he showed us how he disassembled jewellery into bits to restructure it into sculptures and crowns. Necklaces and jewellery were dangling everywhere. On the table were trays and boxes filled with rings and necklaces not yet scavenged. The students ogled and stroked things, and he said sweetly in a low voice that they could each choose one thing to take away as a gift. He said it so gently and quietly that we almost missed what he said. Everyone blinked. I tentatively asked him to clarify and repeat; that I thought I'd heard him right but wasn't sure. With a wave of the hand he said they should help themselves. They were delighted. The girls each took a necklace (floral, swirling) and the boys each took a ring (chunky, rock and roll). You can see some of them on the cover photo, which we took on the balcony that overlooks a spectacular stretch of the Danube, looking from the Buda side across to Pest. From his flat filled with gems, he saw this city as a gem too. We thanked him, over and over, and drifted down the stairs.

Focused loved meeting Mark, and loved his dog too. But even as a dog person, Focused thought the dog didn't like them, because he yapped in irritation a lot of the time we were there. In fact, it may have been the entire time we were there. But Anton often did this. It was not that the dog didn't like them. The dog didn't like anyone near Mark or his flat. He was overly protective and wanted Mark all to himself. Anton was a devoted museum guard, day and night, of the art and of its curator.

We went to a small nearby park and sat down with a big sigh. There was still a month's worth of food budget earmarked for the students. We decided how to split that equally and convert it to a cash gift earmarked for meals on the road and beyond. There followed a rough and complicated sketch of how to do this via a combination of online banking, PayPal and plain cash in hand. It was not straightforward or simple but it forced me to update and expand my banking methods. Suddenly, there were lots of those sorts of tasks. Ten people moving house in a few days! Times like these, one's lists have lists.

We travelled back upriver with a warm, shining sunset across the water to the Pest side and the lavish Parliament building and other outstanding buildings. Here on the Buda side was a pretty stretch of riverside promenade with trees in blossom and contented people strolling across their Sunday afternoon, smiling at the scene. Lots of visitors fall in love with this place. It has charm and magic.

The students were smiling at the scene too. Focused said it was a beautiful city, and he'd miss it. I knew what he meant.

21. Oranges and Distrust in Hungarian History

My new friends and I were getting glimpses of a local issue. Distrust of officialdom is a long-standing issue in Eastern Europe, with its own distinctive flavour. There has been history, to say the least. One of the best and oddest illustrations involves tropical fruit and a very inappropriate environment in which to try to grow it. This episode will give you some of the flavour of this culture, and why cynicism and surrealistic humour have blossomed there – unlike the oranges, which did not.

This part of the saga begins with an agricultural tragedy in the 1950s. On the one hand, it caused senseless loss, starvation and suffering. Much later, the Hungarian orange became an infamous running joke because of the satirical film *The Witness* (*A Tanú*, in Hungarian), based on these times. History sometimes provokes in Hungarians the ability to turn hideousness into weird humour.

The post-WWII Communist regime then ruling Hungary decided with a fervent passion to cultivate oranges and other tropical fruit. They were desperately, absurdly committed to this mission. Their land was not known for tropical weather or any of the right conditions, but they did not waver. The regime decided that the lemon must be domesticated in Hungary. They convened a quarterly lemon meeting in 1951 and appointed a national lemon manager. Special species alleged to be frost-resistant were shipped from Moscow, and 7,000 lemon, orange and tangerine saplings were planted. [1]

It did not work. Farms failed, people starved and it did a lot of damage.

Many have observed that Hungarian history is full of strangely brutal times. Many also say that one of the worst was the reign of Mátyás Rákosi, whose economic policy was infamous, absurd and catastrophic. His era was 1948–1953, years remembered as a time of fear. It was a police state. Disappearances happened routinely. Political prisoners were taken to internment camps for forced labour. Torture, imprisonment and terror were commonplace. Hundreds of thousands were imprisoned, and thousands were executed.

This is when my Great-Uncle Rudolf (Rezső) disappeared without trace. He was exactly the sort of profile who did disappear. The only thing that calms my stomach about that is the fact he is out of his misery now. The Nazis and their collaborators got some of our people, but the Commies got him – allegedly. No death certificate has ever emerged, which is very unusual, but without that document I am not allowed to see his security file. There was a catch-22 feeling about it.

As for agricultural and other policies, Rákosi and company were typical of their time. They never considered the role of the environment. Like Stalin their adored teacher, they too wanted to overcome and conquer Mother Nature. Wherever they built, nature was ignored. More than a few buildings were built on unstable soil, with disastrous results.

In the agricultural area, there were scandals of child labour: over 4,000 young people were sent to work in fields, housed without beds, barely fed, one spoon for every 400 children, and no drinking water at all. A nearby farm offered a hundred litres of wine, and many children got drunk and sick.

There were issues of flooding, disease and environmental damage. Wheat production fell but the population grew, and bread grain had to be imported. This is the legacy of Rákosi.

It's worth mentioning that Comrade Rákosi mustn't be confused with Prince Rákóczi, especially if you're visiting Budapest.

Prince Francis Rákóczi II, in the 1700s, led his nation's rebellion against the oppressive Habsburg Empire from Austria, a spirited but doomed project. It would take a few more centuries and a world war to see the end of that empire and for Hungary to gain independence, but the Prince is credited with getting that ball rolling.

He is depicted in bronze as a larger-than-life figure looming astride a horse rearing up in front of the Hungarian Parliament. There are statues of him in other places too, and quite a few major streets named after him. He can be seen in oil paintings with a grand fur hat and elaborate regalia, with a great dark mane of curly locks and a magnificent moustache. He is a national hero, identified with their passion for independence.

By contrast, Comrade Rákosi (born Rosenfeld), the Communist autocrat and fruit maniac, was another matter altogether. There are no statues of him anywhere, to my knowledge. If there were any that were accurate, they'd show him as almost spherical, neckless and hairless, in a grey suit and with a cold and heartless stare. He was finally ousted in 1956, returned to his beloved Soviet Union, and was never allowed to return to Hungary, where he is generally seen as their ultimate symbol of tyranny and oppression.

Scandals and nightmares to one side, the film *The Witness* actually made a lot of this era funny, especially the fruit-farming debacle. That might be hard to believe, but I was an eyewitness. I laughed in horror and in irony, but I laughed throughout this excellent film.

Many consider it one of the best films from Hungary, as well as one of the best satires about Communism anywhere. I personally consider it to be a gem, by any standard.

Péter Bacsó made the film *The Witness* (also known as *Without a Trace*) in the late 1960s about events in the 1950s. It was made in a tense political climate, when talking about the early 1950s and the 1956 Revolution was still taboo. This film mocked that whole world, and made thinly veiled references to real army generals and other party officials. Unsurprisingly, the film was immediately banned throughout the nation, and stayed that way until the Communists left power twenty years later, in 1989. [2]

The 1981 Cannes Film Festival screened it. As a result of that and other screenings abroad, authorities eventually relented and allowed its release in Hungary. It became a beloved classic and a cult favourite, and a lot of its dialogue entered the national vocabulary.

The loveably soft main character is a sweet, simple guy, the honest and innocent Pelikan, a single dad of eight kids whose wife ran away. He is dragged into the ruling party, but fails spectacularly with every task they give him, goes to prison many times, is almost executed more than once but escapes, sees his house burned down, and when the Danube floods, he and his family are stranded high in a tree. Whichever way he tries to fit in, he is just too nice to master the fine arts of selfish corruption and deceit. In the end, because he's honest, he's sentenced to hang but is released after Stalin dies.

All that befalls him, he accepts calmly, with understatement. He is used to nothing going well. Disasters never surprise him. He accepts sweetly that nothing makes sense, nothing is honest, nothing works correctly. There is no competence, anywhere. But he smiles. He's a sort of absurd hero. It's like Kafka but funny.

A now-legendary scene coined a catchphrase for the nation. It's when our hero Pelikan is assigned to the orange research department.

A feared party leader visits the site where scientists have been unsuccessfully experimenting with orange-growing. Mr High-Up Comrade has come to taste one of these oranges. The scientists have only managed to produce one tiny fruit, but a large public presentation is constructed around it. They hope to hide the fact that this is the only orange they have. Unfortunately, Pelikan's small hungry child eats it, right before the ceremony.

Quickly, they substitute it with a lemon, telling the party official, "It's the new Hungarian orange, a bit more yellow, a bit more bitter – but it's ours." [3]

The party man eats the "orange". It's awful. This was the new Hungarian orange. An icon was born. Thus that sentence and image entered the culture. It became a symbol for the huge and insane gap between sweet party propaganda telling you things are fine, and everyday sour facts proving they are not.

They proclaimed Let There Be A Hungarian Orange – and hey presto, there it was, a lemon re-dubbed an orange. It was no empty promise, just a re-labelling.

It's amazing how the film made these nightmares funny. For those who did not grow up in Eastern Europe, it's hard to believe. Their daily experience of absurd surrealism must go deeper than we outsiders can imagine.

High points of ridiculousness from the film's villains:

"Remember: those who don't trust us, don't trust themselves and those who don't trust us don't trust our bright future, either. And those who don't trust our happy, bright future… are traitors."

"The suspicious thing about spies is that they're not suspicious."

***

In 1989, a weekly magazine called the *Hungarian Orange* (*Magyar Narancs*) was founded.[4] It's still publishing today in 2023. It's jokingly abbreviated to Mancs, which means paw. It was named after the famous orange in the banned-then-unbanned film. Like the film, the newspaper is seriously satirical, blending serious points and humour. Their journalistic style was fresh and new to Hungary at the time: ironic and satirical, using everyday informal language. The articles are mostly about politics, culture, sociology and the arts.

The founders were young intellectuals associated with the Alliance of Young Democrats which later became the Fidesz Party, and which at the time had liberal views. That's hard to believe if you know anything about them now. But, at that time, with the heavy legacy of decades of Communist misery, anything anti-Communist looked liberating, liberal, even progressive. Lefties and pre-democracy types today must shudder at the memory. Or, maybe they make ironic jokes to ward off any shuddering.

The association between that party and this paper did not last long. Fidesz was elected in 1990 but the newspaper soon severed its ties with them. The leftist magazine kept the *Hungarian Orange* name. They both wanted to keep it, but the paper had it first, in 1989. Fidesz has steadily proceeding to the right ever since, but kept the bright orange circle as the theme behind their logo.

They both wanted a bite of the orange. They had very different ways of being anti-red.

One last tragi-comedy with fruit

The tradition of using citrus as social commentary was alive and well in 2012, when a protest group created an inflatable lemon, 5 metres long and 3.5 metres high. They took it to the centre of Budapest, Kossuth Square, the site of the Parliament building and the princely hero Rákóczi's grand statue. They went to a "Peace March" in support of Fidesz. The protesters were hoping to get their "Hungarian orange" (lemon) on camera.

This was not to be. They never even got close. Angry "Peace Marchers" intercepted them and destroyed the inflatable while screaming angry curses at them. [5]

Later the protesters re-entered the rally's grounds, when speeches were over and the national anthem was playing. They took an ironically solemn and sacred attitude, parading their giant lemon's remains, carrying it above their shoulders. They were greeted by surprised but happy faces of their supporters, who proceeded to play catch with it, joyfully tossing their "Hungarian orange" back and forth, around the crowd.

I'm not sure you can trust people without a sense of humour. It's as weird as not liking dogs.

By the way, also on the fruit theme is the fact that Barack Obama's first name, in Hungarian, means peach, and that deserves a mention too.

The sad news is that huge numbers of Hungarian citizens have emigrated, because of all of the above and more than we can ever know. They miss their native land but cannot abide the paranoic, untrustworthy political conditions. And some of them are scared and do not feel safe. Recent refugee guests, like my new student friends, were getting uncomfortable there too, for some of the same reasons, and they were planning their escape.

The good news is that you can't stop happiness and laughter, even in Eastern Europe, where for centuries, that soil has produced more grumpiness than oranges.

22. Fear and Plantain Chips

Monday 23 May 2022

I was the first off the mark in the texting stakes, asking if they were free that day to buy bags and maybe more, plus recce Keleti train station.

I attached a document of Dos, Don'ts and Dangers when travelling these days as a refugee. It was damned lengthy and complicated. I could not bring myself to say, "I know you're up to your ears in exams and feel like you're drowning, along with your entire life being turned upside down, but please will you memorise this tedious list of 700 details?" Unfortunately, I reckoned they might be needing some of them.

There were dangers out there worth warning people about. Those who'd left the country already were vocal in reporting how it went. There were very mixed reports. Paying attention to these accounts was vital. WhatsApp and other chat groups fizzed with exchanged stories, first-hand accounts, eyewitness reports. Mainstream or official info was not the main focus. They were not trusted.

Officially, in theory, the EU declared that anyone fleeing the war in Ukraine could travel free on their trains. In practice, and in time, this faltered, more and more. Regulations changed often and new terms didn't always filter down to the rank and file. Also, some officials simply didn't obey directives and were alleged to be lining their own pockets. It started to become irrelevant, what the official version was. What mattered more was the mood of the official standing in front of you.

Speaker texted that she'd heard from others who went ahead.

> *S* *The two of them that left for Netherlands last week on Friday, they paid 3 dollars each to Germany and 70 dollars to Netherland even after showing their Ukrainian ID. It does not work for everyone, or they may have stopped.*
>
> *E* *Very sorry to hear that. You must be ready for that too. But, might be OK.*

Of course, countries would have to stop these services someday. But whatever the rules from one month to the next, it appeared that individual staff were taking it into their own hands to implement things when they chose – helping these people, but not those. This became another strand on the internet grapevine, which was becoming more and more essential to just about everything. Every question found a village of consultants and fellow travellers. It seemed like no one read the official sites or the mainstream news. They just didn't believe them. They only believed each other. They wanted eyewitnesses.

In this case, multiple postings suggested there might be added costs to the journey, regardless of anything official. As for waves of migrants, those with money had come and gone. Back in March, there were many refugees who were middle class, booked hotels for a while, then flew to Germany or wherever. These were the people so many European and American journalists referred to as not the usual refugees but the acceptable ones. Their tone was that these were not really refugees at all because they were nicely dressed and professional; of course, they were white, and let's not forget the nice suitcases plus they're really into their pet dogs. So, let them through. No fences: open gates.

Back in Obuda, it had not been straightforward for the student group to make plans with each other. Speaker had wanted everyone to travel together, or as many as possible. She felt there was safety in numbers, in case of problems. Not everyone agreed. In fact, some insisted this would draw too much attention. A few clung to the lone wolf idea. There were ten different lives being disrupted. Each had to find their road.

What's more, a mere few months ago, these people had never met each other. They met on the bus to Budapest. They got chucked together only because they were fellow nationals. And soon, they were getting chucked in quite a few different directions, not all of them clear yet.

Certainly, the women should not travel alone, and they did not.

Princess admitted she was partly trying to choose a travelling companion based on his helping carry her luggage. I quietly thought she'd probably carry her own luggage and would learn this in due course.

Overall, it put one in mind of the old saying that if you

want to travel far, travel with a group, but if you want to travel fast, travel alone. They were all making those sorts of decisions.

Eventually somehow things got decided. Some of them were heading to Germany, some to France, and the rest to various parts of the Netherlands. Few other details were clear. Some might travel alone or maybe in pairs. Some now, some later. Speaker thought that on Wednesday, seven people would travel together. They'd need to get their tickets on Tuesday, in person, showing ID. And Monday, today, there were other preparations. And worries. And a constant river of unknowns.

***

We were meant to meet at Nyugati station, but somehow yet again Speaker and I misunderstood each other. She liked to hit the ground running but it wasn't always in the right direction, bless her. I'd asked her to go to a certain bus stop, where I was waiting. I waited for a while, and then I texted.

E I am at the bus stop – where are you?

S I have been looking for you, for 14 minutes.

E Where???

S I walked to this place to look for you ma.

She sent a stack of photos which, again, were too much to download, but I could see that she'd been running everywhere except where I'd asked her to wait. Finally I worked out where she was.

E *OK, stay still, I will come to you. Do not move. I'm there in 2 min.*

S *OK ma.*

Immediately she moved, of course, and ran outside the station, and ran all around looking. Was this panicking? Let's chalk it up to that. It was Focused who found me. I hoped that when Speaker works in a hospital, she can find where she needs to go. I hope when her supervisors give her directions, she knows she must follow them and must go where she's told.

We bussed it up to Lehel market of the chin-scarf tough women, and got Devotion the bag on wheels he deserved, not the cheaper one he'd asked for. He'd humbly said any cloth bag with handles would do. I knew for sure that later he'd want wheels, not to shoulder that weight the whole long way. We outvoted and upgraded him. Then we took another bus to Keleti station, where their journey would begin on Wednesday.

From my journals on the day:

> *We went to see if there was some kind of information centre. The only one we saw was a serious-looking police point. The last thing it looked like was a help centre. We most certainly did not go there. That was exactly what could get you deported straightaway. We all went quiet and proceeded straight to the ticket office, where we didn't exactly know what to do. We sat outside trying to decide.*

It felt like a wasted trip. It was an unusually hot day and a disappointing one too, on top of all their other concerns. They looked tired, stressed and scared, which is how I felt too. I went into the main ticketing area and read everything on those walls, learning that, without a seat reservation, they might sit on the floor the entire way, if the train was crowded. And it was many, many hours from Hungary through Austria and Germany to the Netherlands, a very long journey indeed. The good news was that these seat reservations were a mere one or two euros each, so I could easily guarantee them that much. No sitting in the aisles for them. It wasn't much but it was something. Conveying this news to them did not lift the atmosphere in the least. They were drowning in a sea of details, contradictory advice, dark fog and of course, fear.

By the end of that day, everyone was hot, dehydrated and depressed. However, we made plans to meet here the next day to buy tickets. They all needed to do this in person and present ID.

It was a hassle to arrange a time when everyone was free. Besides the stress, the suspense and the packing, they were still expected to attend online classes. It would never cease to astound me that they did this all the way along, including taking their final exams.

My notes from that day: "Focused is cool-headed, on the case. Speaker must panic less and listen more!" We had discussed this. She was a better leader at the residence, an excellent organiser of people, dynamic, vocal and strong. He was a better leader for the road, fantastically calm under stress, patient, even-tempered and controlled. They were going to need that on this particular journey. It was no time to be volatile, flying off the handle.

There were still some ructions in the group, confusion about who was travelling with whom. They were engrossed in a flurry of texting, and said they'd let me know the next day when all would have to be decided. We went our separate ways, once I got them on the right bus. I went for a long walk, like I often do when I need to think. I went via the international food shop where we once got them a pile of African groceries. I went back inside to buy a small mountain of plantain chips and a sack of groundnuts – their favourites and good comfort snacks for the road.

Later that evening, I sent directions from their place to Keleti station. A few rehearsals were not a bad idea. Perhaps Focused would quietly play co-navigator.

S Hello ma. Thank you so much for today.

E [I was so tired, I probably just sent a heart.]

23. Tickets, Strategies, Spies

Tuesday 24 May 2022

We met at Keleti station and proceeded straight to the international ticket area. We took our numbers and waited outside the ticket room, which was full and frenetic. Inside was buzzing too, with a guardian at the gate. We were lucky to get a bench. There was time to do a briefing and I was glad for a chance to talk to them. I needed to know if they'd read what I sent, if they remembered key points. If they didn't, this was worrying. I wanted to check.

While they were busy studying for exams, I was busy studying online results of others who'd just done what they were about to do. There were now more dangers than they appreciated, than any of us knew until recently.

I don't like situations where I cannot see any way to make a joke, even a horrible black joke. Whenever there's a total lack of a sense of humour, this is usually a very bad sign. However, onwards we stumbled, towards a consideration of their worst-case scenarios, and there were all kinds of new unhappy traps you could fall into.

Here was the new fine print that was easy to miss:

The temporary residency card they received on arrival in Hungary was their main ID here. It was the first thing to offer anyone who asked – officials, ticket sellers, anyone. It said you were allowed to be here. Even before the passport, this was the first thing you showed, always.

That changed, and the change was not widely announced or understood. This ID card now sometimes meant the opposite of before. It might mean you were not allowed to stay here. Deportation of some sort was now imminent, whether you liked the idea or not. This quiet new policy seemed to happen overnight, turning your protection card into a deportation card. In some cases. Allegedly. All rules seemed to change often and it was difficult to keep up. Plus, there were all the rules we'd never see.

Therefore, it was imperative that from this week, they must show their Ukrainian residential ID, first and foremost, and only that. It was imperative they hid the Hungarian cards unless immigration or the police asked, not ticket sellers. Same with passports. With a Ukrainian student ID, they were entitled by the EU to the newly-devised Solidarity Ticket. They could take trains in Europe for free. For now. All going well. If they could skate around grumpies and closet Nazis – and maybe even a few of the out-Nazis too.

But, showing the Hungarian card would probably spell deportation. I am not sure how many times I tried to get this across, but in the general melee, anything could slip through the net. So therefore, as time ticked by, I asked them to get ID out ahead of time and waste no time at all at the counter. The clerks hated it when you were not ready to hand things over.

The four students nodded, reached into their bags, took out a large clear folder with, in full view, all their IDs together: passport, Ukrainian residency card, and right on top was the now-poisonous Hungarian residency emergency card, which I had told them to keep way out of sight.

The lid on my impatience exploded.

I nearly shrieked but instead angrily hissed at them, "Put that damned thing away! Hide it! Do you want to be deported?"

Three remembered, grasped what I meant and corrected things instantly. One did not understand and did not immediately comply, and I worried that could be a liability. But, all complied in the end. Minutes continued to tick by as we waited our turn.

They were chatting about all sorts of things other than what was happening. I kept an eagle eye on the number board. We were almost there. I moved us into the inner sanctum and hovered in eagerness to spring over to the caged window the second it was announced. Being slow can lower the odds of your getting what you need. A lot depended on a good impression, although even more depended on the mood of the clerk, nothing more, and that was always a gamble. Same odds as roulette, red or black: here you got either a Nicey or a Grumpy. There were usually only those two options.

Finally it was our turn and our clerk was not smiling. I presented all four of their Ukrainian student IDs, having already double- and triple-checked that the poisonous IDs were in the very bottom of their bags.

I also presented my request written out in Hungarian, as I often do, and that was crucial in this moment.

Hello! My Hungarian friend wrote this. Sorry, we speak only English. Please – my friends want Solidarity Tickets. They have Ukrainian residency cards. Four people, going to Amsterdam, Netherlands. Tomorrow evening, if available. Thank you very much.

That sort of note has paid off for me time and time again. Very few clerks here spoke English, and even if they did, most of them hated to. Plus, even if you spoke any Hungarian, they were intolerant of the tiniest of imperfections and waved you away like a bad smell. A well-prepared note usually worked better, ideally one that had been pre-checked by three native speakers.

This clerk didn't look happy at all. But she didn't look murderous either. Mrs Maybe, that's who she was. I repeated the buzzword "Solidarity Ticket", which meant refugees did not pay. Without this, it was €100–€200 or more. It was the same if you accidentally showed a passport first, rather than Ukrainian ID. There were traps all around.

Mrs Maybe was grumpy for sure and not hiding it. She understood my English, it turned out, but she was not going to speak any, not a single syllable. So, even with my beautifully prepared, succinct and perfect Hungarian note plus the right buzzword, she'd made up her mind and not in our favour. She ignored my four black friends, never once making eye contact with them. I suspect it was a good idea I was here with them as white sponsor and spokesperson. I suspect they'd have got nothing if they'd been on their own. That's a hunch – a strong hunch. A strong and grumpy hunch.

We pressed on. I asked about trains to Amsterdam and she

said No. Anything in the Netherlands? No. She said No to many things, and finally said "Vienna" in a tone that suggested this was as far as she was willing to go. The truth was, officially speaking, she could and should have provided the Solidarity Ticket all the way to the Netherlands, but she appeared to be personally vetoing this. They got instead four discounted tickets to Vienna, but only guaranteed to the border.

Only guaranteed to the border? What did that mean? It meant there would be some kind of checkpoint and no promises from the Hungarians after that.

Later, that would indeed present us with a snag.

The soonest available tickets were for the following evening. The students were determined to leave as soon as possible. They wanted tickets, any tickets, even these ones that were allegedly to Vienna but really just to the border. They didn't care how dodgy that sounded. They'd work out the rest after that.

I asked them to consider going early the following morning. If they took this first offer, they'd arrive in Vienna late with nowhere to stay, unable to get ongoing tickets until the next morning when the ticket office reopened. They'd have to sleep in the station all night. I wasn't sure your average Austrian cop was inclined to be nice about that.

They hadn't thought of that but it didn't matter. They wanted out, and the sooner the better, so they grabbed those tickets for the following evening. Sleeping in a foreign train station all night with their worldly possessions in two bags under their arms was less scary than trusting Hungarian authorities one more day, in their view. I must admit, at this point, I could see why they felt this way.

I met young aid volunteers who shrugged that this could be

a classic experience for a young traveller, waiting all night in a foreign train station – what fun. Obviously these were white middle-class guys on vacation or a gap year or working online. By contrast, I once had a long wait between trains, after midnight, in Milan train station when I was nineteen and alone, and that was not fun at all. I did not think black refugees in Austria were likely to encounter any sort of frolicsome adventure. Again, this was yet another mere hunch.

At any rate, these were not young students. These were young adults and it was their call. The trip was on. They had their tickets, at least for the first leg of the trip. They had a plan, as far as anyone could have one these days. We were tired and sweaty and went our separate ways.

Focused

> *"The day we went to buy the tickets, it felt kind of sad for me. I was getting attached to Budapest. The city was so beautiful, it looked and felt homely. But I was also eager to leave because of the pressure from the school hostel, and immigration. So now I was travelling to countries I have never been. It was adventurous and also scary, because I don't know what is waiting for us."*

I sat on my bus, rumbling and bumping along, haunted by the fact that they'd arrive in Vienna at 10pm and would be stuck there overnight. I really did not like that picture, not at all. Later, they admitted it had not even crossed their minds because there was so much else to worry about. There was the worry they might not get to Vienna at all. There were so many traps they could fall into, so many ways to put a foot wrong. Then, in one moment, your life can pivot forever in a direction you were praying to avoid.

They could not go back to Ukraine. They did not feel safe going back home. Their own families were warning them it was dangerous to go back. By now I'd read and learned enough that I didn't want them going back, either.

All refugees travelling this route recently only had trouble here, or before the Austrian border, or maybe even in Vienna. Afterwards, things went better, by all accounts. People actually got where they were going – not without tears or difficulties, and in some cases, with several days of exhaustion and zig-zagging. But, most of them got there, eventually. We had to get our group past Vienna.

My own crazy fantasies ensued involving my accompanying them all the way to the Netherlands, renting a house and moving in with them as den-mother for a month before hiring a proper housekeeper, ideally a strong African lady, to watch over them for the rest of their education and possibly for the rest of their lives, helping raise some of their future children. A nice, sweet, crazy dream.

Then came an excellent brainstorm: it was not crazy to accompany them as far as Vienna. That would be easy, in fact. I'd done that route countless times. It was under three hours away. I could stay with the cousins. I knew the city and its stations and could navigate. I could help them, this was obvious. I could and should and would go with them, as far as Vienna, and then I'd shove them in the direction of the Netherlands. It was settled. As soon as I got home, I'd pack my chaperone outfit, which is conveniently my librarian disguise and always at the ready.

Meanwhile, still bumping along on the 76 bus, I texted Cousin Vera in Vienna.

E *Hi, I hope you are OK. This is sudden, I am sorry, but is it possible to stay at your place tomorrow night? One night only. I will explain later but... may I?*

V *Sure! Welcome! We leave tomorrow morning on a bike trip, and come back Friday. The fridge is full. Take what you need.*

How easy was that? I had a key to her place and she had a key to mine. She was that kind of cousin, and this was exactly the time when you needed one of those. Also, dear readers, let me add that this sort of thing went beyond blood ties. This is what many call Chosen Family, meaning trustworthy, true friends, especially in a pinch. These particular ones were always offering a full fridge where you could just take what you needed. A home ready for guests, where their first thought is: take some food, there's plenty of food.

I was very satisfied with this decision, and felt calmer head to toe. I gave myself a food reward, a slice of my favourite pizza from the nice blond dreadlocked guy. I ate it barbarian-style, meaning sloppily, as I walked home. Minutes after getting in the door, I was the proud owner of a one-way train ticket from Budapest to Vienna, the following evening, same carriage as theirs, and was soon packing my bags. A group of black students could only benefit from the smiling presence of a nice little old white lady librarian saying, "They're with me". It worked getting them out of Ukraine, and it was going to work here too.

I also booked them into a hotel. Vienna was extraordinarily busy, so that took some doing. After that, the next morning, if the only train to the Netherlands was days later, we could camp out on Vera's floor, and thank heavens for a good back-up plan. With luck it would not come to that.

I'd already told the students to bring as much food as they could, explaining that Western European trains sold food that was infamously disgusting and insultingly expensive. They were surprised. Perhaps where they were from, and as I'd seen in many parts of Asia, train journeys were usually accompanied by plenty of vendors with cheap, nice things to eat. It was hard to avoid them. It was a very pleasant part of many journeys.

I fell into a fond daydream recalling memories of southern Thailand where long-haul trains stopped at each station for an extra few minutes to allow a stream of vendors to trot from one end of the train to the other, a big basket hanging from their necks, selling as fast as they could walk. You were smart to have exact change to be quick. In a minute or two, you could grab drinks, sweets, fried chicken, rice, veg, mini-meals, fruit, all sorts of goodies. You could assemble an excellent picnic.

However, we were in the land of corporate monopolies and cold-hearted rip-offs. I emphasised the wisdom of taking a picnicking approach and they got it. Again, one saw the need for insider information. Without it, they'd have spent their meagre budget before they ever got there. There would have been more than one bitter taste in their mouths. Then again, they may be shocked by the high Dutch prices compared to Ukrainian ones. Or Hungarian.

I'd booked them rooms not far from the station and also not far from Vera and Andi's place. There was still a chance others of their group would book on this train. There might be seven or eight, at last count. I got a combination of rooms that would somehow juggle everyone concerned into a bed for the night.

I read more reports about people being sent back, and subsequently deported. The most typical scenario was that conductors demanded money when they shouldn't. If they did not get it, they threw people off, or arranged for them to go straight back where they started. This lot had some pocket money but not that much. Somehow I still thought it unlikely.

I was wrong about that.

MAY 2022

Across Europe and the World

24. Five Possible Tickets, One Possible Nazi

Wednesday 25 May 2022

It was the evening of their escape train to Vienna, which we hoped would lead to a train to Amsterdam, which would in turn, we hoped, change their lifetime trajectory to the positive. In the meantime, it was grey, windy, cold and starting to drizzle outside Budapest's Keleti station, where even the Crazies and the Ickies were not by the stone ledge with the hedges, as was usually their custom. Only the smokers were out in force, braving the elements.

I was absurdly early, as is often my custom. I went around the corner to my favourite cute little vegan place with the cute old couple and their cute little flowers and even cuter inspirational quotes. It was shut. I tried to make good my promise to bring the students' favourite fried chicken, but that was shut too. This was somewhat ironic, remembering that in the beginning, they'd had no other food but this, once a day, which was a misery, whereas now it's a welcome choice.

The third place plus some others were shut too, making me

wonder if I'd missed a public holiday. This mystery was never solved. Eventually I got some terrible sandwiches, but they would be offset by the huge amounts of groundnuts and plantain chips already procured: high protein snacks and a nostalgia fix. There would be snacks. Every journey depends on snacks.

Speaker and I had had yet another communications haywire about where to meet. It only took a few tries this time. I persuaded her to come to me and help me carry my load, much of which was food for them. She led me to a side area where they'd cornered a bench and created a small mountain with their things. My smaller overnight bag joined the mountain. I've moved house like this in the past. Leaving home is hard enough, but leaving the country is that much harder.

Here too, they saw I was not there just to see them off. I was going with them, for real, to Vienna, and I was even on the same carriage. Not overbearingly on top of them, but nearby. I'd stick by them on the train. I'd shuttle them to a room at a hotel, and the next day I'd get them onto some kind of train to the Netherlands and some kind of hopeful new future that was far away from all wars, ideally.

Meanwhile we'd all been reading up on Holland, and then learned that Holland and the Netherlands are not exactly the same. Holland is a small section of the Netherlands. We stood corrected. It didn't make anyone feel very ready.

After much wrangling, it turned out there were four people travelling, not seven. Booking three rooms for seven people was now looking partially wasteful. But, there was still some confusion and disagreement about who went when, where and with whom. The group was exploding in all directions, and there would be a few more eruptions to follow.

Then, a similar past eruption came to mind.

A Detour to Second World War Refugees I Have Known

In the late 1940s, after the war, my cousin Andreas had escaped from Hungary and also from Communism, and was living with his wife and baby in the protection of the American Zone's Displaced Persons (DP) Camp in Salzburg, Austria. Previous to that, he'd survived the Nazi death camps as a teenager.

In the DP Camp, everyone was enmired in efforts to find a way out, a way forward. They were scrambling for visas, transport, someplace where they could work, anywhere they could survive.

Andreas eventually ended up in Vienna and spent his whole life there. He spoke Hungarian at home and with friends, German with everyone else, and English with me. But back in the late 1940s, he almost ended up in Brazil in what would have been a disastrous mistake.

This news came to me from him and also from the International Tracing Service, which sent me thirty-five pages of documentation about his search for a life away from Nazis, which he found, eventually, in Vienna.

At the time, there was not much choice, in fact few opportunities, and therefore he hastily agreed to an offer for transport to Brazil from the American Joint Distribution Committee of Salzburg. A friend of his was accepted too.

The friend went immediately. Almost immediately after landing, he contacted Andreas and warned him not to take the offer. Yes, there was a room on a ship. But at the other end, there was nowhere to stay, no one to help, no job, nothing. He was in fact looking for a way to escape what had become yet another nightmare.

Andreas stayed in Austria. He cancelled the trip to Brazil, but not without potentially large consequences.

In that same folder I found a document from the organisation that had given him those tickets to sail to Brazil. They were furious at the refusal. They were asking everyone and all authorities concerned to keep an eye out for this family and to prevent them from receiving any aid, help or services.

"They are quite likely to turn up in Germany as we understand that they have a restitution claim pending. It is possible that they may be registered at Foehrenwald Camp, Germany." None of that was correct.

There were full descriptions of the three of them, including the exact birthday of their toddler daughter (cousin Vera), and that the mother had a distinctive scar.

A copy was sent to several of their departments: Emigration, Welfare, Medical and Social Services, plus one Mrs Kohn, whoever that was.

In the end, the Vienna Technical University employed him. He began work as a researcher and retired as a professor. And rather than getting dumped and abandoned in Brazil, they only had to move from Salzburg to Vienna, which is not far at all, plus they already spoke German.

So far, they have stayed there for four generations, and are still there now, proud Viennese. As I write this, we have plans to meet next month. Andreas just turned ninety-five and all is well – even having never been to Brazil.

War spews out remarkable relocation stories. People survive amazing things, although these are not always the best stories to tell someone right in the middle of something similar. In fact, it's hard to know what to say, which made me perpetually cautious.

Back in Budapest at the train station, in the meantime, our group was about to leave the country quickly and quietly. These were two men and two women: Devotion, Focused, Princess and Speaker.

They had several years' possessions squashed into one or two large bags each. I wondered if young students today even saw or used paper textbooks. It could be, because it was a heavy load, overall. We were moving four whole lives in just what we could carry with two hands each and a backpack.

There were also food-related bags, including some of the kitchen things. This was smart. It was also touching. Only recently, their lives were hell for the simple lack of a cooking pot, plates and spoons. Wherever they might end up as refugees, they would at least not go through that again. I could see cutlery and tinned black-eyed beans poking out of the top of the bag.

It was reminiscent of a Tibetan group who fled the fighting with China, who swore they survived that long trek because one young guy thought to bring a tin kettle. They made fires, melted snow, made tea. But in an emergency, if panicky, in the heat of the moment, people remember and forget to bring all kinds of things that may or may not be useful. A man once jumped from a fire clutching his golf clubs.

With me, it would probably be food. It usually is.

In their food bag, that particular can of black-eyed beans was a sight so poignant that it almost hurt. We'd spoken about how we especially liked these beans, and how they were sometimes hard to find. As was my custom, when I finally spotted some, I usually snagged two. This time, I snagged two for me and also two for them. And here was one of them, ready to go. It's exactly what I'd have done.

I suppose some food had to be left behind, and surely those students or the staff would have found and devoured it, I hope. I hate food going to waste. I applauded bringing as much as they could. The food bag of any day is a central thing, this I know. It's just like the kitchen is the heart of a home. The food bag is the engine of a long and heavy journey, especially an emotional one. This would be a long day and a long journey, and the suspense of their upturned lives was some of the heaviest luggage they ever carried. That and the food bag with the tins and a cooking pot, bowls and spoons.

The boys were away somewhere. Speaker and Princess were the ones to whom I offered up my own food contributions to the project, apologised for the second-rate sandwiches and suggested they were a last resort – desperation food if it came to it, and we hoped it would not. Speaker accepted graciously with thanks and appropriately stowed them in the very bottom of the bag. The groundnuts were seriously welcomed, and there was outright delight at the sight of the plantain chips.

Princess was particularly touched. "Look at this!" she bubbled. "She remembered! She does not have to do a thing and look at this. Look what she did!" The plantain chips went into priority position at the top of the bag. Treats.

I asked them to listen to me seriously. It was a warning. They were about to travel through all of Austria and all of Germany, the very areas where Nazism was born and prospered. It had not gone away, either. They might meet racist people with bad attitudes. I asked them to please be ready for that, and to not, for example, argue with aggressive crazy people, especially the drunk ones. They knew exactly what I was talking about, and they took it seriously.

At that point, the journalist from *Szabad Európa* (*Free Europe*) got in touch. They'd shot and put together the video before the students decided to leave the country. They wanted to double-check things before it was broadcast. Speaker was torn between two lines of action. She wanted to publicise these problems that unfairly affected many people in their shoes. That was the communicator in her, the one who could be a newscaster, the one who wants to tell the story. However, the general circumstances suggested she should only get noisy and noticeable after she was safely over the border and reasonably distant from deportation and another warzone. She changed her name for the report, in any case. The reporter was sympathetic, and the media company delayed the broadcast a little.

The students said they were happy with the video, that it represented the issue well, and they were grateful that *Szabad Európa* was bothering to cover this side of the story. Here's a summary of the main points:

The Hungarian government and other groups offered some support for students to return to their home countries, but Speaker and some of her peers were afraid to go back home, as many were. Her own homeland was considered dangerous enough that she could be granted at least temporary refugee status in Hungary or perhaps elsewhere. She did not want to return home, having heard too many accounts of students who had returned from Europe, were assumed to be from billionaire families and were then targeted by local criminals for intimidation, extortion, kidnapping and blackmail.

"Family, at home, they want you to be protected. They want you to feel safe. That's the main reason we were sent here to study in Ukraine in the first place. Our parents wanted us safer. At home there was a lot going on, Boko Haram, kidnappings, human sacrifices. It's too much.

"The kidnappings, they happen when you land at the airport. You take a bus. They kidnap you from there. Then they call up your parents to say that they have you. The parents must send a ransom of money to get you back. So parents go to the bank to get a loan, but kids were going missing. And people were dying. So, you know, you're living in that kind of tension, and pressure. Your parents give up their land, their house [as collateral], to get a loan to send you out, and now you are forced to go back?" [1]

She was travelling in the hopes of not having to go back. As much as she'd love to see her family and friends, they all told her this was not a good time. And when families do that, it's truly a bad time.

Keleti train station's big echoey lobby had grand arches and domes, bedecked with dramatic murals and mosaics. Focused hovered near the electronic board displaying the platforms. He and I both wanted this information as soon as possible. I warned him that around here, such info was often posted at the last moment, and it was smart to be ready to move quickly. He got it. He always got it. Alertness was one of his strong points.

Our number appeared. Of course, it was the platform furthest from where we were, and the station was crowded and collectively grumpy. We somehow dragged our small mountain from one end of the station to the other through the buzzing yet grumpy beehive. We found the right train carriage, climbed up and dragged things up one by one, which took some time and huffing and puffing. In our hurry, we went to the first storage area we saw, into which to dump it all. This was accomplished in a messy, panicky rush.

Their reserved seats were at the other end of the carriage, it turned out. They changed their minds. They wanted their things nearby. So, there was another kerfuffle as they moved it all again, stowing all of it as nearby as possible and much of it protectively under their legs.

My seat was a couple of rows behind them and opposite. They had a nice foursome table.

Once they were all settled, I too went to retrieve the rest of my things. When I got to the storage area and took my bag, for some reason, I was addressed sharply by an older lady sitting opposite, with her dour, silent husband. They were seated right next to all of our relocation flurry.

She seemed annoyed and barked at me like a small yappy lapdog. I couldn't understand. I was so tired and distracted, at first I assumed she spoke in Hungarian, which I'm bad at. I managed to splutter in Granddad's native tongue that I only spoke a little Hungarian and, please, did she speak some English?

Here she interrupted me, crisply announcing one curt word, "Deutsch!" German.

This was in Budapest, Hungary, by the way.

A nice young smiling woman nearby offered to translate. Old Mrs Deutsch was asking if all my things were there – was anything missing? I said everything was fine. She repeated her question. Really, was nothing missing, really? She asked this while staring hard at my four friends in the corner. She wore a fierce frown, while the translator diplomatically asked if I was sure.

Yes, I was sure, everything was fine. I said that as casually and calmly as I could, while feeling like slapping her. She looked angry, hostile. Later – it's usually later – I thought of things I might have said:

> *Those are my students. We're travelling together. Everything's OK, thanks for asking.*

> *Those four, in the corner? Medical students. Do you need a doctor?*

> *Are you suggesting all black people are thieves, you Nazi bitch schweinehund? (This means "pig-dog" in German.)*

In reality, I did not say any of these things. I probably thanked her sarcastically and the helper genuinely, because, thank heavens, in the nick of time, I recalled that the purpose of this trip was not to antagonise anyone, especially potential Nazis. Hadn't I just warned the students not to do that? Damn, it was difficult to restrain oneself under provocation.

It reminded me that when asked about accomplishments last year, my first reply was that I had not slapped anyone even though I wanted to. There were a surprising number of people who felt the same way. In this instance, it's good that extreme fatigue slowed down my reflexes and shut my mouth.

Princess wore a look of naïve and sweet confusion as she searched in vain for a place to charge her phone. These were old-style trains, so there were no such facilities. She kept searching, sure that there had to be one, but there was not. Focused watched this and smiled like a wise, patient dad. Speaker was organising things like a mom. Devoted was quiet and ready like a big brother. Princess was little sister. They were acting like a family unit.

We settled in. I was only a few seats away. The carriage lurched – we were off! The moment they gave me their four tickets, I became Mrs White Chaperone. By all accounts – which were changing all the time – we just had to get over that border and the rest would be OK.

Some of that was true.

I joined them briefly, repeating yet again the main reminders: Always ask for a Solidarity Ticket. Only show Ukrainian ID, otherwise they'll charge full price, which is a lot. Only show passports to police and immigration. I don't know how many times I reminded them. Of course, it was too much. But it was so crucially important that, like any diligent teacher or elder, I kept checking and checking and checking, and this is why teachers and parents go crazy, in the end. Some younger people do too and there's more on that later.

I curled up on two seats across, grateful for armrests that folded down into a mini-bed. I shut my throbbing, aching eyes. Sleep was impossible but I pretended. My stomach was in a knot, and so was the rest of me, inside and out. But I could smell the nice chicken and rice that they had cooked up for the trip, and that was reassuring. I kept my ears open to their low, relaxed murmuring voices in a friendly card game. The whole carriage was relaxed and quiet. I relaxed a little too.

Then we came to the Austrian border.

Here I was nervous. If anything were to go wrong, it would be here. It would be very easy for a train employee to tell them to go back to Budapest, where immigration was waiting for them.

Immediately after we crossed out of Hungary and into

Austria, a tall silver-haired conductor approached our foursome. Focused indicated I had their tickets, and he stepped over to me. I presented all five tickets. He looked at them and he looked at me. He punched my ticket and looked again at theirs.

C *This is only to the border. They need new tickets.*

E *Yes please, to Vienna, Solidarity Tickets.*

C *That will be 104 euro.*

E *They have Ukrainian Residents' ID and—*

C *I don't know about that.*

E *They want Solidarity Tickets to Vienna, please.*

C *I don't know about that.*

E *It's from the EU, free travel for—*

C *I don't know about that.*

I may have opened my mouth to try again, but he leaned forward with a look that stopped me. His frozen pseudo-polite smile dropped abruptly. The mouth scowled, the eyes narrowed and his voice changed entirely into suppressed anger. He fiercely hissed, "One hundred and four euro. Please." Then he leaned in a tiny bit more, with an unblinking stare, uncomfortably close. He only moved back when I reached for my bag. He rang up the tickets.

My card did not work.

My second and only other card also did not work.

His anger was rising but I had about 120 euro on me and handed that over. He was fastidious about giving me my exact change, almost prissy with precision. He was playing it up with a fake gentlemanly elegance, overdoing it. He was a clichéd movie Nazi and he was enjoying his triumph. The long face suggested Max von Sydow – no, Max was too classy. You'd have to cast someone cheaper. In the film version of his life, he'd be played by a second-rate ham as badly paid as a conductor on a train, for example, like him, fed up watching people pay nothing and glide across the continent by the thousands, when he could barely pay his bills and never went anywhere except working. He may have complied in the first month, but now? Maybe not, according to Max's cheaper nephew who was looming over me.

You can think a lot in a nanosecond. I couldn't risk anything for them so I paid. If I hadn't had that extra cash, he'd have cleaned them out of all their pocket money for that whole trip, right here. That chicken would have been their last food for twenty-four hours and then some. Or they might have been thrown off altogether, as others were, and let's not think about that. From here on, it was likely to be smooth.

We were somewhat wrong about that, too.

In the meantime, they were not aware of this transaction. They were absorbed in their card game and relaxing while keeping a low profile. It was only much later I told one of them. I also told many others about to make that same trip, to warn them, via all the relevant grapevines, that this sort of thing was now to be expected. Generosity was waning, and some of these people were launching their own version of a vigilante campaign. Of course, for some of them it was a straightforward side hustle and business as usual. In wartime, there are always extra racketeers. There were all sorts of nerve-wracking things going on. Some of the stories had a nasty emotional, vengeful edge. The human jungle was barking and snarling more than usual. It was a dog-eat-dog world.

***

Vienna appeared soon and I was so glad we had places to stay. It was late. I looked forward to seeing the cousins, even though it would not be for long, a quick hit-and-run. It was with great relief that the students and I stepped – or rather staggered – down the steps into Vienna's Central Train Station, the Hauptbahnhof, a place I knew fairly well. Welcoming beds were not far away. So far, so good.

We struggled through the massive station, which was surprisingly busy that evening. It had been hard to find rooms, and now we could see why. There were festivals and tourist attractions all over the city, ads and posters galore. There was plenty of pushing and shoving, and we were trying to navigate with our small luggage mountain.

The station was frantic and sweaty. Some people were clearly on vacation or out for entertainment. Some were clearly refugees. A surprising number were impossible to categorise.

We passed a large crowd gathered around some tables with a few volunteers and lots of signs in German and Ukrainian – probably English too, although we were focused on where we were going. It was the local branch of an international charity called Caritas, helping refugees, in this case. There were at least several dozen people waiting for assistance, looking stressed and overladen with luggage.

Escalators became a major learning curve. We had to take it in shifts, in the ancient art of dividing to conquer. One person loaded, another escorted things down, and we looped in relays until everything was downstairs. I was never so aware of the vast numbers of escalators in that place. Yes, there were lifts, somewhere, probably, but in that cluttered, stressed mayhem, we just grabbed the first escalator we saw, where a kindly lady joined us and carried some things. When all the luggage was downstairs, she offered all the students a mumsy hug, which Devotion politely accepted, Focused barely tolerated and the two young women embraced fully, warmly and happily. Mrs Huggy returned to her station with a small group that waited nearby for exactly such moments. They had a small card with the initials JW, which I assume was the Jehovah's Witnesses. They were there, waiting. Not hit-and-run but help-and-run.

Overall, many individuals helped us with luggage all along the way. They could see the struggle, they took a practical view, and with small efforts here and there, they pitched in and made a lovely difference. There was a tremendous amount of practical kindness about. It cost nothing. It was an easy smile. It was charming and it renewed hope, warmth and energy.

***

Close to midnight, we arrived at their hotel. This was cash seriously well invested. Before we got inside, they comically collapsed at the door and laughed about it all, moving a luggage mountain. Speaker and Focused joked about a quarrel before leaving, in the packing process, because she wanted "to take every pin" but she made him carry the heaviest bags. She said it was because he was the man. She was, in fact, a tall, athletic, strapping, strong young woman – but he was the man.

It was very funny, but in the meantime, I was barely upright on shaking knees, about to cry from sheer stress and worry and fatigue, and not really being cut out for this at all. I let them laugh for a while until I lost the strength to remain upright, and cried out, "I am really tired. Please, go in, I need to leave soon!" They snapped into action. I forgot they were young. They'd just been in a warzone, and they just needed one moment of relief.

I asked Focused to test the door key cards and all worked OK. We'd meet the next morning.

Again: so far, so good.

I staggered over to the cousins, a ten-minute walk away, and let myself in. We were all tired and it was late. I quickly explained the situation and they said to use the place as my own. They were leaving early the next morning so it was another case of help-and-run. They were away on a cycling trip for a few days. Andi was thought of by many as the Bicycle Guru of Vienna. His latest contraption had Vera riding in the front. Vera pointed out that she got a great view and also the main danger in a head-on collision. She shrugged that off, and added that if my friends needed a place to stay, that was fine.

Chosen Family came through yet again. Also, Vera was born in a DP (Displaced Persons) camp, in the American Zone of Salzburg, after WWII. Vera understood.

Everybody looked exhausted, and everybody had a big day ahead. I proceeded to their sweet spare room that I knew very well from countless visits. It was ready for me. Logo the cat did not even attack me or complain about eviction. All I remembered was falling towards the mattress, and I was probably asleep before hitting the pillow – feeling safe.

25. Not Quite Amsterdam: Utrecht Red Cross

Thursday 26 May 2022, Vienna

In the morning, the cousins and I staggered towards the kitchen, barely waving hello while imbibing coffee and trying to induce energy production. They were minutes from launching their latest cycling excursion, packing and checking things. There was coffee, there was bread, there was gratitude and then suddenly, they were gone.

There was plenty of time to get to my travelling foursome before 9am. My stomach knot had not loosened much, but it probably would at some later point. For now, my stomach did not intend to trust anything until those four people were on that train. We got through the worst of it yesterday. That we were here at all now was a good sign.

How things can change.

We were in some kind of new phase now that it was coming up to a three-month marker, a whole season at war and another season in view. On the refugee trail, there were more and more reports of problems, ugly encounters, racist anger, demands for payment – survivable but scary. People about to leave were hearing warnings like these on their digital grapevine of information from those who'd already left. This group was glued to that network. The big official networks received no such trust. They had no such details or information either.

E Hello, I'm here.

S Good morning ma [heart]

E Please do not bring luggage downstairs. We check out later. Tickets first.

S OK ma.

E Come downstairs. Bring ID.

Earlier they were so tired and emotional that a detail slipped their mind. A couple of them sprang awake, got ready and brought their things downstairs, only to drag them back up again. We were all a bit tired, but nothing like yesterday when we'd arrived absolutely dog-tired. Focussed said they slept like they were coming from the war front, and he couldn't remember when he's slept on a bed so soft. Today, refreshed, they had a fighting chance and a new supply of stamina. They were showered and ready to go. This was so much better than them staying up all night in the train station. To start a long journey already tired, unslept and stinky is really not ideal.

I was unnecessarily rehearsing worst-case scenarios that included them only getting train tickets many days from now, and me sorting out how we could fill Vera's floors, use rugs and blankets and… I was getting ahead of things.

Thanks to my clever planning (Focused approved), we

were a mercifully short and easy walk to a station where we could buy tickets. We had over an hour to sort that.

I was glad to be familiar with yet another massive station and steered them straight to the international ticket counter. Here we had a very different experience than in Budapest. There we got a Grumpy. Here we got a Nicey. That was not the only contrast. Instead of heavy, dusty, dark wooden doors reminiscent of an ancient dungeon, this was modern, tidy and well-lit.

Our clerk spoke excellent English, explained everything and was pleasant. She looked like she'd just washed her hair. She happily issued their Solidarity Tickets to Amsterdam, and explained they had to get a new local ticket after every border, and after every change of train. They'd have to stand if it was full, unless they bought seat reservations. The students decided to take their chances without those. Later they'd regret that.

That morning, the station was buzzing even more than last evening. This was a hugely busy weekend, with all sorts of big events taking place, and there were slow-moving crowds everywhere. There were absolutely no direct trains to Amsterdam for at least five days, probably more. But there was a train going there with one change, in Frankfurt. It was leaving in just a few hours. The Frankfurt change was awfully quick, in fact extra risky with all their stuff. That was the downside. But it was leaving soon and they leapt at the chance. Under the circumstances, this was very lucky indeed. We enjoyed the nice easy five-minute walk back to the hotel, and checked out in good time.

In the hotel lobby, while the others herded luggage towards the exit, I had a moment with Focused where we could continue a conversation from before about how different people have different sorts of stress reactions under pressure or when confronted suddenly with unwanted surprises. Some people were volatile, others steady. He was steady and even-tempered all the time I'd seen him. In fact, when conversations got heated, he became all the calmer, steadier – more focused. He confirmed this. He said this was his usual way. This was exactly what was needed now, we agreed.

Speaker and Princess were excitable and volatile, I pointed out, which was great and fun, and I loved them, but now was not the time to be loud or noticeable. When you needed strength of character and visibility as a front person, Speaker was ideal. Here, I thought he was the right leader. I hoped they would follow his lead. I hoped they'd meet no Nazis or racists, but if they did, I hoped for calm. Focused nodded in a way that said he knew all too well what I was talking about. I added that soon they'd be on their own, and he laughed like he already knew that too. It was like seeing the future doctor in him – a smart, alert and dependable one. He was another one who'd take seriously any field he chose.

I noticed he held all four of their tickets. He was playing dad for this trip already. All the luggage was organised and better packed. The food bags were much smaller. All my stuff was at home with the cousins so I could share some of the load. Everything was easier than yesterday, with much of the fear and pressure eased.

We set off for the station. We could saunter and not stress, take time to admire Vienna's charming prettiness, which is elaborate and ornate, even frilly. There was time to compliment a lady on her cute dog, and we all gave it a pat. Focused said small dogs like that were his favourites. That's what he'd have if he could. He showed how he'd carry one, hugged to his chest. I could picture it, him as a dad with a dog.

The station was even busier, thronging with people. It was as if every single participant in all those events was trying to use this one corridor. Still, we had time. We found the platform. We were early and we were ready.

At Speaker's urging, there were goodbye photos. She organised a series of them. In some, she was exuberant, kicking up her heels, as if she were going on holiday. I hoped her relative naïvety would shield her from the kind of worry still turning my stomach knot into a painful stone. However, it was a smaller stone than yesterday. It was a living, flexible stone, a stone that could transform and grow. A stone with a future.

For the fifth time, there was an announcement in several languages, saying that a small boy in a green tee shirt was at a distant train station (at the end of this line), separated from his family. It sounded like they did not recognise his language.

The parents had clearly not heard this announcement, and perhaps they didn't understand it either. It was repeated with increasing frequency. Wherever the parents were, it would be at least an hour before they could get to him.

I stood with Speaker as she quieted down for a serious moment. She admitted she was scared. I nodded. I felt fear too. I was scared about so many things. I was scared they'd meet racists who would terrorise them or turn them back, or demand money or punish them for lack of it, or just be scary and hateful. I was afraid deportation would be an on-going nightmare. I was scared that it may be a long time before they saw their families again. I was scared about lots of things and mentioned not a single one of them. I let her speak.

"I'm scared six minutes isn't enough for the train connection in Frankfurt."

I was so glad I shut my mouth, and replied, "Yes, it'll be tricky, so be ready. Prepare ahead. Move your things nearer the door, ten minutes before you arrive. Get your teamwork going."

She nodded in a daze, totally distracted. I made a mental note to text several of them, fifteen or twenty minutes ahead. Princess looked calm but dazed too.

Just before the train arrived, I stood wordlessly next to Devotion. I said I was thinking about their whole journey, the whole last few months. I only saw one season of their lives, that one tough spring in Hungary. At the start, at that first place in Erd, things were so bad for them, one meal a day for weeks – but now I had much more hope for this group.

He smiled one of his pure, excellent, understated, dignified smiles. You'd trust him if he were on your medical team.

The train was packed, and it was a bit of a melee, but everyone got aboard. The four of them stowed their things, and got into their seats and looked OK. The train groaned and started to move and soon they were out of view. That seemed to trigger something in my knees, which went so weak that they shook. I felt I might fall but staggered to a bench, splat myself down and suddenly burst out sobbing. Tears were leaping out of my face while inside I chanted, "Please let them be OK, let them be OK, let them be OK!" over and over and over.

I'd been holding it together to stuff them onto that train, at which point all my nervous fear exploded at once. As for them, the young anywhere have a tough road, but these were taking more than their share. They were on their own now – not without a village, but all their villages were going to be further and further away.

As for my knees, they firmed up in due course, and I was

capable of going downstairs without collapsing, to buy a ticket back to Budapest that afternoon. I could be back by evening. So I returned to Vera's, greeted Logo the cat who was nicely affectionate, and I actually managed to eat something which stayed down. I packed, returned to the station, and was soon on my train, texting the students on their train, as we travelled in opposite directions.

E *Please tell Focused, that bigger piece of paper, THAT is the ticket to Amsterdam, so it's important not to lose that. The smaller tickets are for each separate step of the journey.*

S *OK ma.*

E *[smiley face]*

S *Thanks so much [two hearts]*

E *Just keep sending news.*

S *OK ma.*

E *Try to find a train worker who knows what platform you need when changing in Frankfurt. Maybe start moving the luggage closer to the exit. And good luck!*

S *OK ma. Thank you ma. Good luck ma.*

A little after that, they confirmed the connection went well.

D *We've arrived in Frankfurt ma. Yes, everything is OK. The second train was delayed, making it perfect to move our things [laughing face]. We are currently on the train now.*

E *That's funny. And lucky.*

They were on the train to the Netherlands, and it would be a very long day. There were a few quick checks and all was boring and fine. Devotion was snoozing and the others were relaxing. Before long, I was back in Budapest, had made and eaten dinner and tidied up. I was very tired but kept the phone near my head and laptop on my lap. I did some light reading to stay awake.

A Detour to a Heavenly Newspaper

The Dogs did a spoof version of *Magyar Hírlap* (*Hungarian News*), a newspaper close to the government: government offices subscribe to the paper, and it receives outsized advertising revenue from the state.

"If you read the Magyar Hírlap," they explained, "you'll see that good humour is gone, and what we have now is terror-media."

MKKP knew the paper would sue them, so they set aside most of the remaining funds from their counter-billboard campaign for a lawsuit, leaving the rest for printing costs – about between €4,000 and €5,000.

"The Two-Tailed Dog's edition of the Magyar Hírlap should not only make a mockery of its politics," they insisted, but also imagine a better world. "Wouldn't it be great if things were this way? Why aren't they?"

Volunteers distributed 10,000 copies of their spoof edition of *Magyar Hírlap*. Here was their vision:

They published the winning lottery numbers for the following week, made a weather forecast based on readers' suggestions, and reported that the banks of the Danube would be transformed into a pedestrian zone, while car traffic would be rerouted underground.

More of their satirical stories:

- Turkey agreed to pay reparations for its 150-year occupation of Hungary during the Ottoman era.
- The EU was funding the construction of a black hole in Mr Orban's hometown.
- "More than four people" had repatriated their jobs from Western Europe as part of the successful "Bring Home Your Jobs!" campaign.
- Anonymous donors paid off Greece's national debt.
- Mark Zuckerberg had bought Hungarian citizenship.
- An ad featured a horse wearing a gold watch on each leg: "Gold watches. For horses. From Belgium."

On 30 October, the paper was distributed in several cities.

Reactions:

> *"This is great! If only it were true..."*

> *Another man "nearly threw himself around my neck for joy," said one party member.*

The owner of the paper that had been parodied threatened legal action, but then nothing more was heard. MKKP didn't expect to hear any more about it because that would be like kicking a cute little dog. This dog had some teeth, however, in the form of good lawyers, so it was a smart dog too.

I really do not remember when I shut my eyes, but when I did, two hours had passed in a blink. Suddenly it was not 9pm but 11pm. I awoke, twisted in my day clothes, laptop slid to one side and phone on the floor. I jumped up, saw the time, checked my messages and panicked. I really wish I'd been awake to see this. My stomach sank at the sight of it. First Devotion texted, and then Speaker.

> *D* *Disappointingly we were just asked to come down now. They said the train we entered is 150 euros. We are in Germany now.*
>
> *S* *My phone battery is low. The train guys asked us to leave the train. We are now in Düsseldorf. We don't know what to do.*

I'd been asleep when this happened! I thought everything was OK! I thought they were "home free", at least for a little while – how damned stupid can I be! I messaged right away, however late.

> *E* *I only saw this now. Let me think what to do. Look for Ukrainian signs, groups to help. Stay near the station. Try to find a place to stay – I will start looking too.*
>
> *S* *They sent us out. We're looking for a hostel.*
>
> *E* *Stay together. Which train station? Düsseldorf has more than one. I can book a place for you to stay, which train station are you near?*

That was at about 11pm. No other message came for a while – their batteries were dead. I sent a load of messages, all of which got there much later – useless. I searched for places they could stay in Düsseldorf, opened a map on one screen, opened a room-booking website on a second screen, bounced back and forth between them, and lined up an assortment of options to greet any number of possibilities. I wanted to be ready for anything.

I wondered and tried a million things that did not help, because about an hour after all of the above, their phones came to life again, by which time they'd long left Düsseldorf behind, somehow or other.

Later Focused explained

We experienced a bit of racism. The train conductor said we were not supposed to be on this train. We tried explaining but he wasn't taking it even though his colleague wanted us to stay. He made us get down at the next stop. We went to where they sell tickets, explained and showed ID. They gave us a ticket for the next train to Amsterdam without any delay or charges. That conductor just didn't like that we were travelling free.

All that time, there was no way to message what was happening. Eventually, they got through.

D We are in Utrecht ma.

E Not Düsseldorf?

D We are in Netherlands, ma.

I was so glad they were out of Germany and the Nazi centre of my nightmares. I knew it was old paranoia speaking, but as a granddaughter of the victims of Nazis, I was emotionally and irrationally relieved that they were over that border.

D We are in Utrecht Central station.

E Are you really in the Netherlands???

D Yes ma.

I almost cried with relief.

E Can you find a place to stay? How can I help?

D No ma, the others have gone to find Red Cross.

I'd already sent them the number of the Red Cross. I'd already told the Red Cross they were about to arrive.

E Don't give up, we are with you.

D OK ma.

A long twenty minutes later:

D We've seen them ma, thanks so much ma.

E You found the Red Cross? You have somewhere safe to sleep, yes?

D Yes ma.

E Oh good, please try to sleep, charge your phone, I will text tomorrow morning.

D OK ma, thanks so much ma.

A few hours later, about 3am, I was pinged awake again by nice, comforting news.

D They've provided us an accommodation. Thanks so much ma.

E Good to hear from you!

I think we all finally slept.

26. Shelter: the Netherlands

Friday 27 May 2022

It was just barely Friday morning, in the proverbial wee hours. The Red Cross gave them emergency overnight refuge in a large area with twenty or thirty cots in tidy rows. A bit after midnight I texted Speaker.

E *Please message when you can. Devotion said you are with Red Cross. I hope they have a place to sleep. You are safer now, with them.*

S *They put us in a hall with stretchers, but it is very cold.*

E *Wear everything you have, even a hat. Morning will be better. I must try to sleep too now. The Red Cross in the Netherlands has a good reputation. You are safe.*

S *OK ma. Thank you so very much.*

I thought they might sleep most of that Friday. People

arriving like this often slept for days in recovery. Budapest had been awash with stories of hosts who left trays of food, water, toiletries and fresh clothes outside a guest room from which no one emerged for a few days, other than to stagger to the loo and fall straight back into deep unconsciousness again. This group, however, arrived in better condition.

Focused wrote: "They welcomed us well with warm showers and food. But the next morning, when they were interviewing us, we were a bit scared because a guy was telling us how we will be given documents and will be able to work. We got excited, but the lady in charge heard, and said we shouldn't get our hopes up because we weren't from Ukraine originally. It really broke our spirit and Speaker was panicking, but we kept our cool. It ended well because now we're registered into the system."

They were up the next day, ready to be moved again to temporary accommodation for the weekend. After that, they'd be moved to longer-term accommodation – they hoped so, at any rate. That was yet to materialise. The Friday project was to get moved to the weekend place. I got news later that evening from Devotion.

D Hello ma, good evening ma. How are you?

E Happy to hear you! Please, some news?

D We are now in Dordrecht. We are planning on looking for a job next week.

E You four all together?

D Yes ma.

This was a huge relief. I asked about the others of the

original dozen. Some were in the Netherlands, in Amsterdam or Utrecht. Some went to Germany. Some had not yet left Budapest. They were all in contact with each other. About the same time, Speaker weighed in.

S *Hello ma. Good evening ma. How are you doing?*

E *I am OK – please give me some news?*

S *We are now in Dordrecht, a town in Netherlands.*

E *Is it OK?*

S *It is manageable. We are trying to know what to do now.*

E *I want to buy a Bluetooth that lets me hear you on the phone.*

S *Oh ma, that will be lovely*

.

This wish would take a while, but was indeed achieved, making chats a regular thing in the ensuing months. (And years.)

E *The others in Budapest, did they leave yet?*

S *They leave on Sunday.*

E *Do they know to use the phrase Solidarity Ticket? It's important, please remind them?*

S *OK ma. Thank you so much.*

E *If the ticket people are difficult, they say it's a "Solidarity Ticket" and show them paper and the Ukraine ID. Don't show any passport except to immigration. Please tell them? And never show Hungarian ID.*

S *OK, Ma, I already told them.*

E *OK, sorry – I don't think they need my advice, but you can give them both my number and my email.*

S *Alright ma.*

E *I am sleepy now, good night.*

S *Good night ma.*

Before, I mentioned how teachers and parents go a bit mad on behalf of their youngers, harassing them with repetition. Ironically, madness is also exactly what elders induce. They overdo it and then students and young adults go mad. One can only apologise. It may be part of a madness-cycle that's bigger than any of us, and just keeps getting passed on, with the best of intentions.

Saturday Morning, 28 May 2022

E *Please text here when you are awake, fed a bit, ready to talk. I didn't yet master Bluetooth, but I downloaded WhatsApp to my laptop which I know better, and there, the earphones work very well.*

S *OK ma. Good morning ma.*

E *I tried to video call, did not work, don't know why...*

S *OK.*

Young people really must curse us sometimes when we cannot keep up with the technology, and nobody wants to teach us even when we are willing. This is a challenge. I must up my senior game.

E *Thank you.*

S *UWC ma.*

E *What is UWC?*

S *It means you are welcome.*

I am so old. But fortunately, they are patient. And that abbreviation doesn't make sense anyway. "You are welcome" should be YAW.

Noon, Sunday 29 May 2022

E *Good morning. I hope you slept OK. I am sending good luck wishes for tomorrow when you register for the social security system. Do you have enough food, until then? Is there a place you can cook? Or get something?*

S *We cannot cook here.*

E *This is a drag. Can you eat in the room?*

S *Yes.*

E *I hope you find somewhere to buy a great sack of groundnuts, very healthy, protein.*

S *Yes.*

E *I'm concerned Dutch food prices are high.*

S *Very high.*

They were indeed moved to longer-range accommodation, with kitchens and a feeling of safety. I started searching for supermarkets near them, and ways I could help like before. In the meantime, some of the pressure was off. On another topic altogether, I answered a query.

E *Since you asked, I'll send a link to the book I wrote, "My Secret Century in Budapest". On the cover, you'll see my grandparents from Hungary. My dad is lower left, maybe age ten, with Uncle Eddie and Uncle Albert. I have my dad's nose.*

S *Wow. I love it.*

And later still, to the group, I said I thought that for anyone who wants to work in the healthcare area, it can be a hard but valuable lesson: when people are in need, someone needs to help. You will probably always remember how you needed help when this war started. Now you'll be the ones to help. It's what they call paying it forward.

D *Yes ma we will do exactly that.*

I said that various times, from here on, and usually got hearts in return.

E *Also, please will someone create a WhatsApp group for all five of us, so I can send things to everyone?*

Speaker did this immediately and dubbed it Eileen's Children (with dancing hearts). This made me laugh very hard, doubling over, because we had had more than a few spirited discussions about with me insisting I was not their mother but a teacher and friend. We had many repeats of all that, but she just nodded and said Yes Ma, and went and did the opposite, with her sharp, smart and wicked sense of humour.

S *Happy Sunday ma. How are you doing? I hope you are fine.*

E *Yes I am OK.*

S *Try and eat something.*

I did. It's sweet she noticed, and even sweeter that she asked. I had a much more open-minded stomach these days, now that the students were not sleeping in train stations. They were safe – for now. All of us, any of us can only be safe – for now.

But, for now, that'll do.

27. The Dogs Are Serious

The press was eager to cover MKKP's activities in terms of humour, but not enough about serious things. I was looking for a collection of their most positive, practical achievements. I'd read about bus shelters and road repairs, and heard about their dissolving a local committee that was a sham. I wanted to hear more.

The party's website features an interactive map from April 2019 entitled All We've Done. Here they collect what they have done in four major categories: Action (protests, demos, discussion groups, signage, presentations), Guerilla Gardening, Street Art and Urban Renewal, with maps pinpointing all their projects' locations.

In addition, the website offers online software, links to other websites, apps – some humorous and some serious: a hoax blocker, a game about mega-rich Hungarian businessman Lőrinc Mészáros's enrichment in the style of Super Mario, a website coordinating their urban renewal projects, an article generator parodying the government media, a public procurement watchdog, an app showing public toilets, a game parodying the advice given by Mr O.'s spin-doctor Árpád Habony, a game called 'Who Should We Hate Today?' based on the TV gameshow *Wheel of Fortune*.

On the purely serious side of things, they also publish reports on their political activities, on the work of the Budapest municipality, and a significant number of their political projects are anti-corruption proposals to create transparency.

They publish information about their previous election campaigns, and a detailed list of activities and actions carried out from party funds.

Their website also offers a social club, where they report on their various social actions, which are also very extensive (all-purpose fundraisers, counselling services, consumer protection, fundraising for school equipment, winter social assistance, Stand with Pride).

What's particularly relevant to this story is that they reported on actions for Ukrainian refugees.

MKKP volunteers manned the Help Tent on Nyugati square for 133 days, where they collected and distributed donations of food, clothing and toiletries, and also organised accommodation for the refugees. They helped many thousands of people.

With other civilian organisers and self-appointed coordinators, they had to relocate two or three times at the request of the police, and had to constantly adapt to changing "systems" (chaos) or organising interpreters, drivers and other volunteers and complete strangers who wandered in asking to be helpful.

And yet, in all that chaos, they noted that, somehow, "everyone here lived with so much patience and spontaneous reaction to each other, despite the lack of sleep that had become a habit, that the process worked, developed itself, people got accommodation, food, and information."

They organised refugee accommodation in Obuda for at least a hundred people. They donated substantial sums to hospitals. They delivered aid to Ukraine in the form of requested sports equipment for teachers to distract frightened children. They also delivered walkers, medicine and medical instruments to hospitals, as well as food, warm clothes and carpets to the city's social institutions that supported the needy.

Also, since the war, there has been a severe shortage of laptops, tablets and phones. An estimated 200,000 schoolchildren were studying remotely, and nearly six million had to interrupt their studies. MKKP were the first in Hungary to join the international civil initiative called Laptops for Ukraine, where people can donate either new or old laptops, tablets or phones.

They spent nearly HUF1.5 million (€4,000) in support for civilians helping refugees.

They're also the ones who, at the very start of the war, organised a peaceful protest and projected a light-painting onto the wall of the Russian embassy, which read out the message of Radio Guy – Русский военный корабль, 'иди на хуй, and now you know what that means: Russian warship, would you please be so kind as to remove yourself from the premises?

These examples gave me the feeling anyone could help. Anyone could throw a tomato into the communal soup pot.

These were serious contributions. I'd have to conclude that this party is no joke. [1]

28. Postscript: A Year Later and Beyond

The Migration

An estimated 12 million people in Ukraine were displaced because of the war, according to the United Nations High Commissioner for Refugees.[1] Of those 12 million, about 8 million left Ukraine. Of those, about 2.5 million left via Budapest, a city of under 2 million. Less than 2 per cent of them are still there, a year later, it is approximated.

In Budapest

Migration Aid tearfully announced they'd have to close down the Madrid street shelter in April 2023. They were in the process of resettling families elsewhere and were still neck-deep in this task when they jubilantly announced in May that they'd be open for another few months. This was thanks to their passionate supporters.

Vitae Shelter also had to close in April. The Red Cross stepped in last summer and provided partial funding. But in the last few months, the volunteer pool became the major donors, to the point where they relaunched crowd-funding to claim some of that back. Their main efforts are to help find accommodation for all of the current residents.

Princess

Princess was finishing off her Ukrainian studies online with a final exam in 2023. She had also been accepted to continue her studies in Canada. There was a group of them, African students in the Netherlands, staying in the same facility. They'd discovered a good plan and now more of them were joining in. She was pleased that there was a group, and that they'd all go over together. She was happy and hopeful. She also added that she was applying to a number of places, and was hedging her bets. She had back-up plans. She was not yet sure what she would choose. I felt confident she was a survivor.

Focused

Focused was dismayed to discover that his Ukrainian university would charge him €5,000 to send a transcript letting him transfer to another medical school. He looked around, did a lot of research, and decided on a different path. He was accepted into a university in Halifax, Nova Scotia, Canada, where he changed his studies from Medicine to Public Health (pre-med). All things considered, and with his family on board, he decided that was more worthwhile.

He started in the autumn of 2023, and was seeking online employment. He was getting used to the icy, windy weather of the Canadian eastern seaboard. It'll be challenging. But it'll be OK. This guy is Focused.

Speaker

A year later, Speaker was still studying online but wanted to transfer to a new medical college. She was dismayed at the energy it took to study properly full-time while also working a full-time job.

Her courses sounded gruelling, and she did not find it easy to "be in class" online all day, in a place where there was little privacy and she had to share a room with many others.

By autumn of 2023, she decided to try the same plan as Focused, and arranged to continue her studies in Canada.

Canada offered one very good advantage over most other countries: it allowed foreign students to work. You could earn your keep from the start and the authorities presented no delays or obstacles whatsoever. There was also the hope, floating around informally on the grapevine, that Canada could potentially be open-minded about letting successful graduates stay on and continue working. Overall, with these particular international students, especially those trying to play the long game, Canada represented the ideal place to end up, if they could manage it.

I found an African online supermarket in Canada and sent her a nice crate of goodies, just like before. I sent more for Christmas. We still are in contact, a few times a month. She still calls me Ma, and I still tell her not to, and she answers by saying Yes Ma.

Devotion

Although Devotion's family disagreed with him at first, later they accepted his decision to delay his studies, and seek full-time work – which he duly found. He was saving up to transfer to a new medical school. He was the youngest of the group, just nineteen when the war turned his life around. He wanted more time and more savings before making a decision. Later in 2023, he applied to several universities to study Pre-Med, and was accepted. Now it was a question of saving up the money needed. He once wrote:

> *"I was 9 when I first thought I want to be a doctor. I never considered another profession. My family encouraged this."*

As for me, things had changed. Hungary was unlikely to be my future retirement home, as I'd been pondering. My eyes were now set on a return to Scotland. Due to Brexit, I was no longer entitled to healthcare outside of the UK. Also, my brain could not face learning foreign language number nine. I didn't get far with the first eight. In Hungary, the social climate could be great for those born and raised there, but it was less and less welcoming to anyone from outside. Building walls and fences was in, building bridges was out. Even my local pizza guys were less friendly these days. But my roots and my people are there. I love that city. I like the menu too. And, internationals always find each other. Therefore, I'll remain a regular visitor and, I hope, a good if sarcastic guest.

The Rest of the Warring World in 2023

The war in Ukraine was entrenched and stubborn. Wars continued to be profitable.

Snake Island Update [2]

Russian forces took over on the first day of the war, early in 2022. A few months later, in April, Ukraine sank the Russian warship *Moskva*, that had originally destroyed the island. This was the biggest warship sunk in combat for forty years. Russia said one sailor was killed. Western experts said the real figure was about half of the crew of 450. A few months later in June, Russia abandoned the island, after taking a variety of heavy losses trying to keep it. They called this withdrawal another "goodwill gesture".

So, Ukraine was able to hang onto Snake Island, which meant they hung onto all shipping routes to and from Ukraine via the port of Odesa. By keeping Snake Island, Ukraine kept their main links to the outside world. They kept their independence.

Saturday 8 July 2023

President Volodymyr Zelensky marked the 500th day of Russia's invasion by visiting Snake Island, which had become a symbol of Ukraine's resilience. Wearing a black hoodie and camouflage bullet-proof vest, he laid flowers, thanked all the defenders of the country, and paid tribute to the dead. He said reclaiming Snake Island was "proof that Ukraine will regain every bit of its territory".

> *"May the freedom ... which we have to win now, be a tribute to all those who gave their lives for Ukraine."*

The Iconic "Russian Warship, Go FCK Yourself"

Postage Stamp, and Other Protests

As of summer 2023, the online resale price of this special edition stamp had risen from $100 to $130. Fridge magnets are also available. [3]

Radio Guy's real name is Roman Hrybov and he won a medal.

Tomato Woman's real name is Elena and she's from Kiev.

Elsewhere across the planet

As per the dedication at the start of this story, it can be reported that daisies and hope continue to push through concrete, one molecule at a time, and we intend to continue.

Thanks

Organisations

GASH – Ghana Students Association in Hungary
https://www.facebook.com/GASH4all

MKKP – The Hungarian Two-Tailed Dog Party
https://ketfarkukutya.mkkp.party/

Magyar Narancs (Hungarian Orange magazine)
https://magyarnarancs.hu/

Mária Mandák Church, Budapest VIII
https://jozsefvaros.lutheran.hu/mandak-haz/

MigAid (Migration Aid)
https://migaid.org/en/our-history

Their shelter in Budapest:
https://www.facebook.com/groups/5031142010284558

Szabad Európa, Pablo Gorondi Palkó, Miklós Lipkovski

https://www.szabadeuropa.hu/

Vitae Hostel, Budapest
https://www.facebook.com/vitaehostel

Hungarian consultants

András Bánó, Péter Bánó

Zsófi Heéger, genealogist, translator
Bence Kovács – translator, tour guide, teacher
https://hungaretrace.com/

Miklós Molnár – linguist, retired professor
https://www.fungarian.com/about-us/

Rudolf Paksa, historian, academic, writer
https://independent.academia.edu/RudolfPaksa

Katalin Szlukovény, senior lecturer in English Studies, ELTE
https://www.btk.elte.hu/en/staff/szlukovenyi-katalin

Karesz Vándor – genealogist, tour guide, translator
https://www.hungarianroots.com/

Refugee Aid Volunteers

Adam Cats
Maomi and Daidai
Anne Murray – http://www.annemurrayartist.com/
Gideon Ong, who is still helping people, here:
https://www.gofundme.com/f/ukraine-war-refugee-fundraiser

Bonny Pratt supports this charity:
https://www.facebook.com/RefugeeFoodBankBudapest
Mark Rimmell
And everyone who donated time, money, food, chit-chat, kindliness, their home or anything else

Also

Facebook group Women of Budapest
The Freud Museum in Vienna
All the Vienna Cousins
All the Hungarian cousins
All cousins in spirit including Hanna Asipovich
All Chosen Family
All comedians everywhere

My new friends Devoted, Focused, Princess and Speaker

Editors Tamsin Shelton, Claire Handy, Kim Kimber
Writers group A Novel Approach

All travel blog readers @ Noodle Trails, Eileen Kay, author page:
https://www.facebook.com/profile.php?id=100035141327939

Notes

Chapter 1

1. About the Snake Island guards swearing at the Russian warship Moskva:
https://www.bbc.co.uk/news/world-europe-60554959
In the above clip, the reply was translated as “go to hell”, though later reports said “Get lost”.
The original audio (widely broadcast on many stations): https://www.youtube.com/watch?v=LDrFVdms8yk
with a more accurate written translation here:
https://www.youtube.com/watch?v=_pOLc5QLYTs

2. Comedian Tibor Bödőcs does an able parody of Mr O, but the punchline here can be misunderstood: when English speakers say Bullshit, Hungarians say Horsedick.
https://www.youtube.com/watch?v=K6tAm8ww7jY

3.https://hungarytoday.hu/two-tailed-dog-party-mkkp-protest-demonstration-russia-embassy-snake-island-ukraine/

4. About the students: throughout this book, all quotes from Devotion, Focused, Princess and Speaker are from our letters, texts, chats and interviews.

5. About People of Colour escaping Ukraine but being turned away at the Polish border:
https://www.france24.com/en/europe/20220228-pushed-back-because-we-re-black-africans-stranded-at-ukraine-poland-border
https://www.bbc.com/pidgin/60561669
https://www.theguardian.com/global-development/2022/mar/02/people-of-colour-fleeing-ukraine-attacked-by-polish-nationalists

6. More about Snake Island battle, seizure, re-capture:
https://www.bbc.co.uk/news/world-europe-61406808
https://www.theguardian.com/world/video/2022/feb/25/go-fuck-yourself-ukrainian-soldiers-snake-island-russian-ship-before-being-killed-audio
https://www.reuters.com/world/europe/ukraines-zelenskiy-visits-symbolic-snake-island-mark-500-days-war-2023-07-08/
https://www.abc.net.au/news/2023-07-09/Zelensky-marks-500th-day-of-war-from-famous-snake-
https://www.bbc.co.uk/news/world-europe-60522454
https://edition.cnn.com/videos/world/2022/02/25/ukraine-russia-soldier-exchange-audio-liebermann-dlt-intl-hnk-vpx.cnn
https://www.newsweek.com/one-13-killed-ukrainian-island-live-streamed-attack-1682540

7. About the thirteen Snake Island guards who were presumed dead but were not:
https://www.abc.net.au/news/2023-07-09/Zelensky-marks-500th-day-of-war-from-famous-snake-
https://www.bbc.co.uk/news/world-europe-60522454
https://edition.cnn.com/videos/world/2022/02/25/ukraine-russia-soldier-exchange-audio-liebermann-dlt-intl-hnk-vpx.cnn
https://www.theguardian.com/world/2022/nov/19/russian-warship-go-fuck-yourself-ukraine-snake-island
https://www.cbsnews.com/news/ukraine-snake-island-soldiers-tell-russian-troops-f-you-killed/
https://nypost.com/2022/02/28/snake-island-ukrainian-guards-captured-by-russia-still-alive/
https://www.bbc.co.uk/news/world-europe-60554959

8. Was the government helping or weren't they? Mixed reviews:
Zoltán Kovács (March 3, 2022). Don't let disinformation campaigns fool you, Hungary is welcoming ALL refugees. About Hungary.

9. Lucy Hough (March 3, 2022), Uncertainty for Ukrainian refugees in Hungary as thousands plan their next steps. CGTN.

10. BNE Intelli News (26 February, 2022). Ukrainian refugees start arriving in an unprepared Hungary

11. Chernobyl dogs:
https://www.bbc.com/future/article/20210422-the-guards-caring-for-chernobyls-abandoned-dogs, 23April 2021

https://www.nationalgeographic.com/animals/article/060418-chernobyl-wildlife-thirty-year-anniversary-science
https://www.mamamia.com.au/animals-in-chernobyl
https://www.newsweek.com/what-happening-wildlife-inside-chernobyl-exclusion-zone-after-russian-invasion-1685863

Chapter 2

1. Ghana Students Organisation in Hungary:
https://www.facebook.com/GASH4all

2. GASH and a church welcome refugees, early March 2022:
https://24.hu/kozelet/2022/03/09/orosz-ukran-haboru-afrikai-menekultek-almassy-ter/

3. About racism at the Polish border – same sources as in Chapter 1.

4. About racism on Ukrainian borders and trains, UN and other objections:
https://edition.cnn.com/2022/03/01/africa/africa-condemns-racism-ukraine-intl/index.html
https://news.un.org/en/story/2022/03/1114282
https://www.theguardian.com/commentisfree/2022/mar/02/civilised-european-look-like-us-racist-coverage-ukraine
https://www.vox.com/22962300/ukraine-russia-refugee-racism
Trevor Noah's Daily Show had a good selection, and he added satirical commentary:
https://www.youtube.com/watch?v=Hxzfpx9nSn8

Chapter 4

1. All stories of refugees in this and following chapters, are from volunteers, on public Facebook posts

2. Zelensky's address to the nation, calling men to the army https://www.reuters.com/world/europe/ukraines-zelenskiy-calls-citizens-fight-promises-weapons-2022-02-24/

3. Comedian David Letterman interviews Ukrainian President Zelensky:
https://www.youtube.com/watch?v=liooTXAF5Xo
Also recommended, comedian Jon Stewart interviews MEP and physician Katalin Cseh of the centrist Momentum Party:
https://www.youtube.com/watch?v=t9DPv7RX4QY&t=3s

4. About the nightmare endured by the international student refugees trapped in Sumy:
https://www.theguardian.com/world/2022/mar/08/sumy-international-students-in-ukrainian-city-tell-of-desperation
https://edition.cnn.com/2022/03/03/europe/international-students-trapped-sumy-ukraine-lgs-intl/index.html

5. Ukrainian postage stamp commemorating Snake Island soldier giving the finger to a Russian warship.
https://www.npr.org/2022/04/20/1093764504/ukraine-snake-island-postage-stamp
https://www.independent.co.uk/news/world/europe/ukraine-snake-island-stamp-russian-warship-b2035099.html
https://www.businessinsider.com/commemorative-stamp-ukrainian-soldier-flipping-the-bird-nearly-sells-out-2022-

4?op=1&r=US&IR=T

6. All the primary sources to do with the history of "giving the finger" are here: https://en.wikipedia.org/wiki/The_finger#External_links

Chapter 5

1. The poem on New York's Statue of Liberty is The New Colossus, 1883, by Emma Lazarus:

Not like the brazen giant of Greek fame,
With conquering limbs astride from land to land;
Here at our sea-washed, sunset gates shall stand
A mighty woman with a torch, whose flame
Is the imprisoned lightning, and her name
Mother of Exiles. From beacon-hand
Glows world-wide welcome; her mild eyes command
The air-bridged harbor that twin cities frame.

Keep, ancient lands, your storied pomp!" cries she
With silent lips. "Give me your tired, your poor,
Your huddled masses yearning to breathe free,
The wretched refuse of your teeming shore.
Send these, the homeless, tempest-tost to me,
I lift my lap beside the golden door!"

2. BOK Hall opened to refugees 21 March 2022, to very mixed reviews:
Source: Hungary Today (March 22, 2022). New Humanitarian Transit Point: "This is the coordination we've been waiting for three weeks" . Hungary Today.
https://xpatloop.com/channels/2022/03/hungary-to-provide-facilities-for-refugees-per centE2per cent80per cent93-bok-hall-turned-into-shelter.html
https://hungarytoday.hu/refugees-asylum-war-ukraine-budapest-receive-info-help-bok-hall-keleti/
https://nepszava.hu/3150469_bok-sportcsarnok_ukrajna_menekult_budapest_orban_kormany
https://444.hu/2022/03/21/ez-az-a-koordinalas-amire-harom-hete-vartunk-segitokozpontot-nyitott-a-kormany-a-bok-csarnokban
https://444.hu/2022/03/25/lezart-vece-es-egy-asztal-fogadja-a-palyaudvarokra-erkezo-menekulteket

Chapter 6

1. About the Two-Tailed Dog Party: all unidentified quotes came from their website:
https://kettarkukutya.mkkp.party/, where you may need a translator, but not always – see the next item:
This is a good general history and introduction, in English:
https://ketfarkukutya.mkkp.party/2019/04/22/the-two-tailed-dog-party/

2. A general background of the party:
https://www.theguardian.com/world/2016/jan/06/hungary-two-tailed-dog-viktor-orban

Chapter 8

1. Migration Aid's website
https://migaid.org/en/
https://www.facebook.com/groups/503114201028455 8

2. Why Hungary smears George Soros:
https://www.aljazeera.com/news/2017/11/22/whats-behind-hungarys-campaign-against-george-soros/
https://money.cnn.com/2017/07/11/news/george-soros-hungary-antisemitism-migration/index.html
https://www.haaretz.com/opinion/2020-06-15/ty-article-opinion/.premium/the-key-to-hungarys-infatuation-with-hate-mongering-authoritarian-orban/0000017f-e9f2-df2c-a1ff-fff36cb00000

3. This is the immigration law that stopped people helping migrants:
https://www.vox.com/policy-and-politics/2018/6/22/17493070/hungary-stop-soros-orban

4. All information about the Mandák Mária Evangelical Church came from their website:
https://jozsefvaros.lutheran.hu/2016/02/26/mandak-haz/

Chapter 9

1. All info about the Vitae Shelter is from their own web pages:
https://www.facebook.com/vitaeshelter
https://www.gofundme.com/f/vitae-hostel-ukrainian-refugee-shelter?member=18070057&sharetype=teams
General background also came from here:

https://www.youtube.com/watch?v=g4aGfxPbN6Q
https://host4ukraine.com/l/62c03957-722c-48da-b1e4-530f3abf353d

2. About Tom Rosenstiel:
https://www.tomrosenstiel.com/

Chapter 10

1. About Endre "Teddy" Bánó, graphic artist:
https://budapestposter.com/artists/240
and in Hungarian:
https://hu.wikipedia.org/wiki/ Bánó_Endre
https://www.kieselbach.hu/artist/bano_-endre_7371

2. About news man András Bánó, journalist and broadcaster:
https://hu.wikipedia.org/wiki/ Bánó_Andras

Chapter 11

1. About Dr Semmelweis
https://www.britannica.com/science/antiseptic
https://www.encyclopedia.com/people/medicine/medicine-biographies/ignaz-philipp-semmelweis
https://en.wikipedia.org/wiki/Ignaz_Semmelweis

Chapter 12

1. Anti-immigration policies
https://www.theguardian.com/world/2015/jul/02/hungary-government-condemned-over-anti-immigration-drive
https://www.theguardian.com/world/2016/jan/06/hungary-two-tailed-dog-viktor-orban

https://www.bbc.co.uk/news/world-europe-36753648
https://www.theguardian.com/world/live/2015/sep/15/refugee-crisis-hungary-launches-border-crackdown-live-updates

2. Nearly everything in this chapter is from their website. https://ketfarkukutya.mkkp.party/
This page has links to some of their campaigns, which parody the government's nationwide poster campaigns:
https://ketfarkukutya.mkkp.party/letoltes/
Example of these campaigns:
"Tudta?" [Did you know?] campaign (2016): https://ketfarkukutya.mkkp.party/tudta-kampany/
"Állítsuk meg az Állítsuk meg Brüsszelt!" [Stop the "Stop Brussels!"] campaign (2017) – with a bunch of anti-Putin illustrations (!!!): https://ketfarkukutya.mkkp.party/allitsuk-meg-az-allitsuk-meg-brusszelt/

3. Their poster said "Sorry about our prime minister":
https://hvg.hu/velemeny/20150611_Oldodik_a_plakatmagany
https://www.theguardian.com/world/2016/jan/06/hungary-two-tailed-dog-viktor-orban

4. More about The Dogs:
https://www.theguardian.com/world/2016/jan/06/hungary-two-tailed-dog-viktor-orban

5. More on aid, or not – Dogs v Mr O:
https://www.bbc.co.uk/news/world-europe-37310819
https://www.bbc.co.uk/programmes/p049mn1y
https://www.indexoncensorship.org/2017/03/index-awards-hungary-two-tailed-dog-party/

https://www.theguardian.com/world/2016/jan/06/hungary-two-tailed-dog-viktor-orban

6. Stephan Segal's henchman lookalike:
https://www.youtube.com/watch?v=LSmcW669sOs

7. Other general background material from John Oliver:
On immigration:
https://www.youtube.com/watch?v=umqvYhb3wf4
On the far right in Europe:
https://www.youtube.com/watch?v=eoNaIs-xRxI
About that chicken:
https://www.youtube.com/watch?v=Uu-ahE4y2KM
https://www.youtube.com/watch?v=6ZOpSay4p8k

8. Many primary sources about Mr O can be found here:
https://en.wikipedia.org/wiki/Viktor_Orb%C3%A1n
https://en.wikipedia.org/wiki/Fidesz

9. Richard Prior quote, about greedy people
https://www.youtube.com/watch?v=gKhGA9SMQGM

10. Comedian Tibor Bödőcs does an excellent impersonation of Mr O here:
https://www.youtube.com/watch?v=K6tAm8ww7jY

11. About gutting the entire asylum system, building fences and being criticised by the UN and EU:
https://www.bbc.co.uk/news/world-europe-36753648
https://www.theguardian.com/world/live/2015/sep/15/refugee-crisis-hungary-launches-border-crackdown-live-updates

12. "Jordan Klepper Fingers the Globe: Hungary for Democracy", 22 April 2022.
#DailyShow with Trevor Noah.
https://www.youtube.com/watch?v=O-YuZPT1NzM

13. Jean-Claude Juncker slaps Mr O, May 2015:
https://www.youtube.com/watch?v=Ko995a81UIU

14. John Oliver rejoices about the above:
https://www.youtube.com/watch?v=LSmcW669sOs&t=40s

15. Interview with opposition leader Peter Marki-Zay:
https://www.youtube.com/watch?v=O-YuZPT1NzM

16. All quotes come from here:
https://www.theguardian.com/world/2016/jan/06/hungary-two-tailed-dog-viktor-orban

17. About spoiling voting ballots by drawing penises on them – the rumour was here:
https://www.newsweek.com/hungarys-joke-party-dead-serious-about-election-875196
MKKP did not suggest the above, but they suggested 9 comic but real ways to cast an invalid vote:
https://www.youtube.com/watch?v=PaZFXngC-7A

Highly recommended: Pravda Haha, True Travel to the End of Europe, Rory MacLean (Bloomsbury, London, 2019). Shortlisted for the Stanford Dolman 2020 Travel Book of the Year Award. Part travel book, part contemporary history, wide scope, dramatic, amazingly absorbing.

Chapter 14

1. Much of this chapter came from here: https://www.theguardian.com/world/2016/jan/06/hungary-two-tailed-dog-viktor-orban

2. About the Two-Tailed Dog Party and their animal candidates:
https://www.newsweek.com/hungarys-joke-party-dead-serious-about-election-875196

3. About the chicken man:
https://www.youtube.com/watch?v=6ZOpSay4p8k
https://www.npr.org/sections/parallels/2018/04/07/599928312/hungarys-satirical-two-tailed-dog-party-will-debut-in-sunday-elections

4. John Oliver comments on Mr O, the MKKP's chicken candidate and more:
https://www.youtube.com/watch?v=LSmcW669sOs

5. MKKP protests: "we want them to know they are not alone": https://www.theguardian.com/world/2016/jan/06/hungary-two-tailed-dog-viktor-orban

6.All Jokey and Satirical Political Party material came from Wikipedia, so long as there were primary sources involved: https://en.wikipedia.org/wiki/List_of_frivolous_political_parties

https://www.worldatlas.com/articles/10-funniest-joke-political-parties-of-all-time.html

Chapter 19

1. About Szabad Europa (Radio Free Europe and more)
https://www.szabadeuropa.hu/
https://hungarianspectrum.org/2020/09/24/radio-free-europe-szabad-europa-has-returned-to-hungary/
https://www.facebook.com/szabadeuropahu/

Chapter 20

1. About Mark Rimmell:
https://welovebudapest.com/en/article/2020/2/11/meet-the-crown-maker-of-budapest
https://iamtarajdavis.wordpress.com/2020/02/03/meet-the-crown-maker-of-budapest/
https://www.budapesttimes.hu/people/from-death-on-the-nile-to-life-on-the-danube/

Chapter 21

1. About the general history behind the phrase and symbol of The Hungarian Orange:
https://dailynewshungary.com/the-story-of-the-hungarian-orange/
https://www.boell.de/en/intlpolitics/europe-north-america-protests-hungary-art-16085.html

2. About the film The Witness:
https://nfi.hu/hu/hirek/a-magyar-film-napja-2020
https://en.wikipedia.org/wiki/The_Witness_(1969_Hungarian

_film)
Here's the delicious clip, in which our hero is ordered to say that a lemon is an orange and that this was not subject to debate:
https://www.youtube.com/watch?v=7e4ADpDiYzc
The whole movie:
https://vimeo.com/337248045

3. The beloved Hungarian Orange quote from the film:
https://www.youtube.com/watch?v=7e4ADpDiYzc

4. Website of the satirical magazine Hungarian Orange (almost all in Hungarian only)
https://magyarnarancs.hu/, but there's more in English here:
https://www.facebook.com/magyarnarancs/

5. The day government supporters attacked an inflatable lemon:
https://www.boell.de/en/intlpolitics/europe-north-america-protests-hungary-art-16085.html

Chapter 24

1. About the video feature by Szabadeuropa (Free Europe):
https://www.szabadeuropa.hu/a/a-szuleid-a-hazatokat-a-foldeteket-adtak-hogy-te-elmehess-es-akkor-most-vissza-kell-terned-ugyanoda-egy-nigeriai-daiklany-tortenete/31882232.html

Chapter 27

1. About MKKP's Suzie Dada, then a deputy mayor in

Budapest, "Fighting Hatred With Humour in Hungary", a Witness documentary, 21 March 2022.
https://www.youtube.com/watch?v=haudOBmaOgM

Chapter 28

1. UNHCR regularly updates figures on displaced people:
www.migrationdataportal.org/ukraine
https://data.unhcr.org/en/documents/details/98922

2. About Snake Island, one year after the invasion: how Ukraine got the island back, Zelensky's visit in July 2023, the 500th day of the war:
https://www.abc.net.au/news/2023-07-09/zelenskyy-marks-500th-day-of-war-from-famous-snake-island/102579618
https://www.reuters.com/world/europe/ukraines-zelenskiy-visits-symbolic-snake-island-mark-500-days-war-2023-07-08/
https://www.npr.org/2023/07/08/1186662854/Zelensky-ukraine-war-500-days-russia-turkey
https://www.bbc.co.uk/news/world-europe-61992491

3. About the defiantly obscene Ukrainian commemorative postage stamp:
https://www.npr.org/2022/04/20/1093764504/ukraine-snake-island-postage-stamp

Also by the Same Author

Noodle Trails, a Travel Memoir: Fair Trade, Dung Trade, and Travels in Thailand and Beyond

Failed comedienne and heartbroken idiot flees to a Thai beach hut. Years later from the same hut, come sweet, silly tales of mangoes, lizards, and a whole new life.

For many winters she'd escaped to the Thai sunshine with her importing business, but not now: she's broke, alone and discouraged. This trip could be her last.

She bid farewell to her Fair Trade business partners. No more elephant dung paper, no more brass jewellery from old bombshells, no more utensils from coconuts.

But even an idiot can do some good in the world and this one did.

It's a love-letter to everyone who helped her see that tsunamis, heartbreaks and other losses can be survived.

It's a journey of edible insects, singing lizards, and hopeful transformation – plus an awful lot of elephant dung.

"Engaging, funny, poignant – everything a good travel memoir should be. I laughed out loud, I got very hungry and want to go to Thailand"

Mary Smith, journalist and author.

"She clearly loves Thailand with a passion but she's not oblivious to its flaws. I enjoyed the unpredictability"

Gillian Fraser, journalist and broadcaster.

"Funny, wise and thought-provoking, outspoken, touching, surprising, and mouth-watering. Impressive debut from a refreshing new voice"

Woodstock Books, Oxford.

"Reminiscent of Paul Theroux in the breadth of her writing, but without Theroux's recurring gloom! The best kind of travel writing – engaging, charming, humorous too"

R. H. Pesch

Noodle Trails 2: My Secret Century in Budapest

"Don't ever bring this up again."

Mom and Dad to me, 1977

"This book brings up everything I could fit in."

Me to you, 40 years later

Stubborn, wacky senior crosses the world seeking skeletons in the family closet, embraces long-lost cousins and tells it like a witty thriller.

For her 60th birthday, Eileen Kay finally disobeyed her parents' orders and flew to Hungary, the ancestral homeland. She only had mysteries, rumours and questions to start with, but a massive history opened up.

Three years of tenacious research unfolded like a detective story, revealing a weird and wonderful saga of mixed races, reconciliation and an eccentric cast of thousands - including newly-found living cousins, new friends and a new home.

Some secrets are better out than in.

"Epic yet playful, with a tart intellectualism"

Dr Andreas Weiss, Vienna Technical University.

"Told with wit and a wonderful line in self-deprecating stories, vivid and heartfelt descriptions as she immerses herself in city life while excavating

the archives. If you've not yet been to Budapest, you will want to"

Woodstock Books, Oxford.

"A truly fascinating journey. Through dogged determination, she brings to life personalities otherwise forgotten – a fascinating cast of characters. It is a family of resilience and nowhere is this more evident than in Kay herself. Moving, funny, and a joy to read"

Margot Trevelyan, CBC.

Noodle Trails 3:

Nothing Went to Plan and Other Silver Linings

Did your 2020 go to plan? Did anyone's?

Did your path in life go neatly from A to B? Or did it look like a bowl of noodles?

Her heartfelt wish to return to the UK was crushed by Covid. Where would she get locked down and imprisoned? A jungle hut in Thailand? Her cousin's flat where the cat pees in her bed? Even Albania was an option.

Many things and locations that year was surprising. And confusing. And tangled.

That's a noodle trail, and we all have one.

Highlights and lowlights of that strange year are laced with sarcasm and sense of the absurd.

It's dedicated to everyone who loves a puzzle, and especially to those who don't.

"This author's style is so refreshing yet deeply considered. Her story is laced with sparkling personal anecdotes, ancestral gems and discoveries, satire, humour and (sometimes scathing) wit. Her gift for storytelling lets you travel right beside her. If you love a good memoir with exotic travel and adventure, dive into this one."

Carol Cochrane, novelist

About The Author

Eileen Kay was born and raised in the USA and then went wandering. She has worked as a BBC slave, half of comedy magic double act Dork and Tacky, and KISS-FM radio traffic presenter Carmen Ghia. She's done a stack of odd jobs too.

Her first degree was in Music and English at Oberlin College, USA. Postgraduate studies were in Education at the Suzuki Institute in Japan, then later at London Film School with a Distinction in Editing.

She's lived in the UK for over thirty years, is a dual USA and UK citizen, and now splits her time between Scotland, Hungary and southeast Asia, teaching English and writing as many travel memoirs as possible.

www.facebook.com/Noodle-Trails-Eileen-Kay-1560532710838005

Printed in Great Britain
by Amazon

40863260R00198